Effective Teaching and Learning in Practice

Effective Teaching and Learning in Practice

Don Skinner

The Companion Website relating to this book is available online at: www.continuumbooks.com/Education/Skinner

Please visit the link and register with us to receive your password and access to the Companion Website.

If you experience any problems accessing the Companion Website, please contact Continuum at info@continuumbooks.com.

continuum

Continuum International Publishing Group

The Tower Building
11 York Road
London
SE1 7NX

80 Maiden Lane,
Suite 704
New York,
NY 10038

www.continuumbooks.com

British Library Cataloguing-in-Publication Data
A catalogue record for this book is available from the British Library.

ISBN: 9780826499370 (paperback)
       9781441129239 (hardcover)

Library of Congress Cataloging-in-Publication Data
Skinner, Don.
 Effective teaching and learning in practice / Don Skinner.
     p. cm.
 Includes bibliographical references and index.
 ISBN 978-1-4411-2923-9 (hbk) – ISBN 978-0-8264-9937-0 (pbk)
 1. Effective teaching. 2. Learning. I. Title.

 LB1025.3.S6 2010
 371.102–dc22

2009034281

Typeset by BookEns Limited, Royston, Herts.
Printed and bound in Great Britain by CPI Antony Rowe, Chippenham, Wiltshire

For Gita, Bina and Sheila

Contents

Acknowledgements   ix

The Aims of this Book   1

Part 1   TEACHING AND LEARNING – AN INTRODUCTION

1   **Perspectives on Teaching and Learning**   5

2   **Making Sense of Teaching and Learning**   18

Part 2   THE FOUR MODES OF TEACHING AND LEARNING

3   **Direct Teaching**   35

4   **Teaching through Dialogue and Discussion**   46

5   **Learning through Action and Experience**   57

6   **Learning through Enquiry**   68

Part 3   USING THE MODES IN PRACTICE – FURTHER CONSIDERATIONS

7   **Whole-class, Group and Individual Teaching**   81

8   **Inter-disciplinary Learning, Thinking Skills, Learning How to Learn**   91

Part 4   BACKGROUND THEORY

9   **Learning and Teaching with Information Technologies**   105

10   **Understanding and Developing Pedagogy**   114

11   **Brain Science, Cognitive Psychology and Teaching**   125

Part 5   HOW TO BE REFLECTIVE

12 Developing Teaching   141

Glossary   153
References   165
Index   176

Acknowledgements

In putting this book together I have been fortunate in receiving the support and advice of a large number of colleagues and academic contacts and from family. I would like in particular to offer thanks to my colleagues: Mandy Allsop, Mary Andrew, Dorothy Caddell, David Carr, Pamela Deponio, Noel Entwistle, Heather Ferguson, Barbara Frame, John Frame, Amanda Gizzi, George Hunt, Bob Kibble, Moira Leslie, Lorele Mackie, Gillean McCluskey, Laura Mitchell, Pamela Munn, Nigel Parton, Jim O'Brian, Rachel O'Neill, Lesley Reid, Gillian Robinson, Peter Tarrant, David Thomson, Zoe Williamson, Kevin Wright, Terry Wrigley; to Debbie Downer, Lorraine Denholm and Caroline Maloney for secretarial support at various times and to the Moray House library staff; to Dr Claire Cassidy, Professor Donald Christie, Sanna Rimpilainen and Alastair Wilson at the University of Strathclyde; to Dr Mark Bastin and Dr Jane Haley of Edinburgh Neurosciences and Nicky Greenhorn of Medical Illustration; to Steve Bell and Sallie Harkness of Storyline Scotland. Staff at Continuum – Joanne Allcock, Liz Blackmore, Alison Clark, Ania Leslie-Wujastyk, Bridget Gibbs and Kirsty Schaper – have been enormously helpful and understanding. Above all, I would like to express my heartfelt thanks to my wife and daughters for their wonderful support and encouragement to me in this endeavour.

The Aims of this Book

This book sets out to explain the key ideas and strategies now thought to underlie effective teaching and learning, the debates surrounding them and evidence from research. A good understanding of all this is an important base from which teachers, of any subject or stage of education, can work to realize educational aims and values through professional action in schools and other educational contexts.

The chapters that follow offer:

- a simple, yet balanced and powerful framework for thinking about teaching and learning in the light of educational aims and values
- an outline of the latest developments in thinking, research, policy and practice
- an exploration of the issues practising teachers face in deploying various teaching approaches and strategies, with examples and advice relating to a range of contexts

This first chapter looks at the nature and aims of education and teaching and introduces a variety of perspectives that can shed light on teaching ideas and practices. The next chapter discusses studies that have compared different approaches to teaching and learning and attempted to identify the characteristics of effective teaching. It also explains the idea of distinctive teaching modes.

The successive chapters in Part 2 look in turn at the four basic modes of teaching and learning – direct teaching, learning through action and experience, teaching through dialogue and discussion and learning through enquiry. These chapters consider the nature of the particular mode, research evidence and practical teaching issues.

Part 3 covers wider aspects of teaching and learning. First, it considers policy and research on the organization of learning (whole class, group and individual). There have been significant developments here lately, especially regarding interactive whole-class teaching, collaborative group work and personalizing learning. Secondly, attention turns to inter-disciplinary teaching, thinking skills and learning how to learn. Many countries are witnessing interesting developments in inter-disciplinary (or cross-curricular) teaching, after a period of neglect; and thinking skills and learning how to learn are prime concerns at all levels. In each of these chapters the role and deployment of the various modes of teaching is explored.

Part 4 aims to help teachers make sense of three issues that figure prominently in current educational discussions and writings. The first is the use of information technologies, whose potential for transforming teaching and learning is still far from being realised. The second is pedagogy, a concept that has proved obscure and off-putting to teachers in the past but is now clearly central. The third concerns the educational implications of research in brain science. Popular practical advice on 'brain-based' learning offered to teachers has come under criticism from neuroscientists urging a more cautious approach to classroom application and deeper understanding of research evidence. Many teachers seek a clear explanation of these matters.

Part 5 considers how to develop as a teacher through systematic professional reflection, engagement with research and participation in staff development activities. It outlines the systems and opportunities for further professional learning, considers some of the tensions and suggests how to build a satisfying and successful teaching career through professional reflection and by exploiting the wide-ranging opportunities that are emerging for continuing professional development. These include involvement in local and national research projects on developing teaching and learning.

Throughout the text, examples of applications and illustrations of ideas are taken from every stage of education from early childhood through to secondary education and beyond. The basic perspective is that of education from 3–18. This broad, comprehensive focus is increasingly recognized as important in educational discussions around the world. A prime example is Scotland's 'Curriculum for Excellence' initiative (Scottish Executive 2004), which covers the 3–18 age range in a single policy initiative. Similar ambitions to take a broad perspective and to transcend traditional educational stages are shown by a major educational research project (The Teaching and Learning Research Programme, TLRP) in England (Pollard 2007; Alexander 2008b: 175ff.) and curriculum reform in Queensland (Hayes *et al.* 2006). Each educational stage has much to learn from the others; and while there are some obvious differences between, say, nursery education and later secondary teaching, many fundamental ideas about effective teaching and learning apply to all stages and subjects, including non-formal and adult education, on which this book also draws as appropriate.

One problem in the past has been a tendency to think of primary teaching as very different from secondary, and both from adult and higher education. Smoothing the transitions between these phases is now proving critical to raising educational achievement and this implies close communication and mutual understanding. The strong splits between stages of education – pre-school, primary, secondary, further education – which emerged from the historical development of education in countries like the UK and USA are beginning to be recognized, in retrospect, as possibly an evolutionary mistake. It is by no means a universal rule, for example, that primary education is from 5–11 and secondary from 11–18. Eastern European and Scandinavian countries in fact developed a 'basic school' from 6–15 or 7–16 (while retaining some aspects of primary and lower secondary phases). Moreover, the widening of learning contexts and breaking down of barriers between school and out-of-school learning is a marked feature of the twenty-first century – and one which needs to be taken seriously by those working in school contexts.

Part 1

Teaching and Learning – An Introduction

Perspectives on Teaching and Learning

Chapter Outline

What is Effective Teaching?   5
What Sort of Activity is Teaching?   7
Insights from Philosophy, Psychology and Sociology   10
Practitioners, Researchers and Policy-makers   14
Education, Schooling and Social Justice   15
Summary   16
Key Reading   17
Useful Websites   17

What is Effective Teaching?

To call something effective is to say that it produces the desired end or result, that it does the job expected of it; as Dennis Hayes (2003: 27) notes, effective teaching means that expectations are achieved, or indeed exceeded. Moreover, it is commonly thought important to distinguish effectiveness from efficiency. Peter Drucker (1962: 1–2), for long the doyen of business management, memorably summed up the essence of effectiveness as 'doing the right things' and of efficiency as 'doing things right' – that is, with minimal energy and waste for the task at hand. Teaching may be efficient in the sense of being technically sound and not wasteful of resources but yet not be effective because it does not achieve the intended or worthwhile results.

An important problem in discussions of teaching is that major questions can often be raised about whether we are aiming at the right thing. We can't just assume everyone agrees what the result should be and then use research to judge what teaching methods produce such outcomes. For example, a large part of the recent British and American debate on synthetic phonics in the teaching of reading centres on such questions. Wrigley (2006: 75) condemns the literacy hour and synthetic phonics approaches as a very narrow interpretation of desired ends in literacy and advocates a perspective based on a broader concept of educational aims and values:

Until recently schools rarely used the term literacy, preferring English or reading and writing. The recent change of terminology has encouraged more artificial ways of teaching reading based on sub-skills – putting the parts before the whole [. . .] The most successful young readers have generally had a rich experience of real reading at home [. . .] reading and writing are built on spoken language [. . .] the literacy hour has made it much more difficult for teachers to connect literacy to spoken language [. . .] language development depends on rich experience, but this doesn't fit well with the rigid structure of the literacy hour.

However, many proponents of synthetic phonics justify their approach in terms of promoting equality, and claim research evidence suggests such structured and focused teaching is most obviously effective for disadvantaged pupils (Diamond 2007). Critics of the literacy hour and a concentration on synthetic phonics question the research methods used to investigate such reading schemes and show that they are by no means technically neutral, but often politically and commercially implicated (e.g. Shaker and Ruitenberg 2007), or provide a one-sided account (Wyse and Styles 2007). The debate continues fiercely. Such issues emerge for many curriculum areas and policies.

Moreover, as Hayes *et al.* (2006: 32–3) have noted, despite initially aiming for significant change, teaching and learning reforms often result in structural changes that lead to greater efficiency but not greater effectiveness because the reforms typically fail to penetrate the traditional instructional core of the schools (Smylie and Perry 1998: 983). A related issue is that, while many reforms and developments appear to lead to some improvement, the effort and resources required seem out of proportion to the gains achieved and there are often downsides as well. Questions of this kind are at last beginning to be asked about the cost/benefit of educational innovations and reforms, for example in relation to individual educational plans and some information technology developments.

Reflective Exploration 1.1 – Efficiency and Effectiveness

Try to identify and begin to explore other aspects of teaching where the issue of effectiveness versus efficiency or cost/benefit might be applied, and where issues of aims and values as well as of evidence arise. Consider, for example, health education, personalizing learning, boys' under-achievement and physical education.

Teaching and context

One of the best discussions of the concept of teaching is that of John Passmore (1980) who points out three features of teaching which are indispensable for understanding what it means to teach effectively: to teach is normally to teach something, to somebody, in some context.

Taking account of these aspects is vital because we might be more or less effective in relation to different subjects, different learners and in different contexts (e.g. very informal as opposed to formal ones). We can't just talk about effective teaching in general, with no regard to what we are teaching, to whom and in what situation.

Campbell *et al.* (2004) have recently developed what amounts to an expanded version of Passmore's analysis to take into account a range of differentiating factors in judging teaching effectiveness. Their five factors are:

- the range of role activities in modern school systems – instructional, but also social, pastoral, welfare and leadership of other adult personnel
- different subjects and components of subjects (e.g. algebra as opposed to number in mathematics)
- learner background factors: age, ability, sex, socio-economic status and ethnicity
- learner personality, cognitive style motivation, self-esteem
- cultural and organizational contexts (e.g. school size, urban/rural location)

They argue that we need this more differentiated concept of effectiveness if we are to develop a secure grasp of effective teaching. We need to specify for which set of factors we are making a claim for effectiveness.

It is certainly important to direct attention to such aspects; but there is surely also a danger of limiting conceptions of one's own role, capacity and abilities as a teacher – a danger of pigeon-holing oneself as a certain kind of teacher and not working to acquire the skills and qualities to teach other subjects, groups, and in different contexts. Campbell and his colleagues claim their differentiated model is important and useful for researching effective teaching. However, many studies have attempted to identify general features of all good teaching and the next chapter considers how far these have produced consistent and convincing findings.

What Sort of Activity is Teaching?

Is teaching best viewed as a science, an art, craft, skill, technology, moral practice or what? This question is important because it affects how we work as teachers, make decisions about teaching methods and how we think teaching should be researched and developed. Considering the various ideas that have emerged will help to build a deeper understanding of the professional context of modern teaching and the issues surrounding teaching roles.

In the background to discussions of teaching are issues of aims and values, the nature of education and the functions of schooling. As the left-hand column of Figure 1.1 indicates, many contextual factors and varying perspectives influence educational thinking and action. The right-hand column shows the contrasting conceptions of teaching that have emerged. These have a strong influence on how teachers approach their work. Debate concerning them continues.

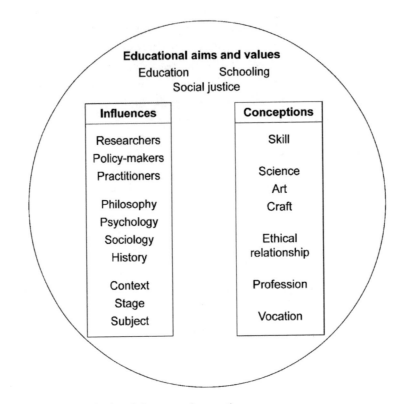

Figure 1.1 Teaching: aims and values, influences and conceptions

As far back as 1890, as psychology was emerging as a science, the father of modern psychology, William James, said that he saw psychology as having little direct application to the classroom because 'psychology is a science but teaching is an art' (James 1903: 7). However, with the rise of behaviourism in education (the idea that education could best be understood through systematic studies of stimulus and response and therefore of what teacher behaviours evoke what kinds of pupil responses) and experimental psychology, confidence grew that teaching could be studied through 'the science of human behaviour'. Cognitive psychology (emphasizing the activity and development of the mind, not just outward behaviour) eventually began to challenge behaviourism, and by the late 1970s the American psychologist Nathaniel Gage was writing about 'the scientific basis of the art of teaching'. His thesis was that while education was an art in the sense that teaching had to be adapted intelligently and with judgement to particular circumstances, underlying such judgements were certain regularities about teaching and learning which could be researched and established by systematic empirical studies (Gage 1978; see also Pring 2007a).

This view has come to be widely accepted by prominent writers on teaching and learning such as Alexander (2000) and Galton (2007). Many educational philosophers however, generally critical of behaviourism, continue to be wary and emphasize the importance of developing an inside understanding of teaching linked to a clear view of the nature of human actions and intentions (Carr 2003a; Pring 2007a). Woods (1996), from a social anthropology perspective on teaching – aiming to interpret classroom interactions in terms of the perceptions and beliefs of teachers and pupils in particular educational contexts – also advocates a more open conception. However, like Gage, such writers argue that, while teaching needs to take account of context, there are some similarities as well as unique aspects – some underlying generalizations about teaching that can be established; and these can and should inform the practice of the art (Pring 2007a).

Not unsurprisingly, educationists from the arts offer alternative views, though one should of course be wary of assuming artists are opposed to scientific knowledge and analysis. The art educationist, Eisner (1979: 153–4) argued that there are at least four senses in which teaching can be considered an art:

> teaching can be performed with such skill and grace that [...] the experience can be [...] characterized as aesthetic [...] teachers, like painters and composers, make judgements based largely on qualities that unfold during the course of action [...] the teacher's activity is not dominated by prescriptions or routines but [...] by qualities and contingencies [...] the ends it achieves are often created in process.

But Carr (1999) has pointed out there is a danger of stretching the analogy too far. Teaching is hardly a full-blown art in the sense of being an open and creative activity in which fantasy and imagination can be given full rein. For Alexander (2000: 274), viewing teaching as an art captures well the unpredictability and problematics of teaching, but he prefers to view it as a craft in Albert Morris's sense – an amalgam of the ethical, aesthetic and practical. Education certainly can be viewed as a craft involving intuition, openness to development through practice, creative mastery of technique, and awareness of context and children. A good analogy is Grimmett and Mackinnon's (1992: 388) account of a ship's captain:

> Whenever I needed to chart my course I pulled out my maps, followed the equations, and calculated my location with mathematical precision. Then I went up on the deck, listened to the wind in the rigging, got the drift of the sea, gazed at a star, and corrected my computations.

Alexander concludes that in practical action teaching has elements of both art and science, but in conception and planning it is a science, which draws also on the collective craft knowledge of teachers. He argues that in England policy-makers have tended to focus on common sense and what works, but operate with a restricted definition of science and of 'what works', conceiving science as implying, centrally, large-scale 'randomized controlled trials' of teaching methods like those used to test drugs in the medical field – an approach which has been hotly debated (Thomas and Pring 2004; Hammersley 2007). Alexander takes a more continental view of science as a systematic body of knowledge, researched in a manner suited to the nature of its particular subject matter, and hence not necessarily based on a physical science model.

Many educational researchers see teaching as an applied science in the sense of a rational activity directed towards certain goals and operating on the basis of evidence, but also emphasize that, in applying research findings, we need judgement to fit the particular context since more variables will be in action than in carefully controlled research studies.

The applied science approach, however, can quickly lead to thinking of teaching as a technology. There are many critics of this so-called 'technicist' view in the field of education, on conceptual and principled grounds. Teaching, it is pointed out, is greatly impoverished and distorted if it is viewed as a mere technology, involving a set of mechanical skills; and this brings us to the question: is teaching a skill?

The problem is that the word 'skill' in now used in a very wide range of senses. Barrow (1990) notes that it has become the generic term for knowledge, understanding, mental capacity, practical competence and interpersonal sensitivity. It is a mistake, he claims, to think of all goal-directed activities as skills. They require understanding and appropriate dispositions, not just practice. Carr (2003a) concurs. Teaching, he argues, is not basically a technical notion, though some aspects can be improved through practice and research evidence; teaching is an intentional activity. Like education, it is more and less than an activity; it is not best regarded as a technical process and can't be reduced to supposedly value-neutral skills and competences. There is a central ethical dimension to teaching and many issues teachers face in classrooms are ethical dilemmas and matters of principled professional judgement.

Teachers need to reflect on teaching, Carr suggests, as an occupational role as well as an activity, taking account of the fact that a teacher has wider professional duties than teaching. Many educational writers promote teaching as a profession, hoping thus to raise standards and the status of the role. Carr urges some caution. He sees teaching as a uniquely complex activity that combines different characteristics of professions, vocations and traditional white-collar service occupations. Teaching involves a wider kind of expertise (requiring sensitive judgement, principled reflection and interpersonal sensibility) than professions based largely on systematic and scientific knowledge (Carr and Skinner 2009) and, at least for early stages of education, seems thus more like the work of nurses, priests and social workers than like law and medicine with their traditionally more impersonal professional–client relationships.

Insights from Philosophy, Psychology and Sociology

In seeking to teach well, teachers can draw not only on professional craft knowledge developed from their teaching experience but also on educational research and thinking involving a range of academic disciplines. The main ones are philosophy, psychology and sociology, though historical and comparative studies, anthropology and economics also have much to offer. One problem, however, with perspectives from the disciplines is that teachers are faced with so many competing disciplines, and several competing schools within each discipline. How can the ordinary teacher be expected to grasp all these, decide among them and use their insights to make decisions about teaching and learning?

It is often tempting to reject all such 'theory' and resort to common sense or 'what works in practice'. This won't do, however. For a start, there is no agreement here either. Moreover, 'common sense' often turns out to be just yesterday's theory or some dubious 'folk psychology' (Bruner 1996) and 'what works' inevitably entails some theory and perspective which can be challenged. When, for example, should children begin learning to read? Some kind of theory about the nature and aims of teaching reading and reliable evidence are surely required. Yet, while Piaget's ideas about reading readiness were widely accepted in the 1960s and 70s, now they are considered mistaken. Similarly, attitudes to aspects of teaching such as 'look and say' versus phonics in reading instruction, mental mathematics, collaborative group work and whole-class teaching have all changed significantly over recent decades.

Practising teachers' ideas about the aims and methods of teaching reading are not merely practical ones. Like many policy ideas, they are based, consciously or not, on conceptions and theories often reflecting now discredited ideas from the past, in the same way that J.M. Keynes (1935) suggested that economic policies are often based on defunct economic theory. We need therefore to be ready to use the range of insights available from various disciplines while maintaining a critical scrutiny of evidence, ideas and underlying assumptions. A wide perspective on the nature and aims of education and schooling is also required, avoiding narrow dogma.

Teachers, however, are constrained by the need to act, and cannot endlessly debate such issues. Fortunately, research results, policies and theoretical backgrounds are now communicated in a much more user-friendly way for practising teachers. But the need to maintain a critical stance remains and there is no avoiding some difficult ideas and problematic aspects of securing and interpreting evidence. Moreover, the issues can't be left to experts or policy-makers who just tell teachers what to do. This is because the ideas behind practices need to be properly understood if new developments are to be used successfully. They can't be successfully put into practice without understanding because they need to be applied with judgement and flexibility. They are not mere technical skills with routine applications.

Similar reversals of practice are common in other disciplines (consider, for instance, medical changes in treatment of heart conditions and stroke over recent decades). Complex fields like education and medicine develop through further research and theorizing as well as through practical initiatives. Contexts change, resulting in new priorities, and new understandings and techniques emerge. Moreover, ideas and practices are subject to inertia, rigid and dogmatic thinking, fashion and political swings. Part of teaching professionalism is becoming aware of these forces and factors and learning to live with them, while seeking a principled, viable and realistic way forward. Adopting a wide perspective can be helpful here (while still focusing clearly) as can being prepared to develop one's stance through further study, critical reflection on experience and collaborative professional development. Education will continue to be complex and raise various issues as practice, policy and research develop in the context of the continuing explosion of knowledge, globalization and other social and economic changes. Responding imaginatively to these is the modern professional challenge for education and teaching and what makes teaching a worthwhile and fascinating field, with an important contribution to human flourishing.

Reflective Exploration 1.2 – Conceptions of Teaching

Try to identify activities or incidents in your teaching that appear to fit the notion of teaching as:

- a skill
- a craft
- an art
- a science
- an ethical practice

With which conception of teaching do you at present feel most comfortable? On further reflection, do you think you should develop your approach to particular teaching activities to give more emphasis to other aspects – for example, to make it more of an art or more of a science, or to conceive it less as a technical skill and more as an ethical relationship or moral practice? What specific changes in your teaching would this imply?

Psychology

Psychology has long been seen as providing teachers with knowledge about how children learn, the operation of memory, attention and thinking; and as offering insight into children's perspectives on the world, their concerns, interests, motivations and relationships.

To teach primary or secondary learners well, teachers need to be able to observe them carefully in the light of a general awareness of developmental patterns and issues, and theories of learning, and come to understand the various influences on their lives and on the attitudes and abilities learners display in class. It is also important to recognize that they are rapidly developing as persons and are learning a great deal outside school as well as in, and that this can have a big effect on their behaviour and functioning in school.

Another important insight from psychological studies is just how much learner behaviour in the classroom depends on the teacher's own behaviour – how teachers interact with learners. For instance, while a teacher (or parent) responding to a child's work with negative criticism only will demotivate the child, indiscriminate praise will not, in the end, prove effective either. But positive, specific praise offered in an open and non-patronizing way will give the child confidence to try new things, not afraid of making mistakes, and to improve performance (Fontana 1995). Though this may seem common sense, the fact is that the first two are by far the most typical responses to children by parents (even well-educated ones) and teachers (even experienced ones). Research like this has uncovered many fruitful strategies teachers can use in interaction with children and has demonstrated that problems might not lie only with the child (see e.g. Dweck 2007).

Psychological research studies have also cast light on how children acquire concepts and skills across the range of curriculum subjects, misconceptions they may develop, difficulties in learning they may experience, the effects on self-esteem, beliefs about intelligence and the role of social factors in learning.

Philosophy

One key role of philosophical thinking is to make ideas clear and explicit, looking critically at the evidence, assumptions behind policies, theories underlying current practice and the logic of arguments. It can influence practice by ensuring assumptions about teaching and learning are tenable and coherent. Often they are not. We live in a world of ideas that shape our practices in many ways. Many questions arise about what we can sensibly mean by learning styles or multiple intelligences, or active learning – in fact about most of the currently influential ideas and educational concepts. Philosophers have a role in pointing up where educational aims and values are contested, where conceptions of teaching and learning are too narrow, and where the very language of educational research proposals limits and distorts the evidence on which the research depends (e.g. Carr 2003a; Pring 2007a).

Educational philosophers along with others have been severely critical of one psychological school, behaviourism, as a theory of human learning, of key aspects of Piaget's theory of stages (as now have many psychologists), and have criticized some fashionable writings on ideas like self-esteem and emotional intelligence (for not acknowledging the contested value implications of the supposed skills of emotional interaction).

Sociology

Sociology is able to offer teachers a wealth of insights into the teacher's role and issues facing schools and society today. Sociological studies of classroom interaction have uncovered how negative teacher expectations can affect pupil performance by becoming self-fulfilling prophecies. They have also demonstrated the unconscious socialization into particular norms and values (linked to class and economic ideologies) through curriculum and teaching methods from nursery schooling upward. Other studies have investigated the ways in which learning tasks are interpreted and negotiated by learners (Doyle 1986) and the various roles teachers and learners can adopt in the classroom 'theatre'. Philip Jackson's classic *Life in Classrooms* (1968) illustrated well the social realities of classroom life. There are broad analyses of the role of educational assessment in society, how it reinforces class divisions, provides differentiation of the workforce and social status, and its effects on curriculum and teaching (Broadfoot 2007) and how learners experience it in classrooms (Filer and Pollard 2000). Sociologists have also painted a rather different picture of childhood from the one which has emerged from psychology, suggesting that development is generally much less individually determined (e.g. Austin *et al.* 2003; Mayall 2003).

There are also more fundamental critiques of the roles of schools in society, of patterns of schooling and of government polices on performance management, curriculum control, bias in relation to class, race, gender, disability and so on (Apple and Beane 2007). These issues need to be taken into account if educational aims and wider goals for education and social transformation are to be realized. Of course, sociological theories themselves entail assumptions about the nature of knowledge, human action and the social world in which we live; and many of these have received sustained critique from within other disciplines such as philosophy and theology (e.g. Milbank 2006).

Practitioners, Researchers and Policy-makers

Recent developments in teaching and learning have shown how important it is to have close collaboration between educational researchers, policy-makers and practitioners. This may seem obvious, but it has not generally been the way educational research, policy and practice have evolved. More typical has been the isolation of each community, each with its own priorities, perspectives and discourses, or languages of communication. These communities have valued different kinds or aspects of educational knowledge. It has been too easy for each group to assume that its perspective is the really crucial one. The result has been that teachers have complained about the apparent lack of clear teaching implications from many research studies and their lack of attention to central concerns of classroom teachers. Researchers have complained about the interference of policy-makers in the autonomy of the research process, the narrow treatment of findings and their expectation of policy-supporting results. Policy-makers have questioned the relevance to policy of much funded research and sought to control teacher performance towards central policy initiatives and priorities.

Yet, clearly, all have a legitimate role in the development of effective teaching and learning and the issue is what kind of collaboration is likely to achieve the best results. In recent years, moves have been made to develop closer collaborative working (Thomas and Pring 2004; Cassidy *et al.* 2008), to communicate better and to involve teachers in consideration of research priorities, in research itself and at the implementation stage of policy development. Some multi-disciplinary communities of educational enquiry have been formed. It is not easy to establish or sustain these collaborations, or to ensure space not only for applied but also for pure research, so crucial for fundamental understanding which can eventually lead to improved practice (Hammersley 2002; Munn 2008). The years ahead are likely to see even closer collaboration, electronic and otherwise, with increasing involvement in policy formation and research,. More account is likely to be taken by research of actual classroom conditions as well as innovative developments (Baines *et al.* 2007; Alexander 2008c), building the capacity of teachers and others to understand and use research results (Munn 2008) and to understand and become involved in policy-making. All this is a challenge for all three communities.

Education, Schooling and Social Justice

Philosophers like Carr (2003b) suggest that one route to better thinking about teaching issues is to make a clear distinction between education and schooling. Briefly, 'schooling' is a term for what goes on in schools. Some of this might be, and much of it clearly should be, broadly 'educational' in aim. But schools also have other aims like socialization, childcare, development of the economic workforce and functions such as certification and selection for further training and occupational roles. Schooling in this sense is clearly important. By contrast, 'education' involves being introduced to activities with their own intrinsic value, with an emphasis on understanding and cultivating broad intellectual and other perspectives. Many teachers and educationists see themselves as engaged in a constant struggle to direct teachers and policy-makers to these issues and values. Educational thinking, they argue, should not be reduced to the mechanical interpretation of standards, pursued through a narrow set of technical teaching skills, focused essentially on preparation for economic roles. Balancing and reconciling the claims of education and schooling is problematic but the conceptual distinction can at least help clarify the issues.

A major thrust of both recent government policy and theoretical debate and research concerns the school's role in promoting social justice (Carr 2003a; Lingard *et al.* 2003). Writers like Lingard argue that teachers, recognizing the extent of injustice in society, need to consider what part schools and teachers can play as social change agents. This means interrupting the cycles of oppression, challenging them and developing effective strategies to counter injustice in schooling processes as well as contributing through the process of education and schooling to higher attainments for all – irrespective of class, race, gender, disability and so on. Schools, it is pointed out, routinely, and often unconsciously, reinforce discrimination through curriculum, teaching approaches, interactions and casual talk with learners.

Teachers will want to take steps to inform themselves, to understand how injustice operates, and to seek practical ways in class interactions to realize equality aims and support marginalized groups. This implies an awareness of peer interactions among learners and clarifying and following through what a commitment to social justice should mean in school contexts. As various sociological studies have demonstrated (e.g. those of Bourdieu, Bernstein and Foucault – see Palmer 2001), schooling does not take place in a social vacuum and schools tend to reproduce inequalities and disadvantages. Moreover, as Freire (1970) emphasized, teaching is always a political act, never a neutral one.

The point most relevant here (Lingard *et al.* 2003) is that pedagogy – teaching interactions and their underlying assumptions – is a social justice issue. While there are major social forces, in and outside schools, at work making for inequality, teachers can make a decided difference, playing a positive role in promoting social justice. Keddie and Mills (2007) provide detailed examples of possibilities here in relation to gender justice, showing how equity concerns, interactive strategies, educational aims and social values and conceptions of gendered equality intermingle in producing teaching that is either helpful or unhelpful in this area. Attention to more 'productive pedagogies' (see Chapter 10) involving practical changes to teaching approaches and interactions can make a real difference to the way learners are treated by peers and teachers, to their educational opportunities, and can reduce feelings of being devalued, ridiculed, threatened and abused.

Another relevant question needs to be asked here. Is good or effective teaching effective teaching for all, or do particular needs require particular specialist approaches? In contrast to some past thinking, the modern trend is to highlight the commonalities of all good teaching for all learners while also acknowledging that for particular disabilities some specialist teaching approaches or adaptations will also be crucial (Lewis and Norwich 2005; Daniels and Porter 2007).

Summary

This book offers ideas, evidence and practical suggestions for effective teaching and learning across the whole range of the school system. The intensely practical nature of teaching as a professional activity needs to be recognized; the craft knowledge of practising teachers is an important source for understanding what makes for effective teaching and the need to adapt teaching to particular contexts. Effectiveness, however, needs to be considered in a wide framework of educational ideas, aims and values, including issues of social justice. Different disciplines – mainly philosophy, psychology and sociology – can illuminate teaching issues; each makes a different, though sometimes an overlapping and sometimes an apparently conflicting, contribution.

Systematic research has an important role in developing understanding and evidence about what kinds of teaching can be effective. Teaching is likely to be advanced if researchers, policy-makers and practitioners collaborate more closely, recognizing each other's legitimate perspectives and roles in researching teaching issues, building policies and developing classroom practice.

Teaching is as much an art or craft as a science; and it is much more than a mere set of skills, even in a wide sense of 'skill': it is a moral enterprise. It also has an important role in promoting social justice through skilled, insightful and principled teaching interactions. As an occupational role it has many aspects of a profession but also of a vocation. Practising teachers need to consider, aims, values and the claims of 'education' in a wide sense as well as of 'schooling' – which has legitimate functions, such as selection, other than 'education'.

Key Reading

Alexander, R. (2000) *Culture and Pedagogy.* Oxford: Blackwell.

Carr, D. (2003) *Making Sense of Education.* London: RoutledgeFalmer.

Keddie, A. and Mills, M. (2007) 'Teaching for gender justice', *Australian Journal of Education,* 51(2): 205–19.

Passmore, J. (1980) *The Philosophy of Teaching.* London: Duckworth.

Pring, R. (2004) *Philosophy of Education.* London: Continuum.

Slater, A. and Bremner, G. (2004) *An Introduction to Developmental Psychology.* Oxford: Blackwell.

Thomas, G. and Pring, R. (2004) *Evidence-based Policy in Education.* London: Routledge.

Useful Websites

www.primaryreview.org.uk

Website of the recent independent review of primary education in England. Many useful practice, policy and research reviews.

www.education.qld.gov.au/corporate/newbasics/

Website for Queensland's innovative New Basics curriculum reform. Papers and classroom examples.

www.curriculumforexcellencescotland.gov.uk

Website for the 3–18 curriculum framework in Scotland. Curriculum reform documentation and links to revised classroom practice.

2 Making Sense of Teaching and Learning

Chapter Outline

How do Teachers Normally see Teaching?   18
Research on Teaching Styles and Strategies   20
Are there Common Features in all Good Teaching?   21
The Idea of Teaching Modes   23
Learning Styles   27
A Note on Teaching Style   29
Summary   30
Key Reading   31
Useful Websites   32

How do Teachers Normally see Teaching?

Teaching and learning are varied and complex. There are different contexts, subjects, learners, teachers and educational aims. While it is important to keep alert to this variety and complexity, it is equally important to find some simple but powerful way of making sense of teaching and learning. Yet the more research has been conducted into what is effective, and the more ideas have been developed, the more complex the issues have appeared. There is no consensus even on the most suitable overall framework for thinking about teaching and learning. It may be useful, therefore, to begin our review of possibilities by considering research on how teachers generally see teaching.

Brown and McIntyre (1993) found that a sample of secondary and primary teachers tended to think about classroom teaching in terms of three main aspects:

- normal desirable states of activity
- progress
- conditions

Normal desirable states of pupil activity (e.g. working well independently or listening carefully to the teacher, participating sensibly in the lesson) varied according to the stage of a lesson and the teacher's classroom style preferences. They were states that had to be established and maintained and could not be taken for granted.

In addition to these normal desirable states, teachers all tended to have expectations of desirable progress in terms of developing knowledge, skills and some sort of product (perhaps a completed exercise or performance). Finally, the teachers were aware of factors that could affect the work of learners and modify teacher expectations, for example if a pupil proved very shy, or if it was a Friday afternoon.

This is a valuable perspective but a caveat is necessary. What teachers currently do or did in the 1990s is not necessarily the most desirable practice, then or today. For example, Brown and McIntyre found teachers gave little attention to clarifying learning outcomes, a finding which reinforced those of Clark and Yinger (1987) in the USA. More recent research and policy development, however, has emphasized the value of having clear learning outcomes and sharing these with learners (Black *et al.* 2003). In open and creative learning contexts, admittedly, too precise a specification and too strong a focus on outcomes may be unhelpful (Howard-Jones *et al.* 2008). But, generally, having and sharing clear outcomes is now widely recognized by theorists, researchers and teachers as central to effective teaching, being linked to a deeper understanding of how learners learn, at least in many contexts. Teachers everywhere are now normally expected to share intended learning outcomes appropriately with learners. Relying solely on standard craft knowledge is not the best way to develop teaching; research and theory also make an important contribution.

Teachers will inevitably need to develop further understanding, teaching skills and strategies as research and development challenge current practice. There is much more to think about than the three aspects identified in Brown and McIntyre's study. Merely becoming socialized in schools into a natural pattern of thinking about teaching is no longer defensible, though it will always be essential to base teaching on classroom realities, addressed with educational imagination.

Aims and values

Judgements about context

Teaching strategies and skills   Effective teaching and learning

Subject knowledge

Environment for learning

Figure 2.1 Factors influencing conceptions and realization of effective teaching

> Conceptions of effective teaching depend very much on aims and values. Within any given conception, effectiveness depends on teaching strategies and skills, subject knowledge and the ability to develop a suitable environment for learning.

Research on Teaching Styles and Strategies

One early influential research study (Bennett 1976) compared traditional and progressive (or 'child-centred') teaching approaches in primary schools. It began by working with a spectrum of 12 different styles or strategies ranging from very traditional to very progressive. The difficulty of making such fine distinctions among teachers' approaches led the researchers to reduce their categories to three groups – 'traditional', 'progressive' and 'mixed' (Entwistle 1981). Bennett found that children in formal (traditional teaching) classrooms made more progress in mathematics and language than those in informal (progressive) ones, though some of the best results came from an informal classroom with a well organized, experienced teacher who devoted considerable time to these subjects. It also appeared that formal teaching was more helpful for anxious children.

A study of classroom interaction styles (Galton and Simon 1980) in English primary schools isolated four main approaches: class and group enquirers, group instructors and individual monitors. Galton's research findings, like those in other similar studies, inevitably relate to particular times, contexts and policy developments; but they were very usefully followed up over a 20-year period (Galton *et al.* 1999). The 1980 study found that the most effective interactive teaching occurred in whole-class discussions. But in recent years, following the introduction of the National Curriculum in England, it is precisely this – whole-class discussion – that has been considered to be of low quality and in need of radical improvement (see Chapter 4).

A general and lasting insight that did emerge from Galton's research was the poverty of teaching interactions in classes with complicated group organizations. These were dominated by managerial interactions at the expense of instructional ones. However, in the end the debate between traditional and progressive teaching proved to be as much about aims and values as about the effectiveness of different methods for reaching the same goals; and both Bennett's and Galton's research served to show the complexity of teaching issues.

This point is further reinforced in the scheme developed by Joyce and Weil (1986). Joyce (1978) claimed that in the research literature over 80 different teaching strategies could be detected. Joyce and Weil advocated thinking in terms of distinct models of teaching and provided an account of 20 models, grouped into four main families (behavioural, information processing, personal and social) reflecting their underlying learning theories. For effective teaching a basic repertoire of six to eight models was recommended and it was envisaged teachers would later expand significantly on this. This 'model of teaching' approach has not been taken up to any great extent by researchers, other theorists or practitioners (though see Hopkins 2007; Harris 1998; DfES 2007). The large number of models is perhaps one negative factor. Another is that the family groupings seem little help in decision-making and Dillon (1998) has queried the compatibility of different models. Moreover, the models relate to varied levels of practice; some are general principles, others specific techniques. They do, however, emphasize that there is not just one best way to teach.

Are there Common Features in all Good Teaching?

A model for general teacher effectiveness was developed by the Hay McBer consultancy in 2001 on behalf of policy-makers in England (Hay McBer 2001). Effective teachers, it claimed, could be found in all kinds of schools and had diverse backgrounds, ages and qualifications. The rationale was that if the practice of effective teachers could be analysed and broken down into specific, describable behaviours then these could be modelled, taught, learned and practised.

The model claimed that effective teaching involved three interacting dimensions, all within the teacher's control and all affecting pupil progress:

- teaching skills
- professional characteristics of the teacher
- classroom climate

Each of these dimensions was further differentiated in the model. Professional characteristics, for example, were divided into five clusters (professionalism, thinking, planning and setting expectations, leading, relating to others) of 16 traits. Classroom climate was said to involve clarity of purpose, order, clear standards, fairness, opportunities to participate, emotional support, safety, a perception of the classroom as an interesting place and a comfortable environment.

Pollard (2002) argued that the Hay McBer model was context-bound. Perhaps it was appropriate for English education in 2000 with its centralized national curriculum and legally defined assessment procedures, but more open systems and less well-resourced ones might have different requirements. Rapid changes in technology and policies might also affect the model's validity. Questions were also raised by research bodies (BERA 2001) about the nature and methodology of the research and criteria underlying the model, and its link to performativity developments.

Borich (2006: 9–19), reviewing a range of American research studies over the last few decades, points out that five teaching behaviours have shown consistent evidence of being correlated with high pupil attainments. These are:

- lesson clarity (use of examples, stating learning outcomes)
- instructional variety (using questions, not just direct exposition)
- teacher focus on the learning task (as opposed to pupil management)
- engagement in the learning process (time on task)
- student success rate (the extent to which learners complete tasks)

Mortimore's 1988 British survey (Muijs and Reynolds 2005: 3) identified the importance of a focus on curriculum, interaction with learners, amply challenging work, a positive atmosphere, praise and encouragement and structured teaching.

The question that arises from such studies is how far they point to common features of all good teaching and how far they merely identify effective direct teaching as opposed to weak enquiry, unfocused discussion and badly organized activity methods or project work. In the absence of detailed evidence this question remains open. It is an important one, however, as the discussion of teaching modes below will hopefully make clear.

The Teaching and Learning Research Programme (James and Pollard 2006) in England recently distilled from its research studies ten teaching principles. These are that effective teaching and learning:

- equips pupils for life in its broadest sense
- engages with valued forms of knowledge
- recognizes the importance of prior learning and experience
- requires teachers to scaffold learning
- needs assessment to be congruent with learning
- promotes active engagement of the learners
- fosters both individual and social processes and outcomes
- recognizes the significance of informal learning
- depends on teacher learning
- demands consistent policy frameworks with support for teaching and learning as their primary focus

This mix of aims and principles, supported in various ways by research, is likely to find wide acceptance. What stand out are the emphasis on teacher learning, the role of informal learning in schools, and teacher support.

To sum up, there may be some sense in the notion that all good teaching has some common features (possibly such as being well prepared, focused and enthusiastic), though as soon as any are suggested exceptions come to mind. However, national curricula have a wide range of aims and it is unlikely there is one best method or teaching strategy to realize them. Other, surely misguided, assumptions are that there exists some generalized approach for each curriculum subject ('This is how we should teach art or literacy or religious education …') or that some particular theoretical stance (one of the varieties of constructivism, say – see Chapter 6) needs to be the starting point of discussions about teaching. Teaching is more complex and varied than early studies suggested and 'one best way' solutions (which keep appearing) are unlikely to prove satisfactory.

Teaching Development Activity 2.1 – Classroom Climate

Consider the various aspects of classroom climate (in the sense discussed above) that at present characterize your teaching context. How would you like to improve it and which aspects are open to your action? Make the necessary changes. Observe the reactions of your learners to the new climate and any changes in the quality of their learning.

The Idea of Teaching Modes

In the light of the above discussion, it can be argued that the teaching profession at the present time needs a simple and flexible classification of teaching that is both theoretically powerful and practically useful. The theory of teaching modes, which provides the main framework for the analysis in this book, arguably meets these criteria. The key idea is that there are some fundamentally different kinds of teaching and that understanding and recognizing these differences is crucial to understanding modern teaching roles.

The theory claims that four basic modes (forms or structures) of teaching and learning can be distinguished. These might best be labelled:

- direct teaching
- teaching through dialogue and discussion
- learning through action and experience
- learning through enquiry

In this view, the effective teacher is someone who has a mastery of each mode – a clear grasp of their differing requirements and the ability to deploy them in a skilful, balanced and flexible way.

Each mode entails a different 'means of learning' and this central difference leads to other characteristic differences in:

- organization and resources
- teacher and learner roles
- teaching skills
- typical assessment

These features are what distinguish one mode from another.

Thinking about a learning activity in terms of mode directs attention first to the particular means of learning involved; and a teacher can then switch quickly into characteristic organization, resources, teacher and learner roles, specific teaching skills and appropriate assessment procedures. Moving to another mode for another learning activity typically requires changes in all these five aspects.

Two features of the modes theory make it immediately worthy of attention. First, it is valid at the level of common sense. According to Powell (1985) there are, at root, four basic ways of learning something:

- having something explained directly
- by reason and argument
- by direct experience
- finding out for ourselves

In short, the four modes identified above. Secondly, all four modes have deep roots in the history of education, for example in the standard range of teaching approaches in higher education:

- lectures
- seminars
- practicals
- projects and dissertations

Once more these are, essentially, the four modes.

The theory of teaching modes does not deny that all effective teaching may have some common characteristics, but it focuses on the differences between the various approaches. To teach effectively it is important to understand just how different are teaching roles, means of learning and so on from mode to mode. There is also a need to learn to switch roles, organization, assessment tasks and so on as teaching moves from one mode to another. One of the problems in recent years has been the tendency to carry over the norms, assumptions and techniques of direct teaching to modes like discussion and enquiry. Another is to fail to recognize, say during whole-class interactive teaching, when one is in direct teaching mode – presenting ideas, informing, explaining and checking understanding – and when one is undertaking a whole-class discussion which requires quite different skills and interactive moves (see Chapters 3 and 4).

The value of the modes theory

The modes theory is simple, powerful, balanced and open. It is admirably simple in the sense that we have to come to terms with only four modes not six, or 12 styles or 17 models. But it is also powerful in that it gets to the heart of the decisions teachers need to make – about aims, teaching and learning roles, assessment and so on. These are quickly brought into a single perspective; for example, assessment strategies can be quickly checked for consistency with other features of the particular mode.

Moreover, it is clearly a balanced theory. It does not say there is one best way to teach, nor does it try to arbitrate between traditional direct teaching and progressive open enquiry, or between instruction and construction. It gives both a clear and valuable role. The effective teacher needs to deploy all four modes in a balanced way to meet the range of contexts, subjects (and their different aspects) and teaching aims. It is also an open theory, open to development in response to further thinking and research. In education, the arts and social sciences, ideas are more open, contested and problematic than we may at first assume or are initially comfortable with. Learning to think about teaching and education precisely involves coming to terms with this complexity, while using powerful but inherently open and often problematic ideas to help make sense of teaching. In a related context, Stenhouse (1975: 85–6) offered the analogy that historians and students of history use concepts like cause and revolution to understand, say, the origins of the First World War or the French Revolution and, in doing so, they come to understand more deeply concepts like cause and revolution and their complexities.

'Mode' is also different from 'class organization' (whole-class, group or individual teaching); it is much more than a means of grouping learners. Class organization has sometimes been used as the basis of various classifications of teaching (in higher education, 'small-group teaching' is a common category) but grouping is a separate issue from the basic means of learning that is the key to differences between modes. Collaborative group work, for example, could involve, as its essential mode, enquiry, action learning or dialogue and discussion. Similarly, whole-class teaching could be direct teaching or a class discussion or, if very carefully planned, a short, whole-class enquiry. Thinking that small group work (or even collaborative group work) is all of a piece fails to recognize the most important differences among forms of teaching.

The theory of teaching modes was first articulated by Arnold Morrison (Peacock 1990), was further developed by the present author (Skinner 1994, 2005) and has had some recognition in official Scottish educational policy documents since the 1980s. Teaching mode is not yet a commonly used term outside Scotland but it does relate to ideas which can be found in a range of books and articles on enquiry methods, action learning and teaching through discussion (e.g. Pring 1976; Dillon 1988; Beard and Wilson 2006) and is discernable in various general discussions of teaching (e.g. Wragg and Brown 1993; Petty 2004). Alexander (2008a) has recently emphasized the variety of teaching within an overall analysis of 'dialogic teaching' (see Chapter 4), focused on classroom talk as the basis for learning. The modes theory is offered here as a further step in the development of a suitably comprehensive framework, taking account of key features of experiential and enquiry learning other than talk.

A longstanding problem is that it has proved very difficult at any level to move far away from direct teaching approaches and traditional assumptions about roles and procedures. This may relate closely to concerns about teacher control of learning, reinforced by pressures from pre-set outcomes based on National Curriculum targets and reaction against some excesses of progressive education. The modes theory offers a way forward.

Each of the four modes is considered in the chapters that follow, using the five differentiating features noted above. This should help to point up their distinctive aspects, what it means to teach using them, and what issues call for further study and research.

The analogy with forms in the arts

Since a teaching mode is a form or structure of teaching, an analogy with forms or genres in the arts might help. In literature it has proved useful to distinguish modes (or forms or genres) like tragedy, comedy, romance and so on. In music there are different forms such as fugue, sonata and rondo. Not all music is the same, nor is all literature. Nor is all teaching: there are distinct forms and these operate in quite different ways.

Stenhouse (1977: 239) argued that teaching 'at its best is an improvisation on a form, the form structured by theory'. He maintained that, to realize their educational aims, teachers would need to experiment with a range of teaching forms; and in the Humanities Curriculum Project (Stenhouse 1975) he developed the teacher's role as a neutral chairman for the discussion of controversial issues with secondary school learners. A key point is that forms in the arts are not static (as, for example, the extraordinary development of the piano concerto under Mozart or by other composers since his time amply demonstrates) and nor should they be in teaching. They need to be deployed creatively and develop as educational ideas as contexts change. In Chapter 3 we will see this clearly in relation to direct teaching.

Alexander (2000, 2008b) has developed this analogy in detail, drawing especially on musical form ('music [...] is a performance in time and teaching, like music, is performance'). Alexander (2000: 315–18) views lessons as 'planned performances in culture and pedagogy' and highlights the importance of trying to see the whole as well as the parts. He points out that 'it is the act of submitting to but then testing the disciplines and boundaries of forms to and beyond their apparent limits that unites some of the greatest composers, writers and painters'.

In teaching, while there is an important place for pure forms or modes – for example a sustained, open discussion of an educationally worthwhile topic – many units of teaching clearly involve a mix of modes; and at the border one mode may shade into another. Many of the important educational questions arise by working at such boundaries between forms. At times it will be possible to view a piece of teaching as either, say, enquiry or as learning through action and experience; or indeed both – if for instance the enquiry is pursued through trial and error.

Some think that because of such difficulties or because, at the borderline, it is difficult to distinguish, say, question and answer (in direct teaching) from discussion (a different mode), the theory falls down. But consider for instance Shakespeare's play, *The Winter's Tale*, which has elements of tragedy and comedy (and indeed romance and pastoral) without making the idea of dramatic modes redundant. The modes are very helpful in understanding plays, perhaps particularly where plays are a mix of several modes. Drama, like teaching, is complex. The same point could be made about musical forms. To appreciate Mozart's *Jupiter* symphony it helps to understand the interplay of fugue and sonata form. Mozart certainly needed to understand them to decide what would best serve his intentions with the symphony.

Recently, it has become clear that the idea of the lesson (traditionally the main unit of planning and analysis) requires reconsideration. The idea of teaching modes can help here. In England's National Literacy and Numeracy Strategies, whole-class interactive teaching is structured into distinct phases and these seem to imply different modes. Muijs and Reynolds (2005: 67) suggest one possibly useful structure for 'constructivist' lessons: start phase, exploration phase, reflection phase, application and discussion phase. This still bears a clear resemblance to the traditional five-phase direct teaching lesson whose roots clearly lie in the nineteenth century in Herbart's famous five steps of traditional teaching: preparation, presentation, association, generalization, application (Lawton and Gordon 2002: 206).

But once the modes conception is taken to heart, all sorts of possible combinations emerge for planning units of work. For example, there is no need for direct teaching to come first, before active work. In some science units an enquiry phase may prove the best start but there need be no set pattern, centrally approved or promoted. Consider the review phase of a unit in terms of teaching modes. Is it conceived as an open discussion, direct teaching in which the teacher summarizes key points, an active reflective presentation by a group of learners, or some mix of these? Thinking in terms of teaching modes can give power and direction to planning and interacting. A standard lesson structure of introduction, development and conclusion seems impoverished by comparison. Different units of work of different lengths and different combinations of modes can be envisaged to suit varied educational contexts and purposes.

Learning Styles

This has been a key theme in recent staff development and classroom practice, taken up enthusiastically in many quarters. However, strong criticism has now been made by educationists and researchers, including neuroscientists. The research and evidence basis for these popular developments has been shown to be deeply suspect, and the practical advice and ensuing practice unsound in logic and educational principle. Yet the question of learning styles is undoubtedly a very important aspect of learning and teaching and needs to be thought through.

Consider first the idea of learning style, which we can define as a habitual, preferred way of approaching a learning task. Are styles in this sense inborn, fixed, strong preferences or can you readily change your approach to suit circumstances? Research studies (Entwistle 1981) suggest that individuals do have strong, and apparently deep-rooted, preferences about how they approach a learning task or activity. Given a free rein, different people approach the same task in quite distinct ways, whether it be making sense of a textbook, tackling a mathematical problem or constructing an essay. The concept of learning styles emerged from earlier work on cognitive styles – preferred ways of processing information – and the terms are often used interchangeably. Two well established differences are between verbalizers and imagers, and between holists and analysts. Verbalizers prefer to use words to think and describe. Imagers prefer pictures. Holists like to see the big picture first and work towards a conclusion from there. Analysts like to start with the detail and consider it bit by bit, gradually building up a picture of the whole area. One can often recognize one's own style when one finds oneself working on a task with someone who is the opposite.

Each approach has advantages and disadvantages. Holists see the whole wood, not just the trees, but can miss important detail and jump to conclusions on an overall impression. Analysts can get bogged down in fragmented detail, but they can eventually build a well-integrated, comprehensive understanding. Such preferences appear to be independent of gender, intelligence and personality. Some have very strong preferences and find it difficult to work in another mode. Others seem to be able to switch more easily as the occasion demands, even though they have a preferred style.

Styles in this sense differ from particular management strategies one might turn on to suit circumstances, such as a sensitive 'softly, softly' approach to interaction as opposed to a formal, imperious commanding style (de Bono 1991), though natural strengths and preferences may exist here also.

The early systematic research in cognitive style, one source of the development of thinking about learning styles, showed how complex, intellectually demanding and difficult to research this area is – not one to yield easily to research probes or policy pronouncements, and promising no immediate practical policy advice (Entwistle and Peterson 2004).

These considerations, however, were swamped in teaching circles in recent years by assertions from advocates of accelerated learning. A key claim (see Sharp *et al.* 2006) was that learners could be classified as having one of three learning style preferences:

- visual
- auditory
- kinaesthetic

It was assumed that learners, including young children, could be readily and reliably measured in relation to what were commonly referred to as their 'VAK' preferences and that teachers should adapt teaching to match each child's preferred learning style. Staff development materials (often highly commericalized) spread rapidly.

In fact (as with 'thinking skills' – see Chapter 8) an extraordinary range of classifications of learning styles has emerged. One study (Coffield *et al.* 2004) noted over 70. It is obviously very difficult for practising teachers to decide among these. More illuminating and useful for teachers is the suggestion from Entwistle and Peterson (2004) that any learning style scheme adopts one of three conceptions of style:

- a way of representing information (for instance, whole/parts, concrete/abstract, words/images)
- a specific modality of sensory input preference – visual, kinaesthetic, aural
- a set of environmental preferences (lighting, heating, comfort and so on)

Thinking about learning styles has now been now exposed as heavily subject to 'neuromyths' concerning 'brain-based' learning (see Chapter 11). Neuroscientists like Geake (2008) have strongly criticized the VAK approach as based on a wrong model of how the brain learns. Geake argues that evidence from neuroscience indicates that the brain operates in a connective and multi-modal manner, not just through a single-channel (visual, auditory or whatever). Another main criticism is that the logic often implied for practice is untenable: there is a case for developing weak points of learning as well as playing to strengths. Thirdly, it deals with only one dimension of learning; but learning depends on a number of factors and, given the variety of learning tasks and contexts, the aim should be to make learners as versatile as possible.

It is not clear that differences in learning styles are reliably measurable, especially those based on self-report questionnaires from young children. Moreover, observant teachers have quickly realized that such 'preferences' are often not stable and that most tasks require more than one of the VAK elements. Geake (2008) notes that multi-sensory pedagogy has long been established in infant education for literacy ('look and say') and such established craft knowledge is undermined, not supported, by the VAK approach. Another criticism is the emphasis on the ease and enjoyment of learning to the neglect of developing traits like persistence, intellectual challenge, effortful approaches and so on. Also, the emphasis on VAK neglects other worthwhile developments. Research in higher education on approaches to study (deep, surface, strategic) is beginning to be applied to secondary learning (Haggarty 2002; Bartlett and Burton 2007) and there is no reason why it should not prove useful in upper primary at least. Finally, there is no independent hard evidence that all the attention to VAK styles has led to significant improvement in educational achievements.

The recent debacle over the promotion of learning styles in schools is a salutary case study which highlights the need for careful collaboration between neuroscientisits, educationists and teachers, care over rapid commercialization of staff development initiatives, the need to consider individuality in learning and the inadequacy of traditional one-sided approaches involving a diet of largely verbal, didactic teaching. Some practical suggestions that might be drawn out of this sorry story are:

- try to become aware of individual differences and preferences in approaches to learning tasks
- aim to make learners versatile and able to adapt to the context and nature of different learning tasks
- help learners to become aware of themselves as learners
- remember any particular style will have advantages and also disadvantages in relation to a range of learning tasks and that many tasks involve more than one sensory mode
- remember that identified preferences may not be stable, reliably measured and may not relate to learning as opposed to enjoyment of learning

A Note on Teaching Style

How far is it desirable for teachers to seek to develop (by analogy with learning style) a broad, individualized teaching style in the sense of an overall approach to teaching organization and interaction? According to Entwistle (1987), the main differences in overall style appear to be between those who favour an informal approach and those who favour a formal, structured one. Such teaching style preferences presumably have links with basic organizational and interactive attitudes. Another issue is how far do teachers teach the way they prefer to learn themselves? Hard evidence here is lacking. Entwistle (1981: 238) noted 'a consistency between educational philosophy and teaching method, but no more', and strong parallels between accounts of differing characteristics of formal and informal teachers and accounts of general differences in cognitive styles. For example, Witkin *et al.* (1977) found that 'field dependent' teachers tended to adopt informal, discussion methods and 'field independent' teachers (those not easily distracted by background in perceptual tests) were more likely to prefer more tightly structured methods of teaching. This may link to differences between holist and analytic thinking styles (Entwistle 1981). However, these hints from research in the 1970s were never pursued as the focus shifted to pupils' learning style preferences and how teachers could adapt their teaching to these.

Another problem is that writings generally fail to distinguish clearly between overall organizational and interactive style and the use of particular teaching modes such as direct teaching, enquiry and discussion. For example, Capel *et al.* (2000) appear to assume that teachers have a preference for either a directive style or an enquiry style of teaching. This may reflect the early research discussed above on traditional and progressive methods. But since that debate has moved on it seems important to consider how far it is useful and possible to distinguish overall interactive style preferences from teaching mode deployment issues. Maintaining an individual style preference, it can be argued, is a separate question from deploying a balance of teaching modes. A teacher, surely, might have a strong preference for tight organization and clear structure yet still deploy open discussion, enquiry and learning through action as well as direct teaching. An informal teacher might still be effective in deploying direct whole-class teaching when appropriate but do so in a more relaxed and loosely structured way than a formal teacher.

To insist that all teachers teach national curricula in a prescribed manner is unlikely to be healthy for pupil motivation or the advancement of teaching. Part of the deep enjoyment of teaching, and motivation for developing it, comes from using one's personality to the full in communicating learning, while being sensitive to differences among learners. Official policy-driven strategies and manuals, based on a technicist model of teaching, stressing the delivery of centrally produced lesson plans, have tended to iron out individuality of approach and squash personality and the creative momentum which is surely the lifeblood of effective teaching interactions. While there are dangers in the charismatic teacher approach (Moore 2000), teacher-pupil relations are fundamental in teaching (Morgan and Morris 1999).

Do teachers tend to teach the way they were taught? Probably, but evidence is scarce. Strategies will also probably depend on the models observed among colleagues. These can often suggest a range of possibilities for teaching well. Some teachers do appear able to change their overall approach when they encounter obviously more successful ones. However, all these ideas must remain tentative hypotheses requiring more systematic study. It is time for a resurgence of studies of teaching style preferences.

Summary

Educational researchers and theorists have tried to make sense of the obvious variety and complexity of teaching and learning in a number of ways. Studies of how teachers commonly think about teaching suggest that practising teachers tend not to be concerned with conscious, specific learning goals, but rather think in terms of regular activities; and they soon learn to identify 'normal desirable states' of classroom activities and to judge pupil progress in relation to a range classroom factors that affect teaching and learning.

Early research on comparing different strategies showed the complexity of teaching and various classifications of strategies have been developed. None has provided a fully satisfactory overall framework for thinking about teaching and learning. Attempts by researchers and policy-makers to identify common features of all good teaching have largely researched direct teaching contexts (which represents the majority of teaching contexts) and for these have found reasonably consistent results emphasizing aspects such as clear goals, structure and focus on teaching interactions.

Studies comparing the effectiveness of different teaching strategies have not proved conclusive. They have shown that different strategies serve different contexts and purposes and suggest that those that entail over-complex organization at the expense of teaching contacts and interactions are usually counter-productive; and that dogma and disputes about aims and values, rather than conflicts of evidence, explain many controversies about teaching strategies.

A case is made for the idea of teaching modes as a powerful way of making sense of the variety and complexity of teaching and learning. This is the theory that there are four basically different kinds of teaching each with different means of learning, different teacher and pupil roles and typical differences in resource requirements, organization and approaches to assessment. This provides a framework for detailed exploration of the different modes in succeeding chapters.

Academic research on learning styles raises critical questions about recent commercial and popular accounts and shows the need for caution in classroom practice, while suggesting that many people have decided preferences in approaches to learning. The origin, neuropsychological basis, flexibility and modifiability of such preferences remains a problematic area requiring careful further research. But these aspects are clearly important for better understanding of learners as individuals, developing more effective approaches to study and enhancing learning environments.

The implication is that teachers should look critically and carefully at their learners' approaches and seek reputable studies in the area. There will be no simple solution here but rather a growing understanding of the variety of individuality in learning. It is, however, important to note commonalities as well as individual differences. Ensuring that learners experience a range of contexts and study requirements will prepare for later-life situations, as will learning to reflect on their own learning.

The idea of teaching style preferences among teachers requires further exploration, earlier inconclusive studies having been sidelined as interest in learning styles grew.

Key Reading

Borich, G. D. (2006) *Effective Teaching Methods*, 6th edn. Upper Saddle River, NJ: Pearson Education.
Brown, S. and McIntyre, D. (1993) *Making Sense of Teaching*. Buckingham: Open University Press.

Entwistle, N. and Peterson, E. (2004) 'Learning styles and approaches to studying', *Encyclopaedia of Applied Psychology*, Vol. 2, pp. 537–42.

Galton, M. (2007) *Learning and Teaching in the Primary Classroom*. London: Sage.

Hay McBer (2001) 'Research into teacher effectiveness', in F. Banks and A. S. Mayes (eds) *Early Professional Development for Teachers*. London: David Fulton, pp 193–209.

James, M. and Pollard, A. (eds) (2006) *Improving Teaching and Learning in Schools: A Commentary by the Teaching and Learning Research Programme*. Swindon: ESRC.

Muijs, D. and Reynolds, D. (2005) *Effective Teaching*, 2nd edn. London: Sage.

Useful Websites

www.tlrp.org.uk

Website of the Teaching and Learning Research Programme in England. Many useful research reports and commentaries on teaching and learning.

http://dww.ed.gov

The 'Doing what works' site launched in November 2007 by the US Department of education, focused on evidence-based teaching.

www.ofsted.gov.uk

This contains a wealth of information from the Office for Standards in Education (Ofsted) relating to research and inspections, including consultations, thematic reports and statistics. It offers useful insights into the thinking of the inspectorate in England on current teaching and learning issues and many ideas for strengthening teaching and learning.

www.geoffpetty.com/

This is the website of Geoff Petty, writer on modern teaching methods (see References). Contains useful downloads and links to many ideas on methods, including information on evidence-based teaching.

www.successforall.net

Website of the Success for All Foundation (SFAF), an organization whose goals are the development, evaluation and dissemination of evidence-based teaching methods. Emphasis on approaches to teaching reading.

Part 2
The Four Modes of Teaching and Learning

Direct Teaching 3

Chapter Outline

Features of Direct Teaching   35

The Mixed Fortunes of Direct Teaching   37

Explaining, Demonstrating and Modelling   38

Whole-class Direct Interactive Teaching   39

Questioning and Formative Assessment   41

Summary   44

Key Reading   45

Useful Websites   45

Features of Direct Teaching

Direct teaching centrally involves the direct presentation of ideas and skills (increasingly now mixed with active participation by learners) with strong teacher control of the direction of learning. After a long history as the dominant mode of teaching it has recently experienced mixed fortunes. 'Direct teaching' has been chosen as the most meaningful and commonly used term for the mode. No term is fully satisfactory, however, and there is a need to be alert to frequent overlaps and ambiguities of terminology in educational writings, not least in the discussion of teaching approaches. Related terms here include exposition, reception learning, transmission teaching and, in the USA, direct instruction and recitation. 'Whole-class interactive teaching' is one modern version of direct teaching.

Means of learning

In direct teaching the means of learning is attending to and absorbing, critically, the direct presentation of ideas, skills and information.

Organization and resources

Naturally, the best arrangement is to ensure that learners face the teacher and that the teacher has access to appropriate presentation aids. Traditionally this meant rows and serried ranks. Schools today have more informal seating and in the early years children now often sit on the carpet. Group table settings in primary schools are not naturally conducive to whole-class direct teaching and with the official promotion of 'whole-class interactive teaching' in the mid-1990s, seating patterns in some UK schools began to change back to rows or introduce 'horseshoe' arrangements. Increasingly, interactive whiteboards are now used, replacing chalkboards and overhead projectors. However, textbooks and practice and assessment worksheets remain important in many contexts.

Teacher and learner roles

Traditionally in direct teaching the roles of teacher and learner were strongly differentiated – basically, giver and receiver (hence 'reception learning'). The teacher's role in direct teaching can be further defined as:

- structuring knowledge for learners
- presenting, explaining, demonstrating, modelling
- checking understanding as the teaching proceeds
- motivating, controlling
- encouraging appropriate participation and critical reception
- maintaining strong direction of the course of learning

The learner's role can be expressed as:

- listening carefully to the teacher's presentation (possibly taking notes)
- active, critical reception of ideas and information
- answering questions from the teacher
- participating as directed or encouraged by the teacher

Key teaching skills

A range of teaching skills is required: gaining and maintaining attention, motivating, explaining, demonstrating, modelling, encouraging participation without losing the focus of the teaching, questioning to check understanding. Teachers also need to be able to devise application tasks and appropriate assessment activities.

Assessment

Typical assessment approaches involve tests of knowledge, understanding and application. This is often through oral questioning at the start to ascertain prior knowledge followed, as the teaching proceeds, by worksheets or practice tasks that provide assessment evidence along with reinforcement through application of knowledge presented in the direct teaching phase. Increasingly, electronic assessment methods are becoming available. The most significant development is the radical change to questioning strategies to incorporate ideas from research on formative assessment (see below).

Issues

The questions direct teaching faces are what role it should now play in the mixed economy of teaching methods that education requires – for example balancing direct presentation with active participation or with phases involving other teaching modes – and how it can increase its effectiveness by exploiting advances in information technology.

The Mixed Fortunes of Direct Teaching

Direct teaching has long been the dominant mode of teaching (except in some early education contexts and adult education where, however, it is far from absent in some form and, arguably, needs to be strengthened in appropriate ways). It is what most people, including most professional teachers, instinctively think of when they think of teaching. Some, indeed, appear to find it hard to use the term teaching to denote other kinds of teaching roles, structures and interactions.

Direct teaching has a clear place in pre-school education, for example in the widespread practice of teaching songs and rhymes and giving instructions in safety, hygiene and toileting (Siraj-Blatchford 1999: 28). This has too rarely been acknowledged by early educators, reluctant to talk about 'teaching' as opposed to learning. There is also a role for brief direct teaching when interacting with children at play – giving a brief explanation, for example, of the behaviour or features of a snail. Earlier dogmas about not teaching directly are being questioned as the value of 'shared joint thinking' has become apparent, though sensitive judgement is needed about balance and ensuring that children's initiatives and thinking in conducting their own enquiries are not squashed. In adult education also, despite the emphasis on self-directed learning, the role of quality explaining by teachers is now more recognized; and it has of course long been acknowledged by anyone who has attended an evening class, be it on a language, photography or cookery.

Direct teaching in the form of whole-class teaching was considered suited mainly to the expressive arts in the 1970s in Scotland. Language and mathematics were said to require differentiated group work, as was much of environmental studies (Skinner 1994). However, in the resurgence of direct whole-class teaching with the advent of national curricula from the late 1980s, it was precisely these core subjects of language and mathematics for which direct whole-class teaching was now officially promoted (Muijs and Reynolds 2005: 37), only to be again under suspicion following evidence of low quality class discussion and the advocacy of dialogic teaching, which some (but not all – see Alexander 2000, 2008b) think is more suited to group work. It is important here to separate out questions of direct teaching versus other modes from questions of whole-class versus group teaching (see Chapter 7).

Direct teaching has frequently been criticized in relation to its practical effects (tendency to encourage passive, dependent learning) and in terms of theories of how people learn (the need for active construction of knowledge and understanding). Yet it is the mode on which most systematic research has been conducted and this has consistently provided support for its general effectiveness and efficiency, when well conducted (see Chapter 2); and it remains the most commonly used mode.

The questions that need to be considered are how far the use of direct teaching is a necessary compromise in view of the realities the of class sizes and pressures for curriculum coverage, how far it is still used because of the difficulty of developing the skills required for other modes, and how far it is needed because it is recognized as effective for some important educational goals and contexts. The argument of this present chapter is that the issue is not whether direct teaching should be employed but in what contexts and for what purposes; and how it can be most effectively modernized to exploit information and communication technology (ICT) and encourage active engagement.

Explaining, Demonstrating and Modelling

Wragg and Brown (1993) neatly explain 'explaining' as giving understanding to a learner. They also distinguish three main types of explanation:

- interpretive (which explains meanings of ideas and concepts)
- descriptive (which explains mechanisms, structures and processes)
- reason-giving (which explains causes and effects)

'Descriptive' might be better called 'analytic' if, as is often desirable, there is more than mere description of the structure or process. Explanations can be at different levels of analysis – for example, in history common-sense categories and folk explanations can give way to explanations in terms of social structures, institutions or power – depending on the level of learners' conceptual development.

Wragg and Brown focus on using questions to structure indirect explanations in school contexts. Galton (2007) emphasizes the teacher's role in encouraging learners to give explanations to their peers and the elaboration of answers, which is certainly important in collaborative group work. It is also important, however, to emphasize the need for teachers to develop the ability to explain *well*.

Factors in effective explaining include clarity of language, use of motivation, memorable and meaningful examples and pacing so that learners can take ideas in. Leinhardt (2001) shows how important subject knowledge is to explanations. Subject matter knowledge and 'pedagogic content knowledge' (knowing useful ways of teaching a subject – see Chapter 10) are the basis for effective explanations, which make links in two directions – towards the subject discipline and towards everyday life and applications.

Along with explaining and structuring ideas for learners, demonstrating and modelling skills and processes is crucial to effective direct teaching. These skills are called on across the curriculum from mathematics to music and sport. Study and learning skills can be modelled, enthusiasm conveyed and engendered, and learners shown how a task can be broken down and made manageable.

Whole-class Direct Interactive Teaching

According to Petty (2004) this is highly structured, with strong teacher control, but learners are actively engaged. He notes the tension and need for balance between structure and interactivity. He argues that whole-class direct interactive teaching is in fact an amalgam of strategies, many of which fit 'constructivist' principles (see Chapter 6) such as sharing learning outcomes, learner activity and formative feedback. In England it has become particularly associated with the national strategies for literacy and numeracy. Critics have complained about the vagueness of the idea and there is a case for viewing it not as pure direct teaching but as a teaching unit incorporating phases of dialogue and discussion as well as direct teaching. A typical approach for the literacy hour is to have an introductory exposition and final plenary between which are sandwiched a whole-class discussion and some group or individual 'seat work'. For mathematics, England's National Numeracy Strategy advocated that teaching should be oral, interactive and lively. Teachers should somehow combine directing, instructing, demonstrating, explaining and illustrating, questioning and discussing, consolidating, evaluating and summarizing.

As Hayes (2008) notes, worksheets – the essence of 'seat work' and often criticized as leading to routine and passive learning – are being modernized through ICT and a range of imaginative activities is now beginning to be exploited: investigation, application tasks, information sheets, practice examples. They are used partly to provide differentiation, though this has its attendant danger of lack of challenge and poor progress for low attaining individuals.

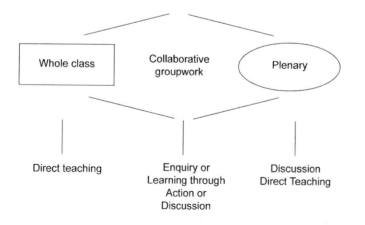

Figure 3.1 Deployment of teaching modes in a phased lesson structure

> The phased lesson structure in Figure 3.1 shows how a range of teaching modes can be judiciously employed to enable learners to experience sustained learning in relation to defined objectives.

Why direct teaching works

It has become clear through various studies (see Petty 2004; Muijs and Reynolds 2005) that one of the main reasons for direct teaching's success, compared, for example, to some of the complex group organizations of primary teaching of the Plowden era, is that teachers using direct teaching have more teaching contacts and spend more time on teaching interactions with learners. But there can be a great difference between well worked direct interactive teaching and poorly worked versions. Badly prepared and delivered direct teaching can soon lead to boredom, lack of understanding and passive learning. Effective direct teaching requires significant teaching skill and commitment.

Critical reception learning

As Biggs (2003: 4) has noted, in direct teaching contexts there can be large gaps in understanding between critically engaged learners and those who remain passive. Understanding can vary widely, whereas in enquiry mode activities, such as problem-based learning, active critical thinking is forced on all learners, reducing the understanding gap between learners.

There has been an unfortunate tendency in some quarters to dismiss direct teaching as inevitably resulting in passive learning. In relation to this, the approach adopted by learners in Confucian heritage cultures like China, Korea and Japan is illuminating. Ausubel *et al.* (1968) make a clear difference between rote and meaningful learning and argue that it is perfectly possible to have critically engaged reception learning. Biggs (2003: 125–7) suggests the need to make a further distinction between rote and repetitive learning and cites evidence that Confucian heritage learners, who appear to rely on repetitive learning, achieve very good, and deep, not surface, understanding – often better than western students. One factor appears to be that they are given more effective, structured teaching. Another is the approach to memorization. It is often assumed by UK educators that rote learning means passive absorption with little understanding. But while many learners in the West have fallen into this trap, other traditions emphasize rehearsal and consolidation of understood material and memorization as a way of gradually developing understanding and enabling the consolidation of conceptual frameworks. Repetition can be a good basis for understanding; once one has memorized, one can focus on meaning; and deep memorizing helps cope with complexity and aids recall. It is far from the mindless and passive rote learning criticized so dismissively in many western educational writings (Xu 2007).

Direct teaching is not an all-purpose tool. But young children as well as older learners can gain a lot from listening to and watching a teacher. The general consensus (e.g. Kyriacou, 1995, 2007; Petty 2004, 2006; Galton 2007) is that direct teaching is well suited to introducing concepts, presenting set knowledge, demonstrating a procedure and teaching a discrete point or skill. But much teaching requires just these things. It is less effective for generating deeper conceptual understanding, open, complex learning and more experience-based, personalized understanding and problem solving. Moreover, in direct teaching it is often not always easy to arrange for learners to learn things in a context of use – when they make more sense to the learner. Direct teaching can also tend to make learners dependent on the teacher for learning – though this can apply to other modes.

Questioning and Formative Assessment

The roots of many of the problems facing direct teaching lie in the role questioning now plays. Three main distinctions can be made among types of question used in teaching. These are:

- closed versus open questions
- recall versus higher-level questions
- different kinds of higher-level questions

Closed questions are ones with a right answer, for instance, 'How many legs does a spider have?' The teacher knows the answer and is checking if pupils know it. Most, but not all, closed questions are simple. Some, though, require pupils to work through the logic of a situation and apply an idea to a new context. The basic point, however, is that in a closed question there is a right answer.

Open questions have no single right answer. There may be several good answers (e.g. 'How could we test if this material is waterproof?') or the issue might be one where people disagree ('Should fishing be banned?'), or the teacher may be just asking pupils to offer their perspective ('What types of novel do you like?'). Such questions are used to get pupils to think for themselves about what are usually more open problems than in the case of closed questions. Moreover, the teacher can respond to pupil answers in a way that develops or challenges their thinking as indicated by their response.

A second distinction is between simple recall and higher-level questions. Recall questions are simple closed ones like asking pupils to name the capital of Australia or the hero in a novel, or to give a simple definition. Learners would be expected to know the answers from memory. Higher-level questions are ones that require more complex thinking. Many, but by no means all, of these will be open questions.

A third distinction relates to the different kinds of higher-level question. One famous classification of elements of learning, Bloom's taxonomy (Atherton 2009), suggests teachers can ask a range of question types, from simple recall through basic understanding and application to higher-level questions involving analysis, evaluation or synthesis. Other writers point out other differences among higher-level questions. For instance, educational philosophers have emphasized a distinction between factual, value and conceptual questions, each requiring a different approach to finding an answer (respectively, factual evidence, justification of value stances, clarification of meaning, appropriate distinctions and usage). In discussing a novel, a teacher will often ask a range of higher-order questions, for example, questions of deduction ('Why was the farmer angry?'), of imaginative speculation ('What would you do in that context?') and of evaluation ('Was it fair to keep the money?').

To use questioning to develop sustained subject understanding and thinking and test understanding, teachers need to be aware of the range of question types and be able to generate them in relation to the teaching content. Many studies of questioning, however, demonstrate that teachers spend most of their time asking low-level recall questions. They ask few open or higher-level ones.

One of the main reasons teachers ask questions at the start of direct teaching is that it seems vital to find out what the pupils know. Simple recall questions seem to work well because they give the appearance of participation, thinking and involvement and enable the teacher to move the lesson along a predetermined path. If a teacher asks more complex or open questions, control of the flow and direction of teaching can easily be lost. Hence a step towards using higher-level questions might be to separate the explaining from the testing phases of direct teaching. The idea would be to base focused explanations on direct telling, not questioning, and to reserve questions for deep probing, using a balance of closed and open questions, or a quiz to recap the main point after the explanation.

If questioning is used to structure direct teaching, several strategies are available, such as: focusing on a line of thought, allowing limited digression; or starting with a few low-level, recall questions to ascertain the pupils' knowledge base before moving up to more penetrating questioning; or moving in an indirect route towards central questions, gradually building up a picture of issues and factors (see Wragg and Brown 1993).

Dillon (1988a) advises teachers to ask just a few well chosen questions and to:

- prepare the questions
- ask them 'nice and slow'
- listen to the answers

This seems simple and obvious but many research studies have shown that often teachers don't prepare even a few questions carefully, that they ask questions in rapid succession, especially if no answer is forthcoming, and often don't really consider the answers they receive.

Many successful learners enjoy being questioned and providing answers, and it gives them further confidence as learners. But for others it is an unenjoyable, even stressful experience, leading to feelings of failure and disaffection from school. Many teachers shy away from explaining that answers are wrong, afraid to demotivate learners; but the problem is that it is usually clear to the learner from the teacher's demeanour that the answer is not what is wanted. Another problem is that it is uncertain how far successful learners are learning to think by answering questions as opposed to just demonstrating what they already know.

Formative assessment

Recent research and development work on formative assessment and the 'Assessment is for Learning' initiative (Black *et al.* 2003; Thomas and Pring 2004; Hutchinson and Hayward 2005) has provided teachers with a radically new approach to using questions to test understanding and to inform and motivate further learning. The assessment for learning approach removes the idea of one right answer and competition between learners, and increases wait time. Learners are asked to think more carefully, perhaps in pairs or trios, and to work towards a *best* answer. A ground rule is 'no hands up'. This enables the teacher's questions to become more probing and open and to genuinely test understanding.

Teaching Development Activity 3.1 – Explaining, Questioning and Assessing

Explaining
Work out a really good way to explain something your learners are finding difficult. Note how this differs from your typical practice. Provide the explanation and then observe how your learners receive it. Reflect on the response to your explanation in terms of your learners' understanding and interest; on your own professional confidence and satisfaction in giving the explanation; and on ideas for further development of skill in explaining.

Question and answer
Try to follow Dillon's strategy for effective questioning in preparing a 'question and answer' session as part of a lesson centred on direct teaching. This means carefully preparing just a few really telling questions, asking them 'nice and slow' and really listening to the answers before responding, probing and so on.
    What difficulties did you encounter in doing this and how would you assess the results in terms of learning achieved?

Assessment for learning
Try out strategies recommended by Black *et al.* (2003) for effective use of questions for formative assessment. For example:

- no hands up
- increasing wait time
- anyone can be asked to respond
- 'I don't know' is an acceptable answer
- pairs or trios work towards a good answer before responding

Reflect on their effects and read further on formative assessment.

Summary

Direct teaching involves the direct, well-structured presentation of information, ideas and skills, with strong teacher control of the direction of learning. It increasingly uses ICT to aid presentation, interaction and assessment and incorporates some active learner participation. It has a long and continuing history as the dominant teaching mode, despite criticisms about passive learning, a tendency to view knowledge as a commodity to be simply transmitted, and problems of motivation and control, and of coping with mixed groups of learners.

In recent decades direct teaching has experienced mixed fortunes. In the UK, from the mid-1960s official reports (like Plowden) strongly advocated group and individual work, but by 2000 'whole-class interactive teaching' was officially promoted as the key to raising attainment standards in schools. While this meets many of the criteria of effective teaching supported by research studies (clear focus, structure, sustained engagement), supposed support from international studies of attainment has now been questioned and the low quality of dialogue, the typically narrow conceptions of literacy and numeracy evident, and difficulty in meeting diverse learner needs criticized.

Direct teaching works well for presenting information, introducing conceptual frameworks and demonstrating skills and procedures but has not proved so effective in the West for developing deep conceptual understanding or problem-solving; these need more dialogue, discussion and experiential learning.

This mode requires effective matching of content to learner attainments, and clear structuring, explaining and demonstrating. While progressive critiques of traditional teaching led to systematic explaining and presenting skills becoming less valued and practised, their importance is being acknowledged once more. High-quality, stimulating presentation and explaining requires sound subject understanding, the ability to make imaginative links to everyday life and application contexts, and to the nature of the discipline involved. Explanations and expositions now tend to be shorter and encourage some learner interaction. Active, critical reception learning from direct teaching is important and memorization can aid understanding. Traditional low-level questioning for active participation, or as covert structuring of an explanation, is not recommended. Radically revised questioning strategies emerging from research on formative assessment offer a better approach to checking understanding, along with motivating application tasks involving supervised practice.

Many see the common teaching of key ideas and developing a whole-class identity as an important contribution of direct teaching. Its importance and effectiveness for particular purposes and contexts for all subjects and stages, its economy and the realities of class sizes, along with curriculum coverage pressures mean that direct teaching, increasingly aided by technology, will surely always have an important place in schooling. Direct teaching by proxy, for example, through peer teaching and computer models and simulations of scientific phenomena and processes, can also play a useful role.

Key Reading

Black, P., Harrison, C., Lee, C. Marshall, B. and William, D. (2002) *Working Inside the Black Box*. London: King's College.

Dillon, J. T. (1988) *Questioning and Teaching. London: Croom Helm.*

Fox, R. (2005) *Teaching and Learning.* Oxford: Blackwell.

Hayes, D. (2008) *Foundations of Primary Teaching*, 4th edn. London: Routledge.

Kyriacou, C. (1995) 'Direct teaching', in C. Desforges (ed.) *An Introduction to Teaching.* Oxford: Blackwell, pp. 115–31.

Kyriacou, C. (2007) *Essential Teaching Skills*, 3rd edn. Cheltenham: Nelson Thornes.

Petty, R. (2006) *Evidence-Based Teaching.*Cheltenham: Nelson Thornes.

Wragg, E. and Brown, G. (2003) *Explaining in the Secondary School.* London: Routledge.

Useful Websites

www.geoffpetty.com
A website devoted to different teaching methods.

http://assessment-reform-group.org/
Useful information concerning new thinking about assessment

http://www.qca.org.uk/
Website of the Qualifications and Curriculum Authority (QCA) in England. It contains many useful resources, including guidance and case studies of teaching where everyday assessment is used to improve teaching and learning.

www.standards.dfes.gov.uk/
This site offers a large range of useful ideas and information about, for example, personalized learning, pedagogy, advanced skills teachers, primary and secondary teaching, and thinking skills.

www.literacytrust.org.
The website of the National Literacy Trust provides analysis of current policy and summaries of research and implications for practice.

4 Teaching through Dialogue and Discussion

Chapter Outline

Introduction	46
Developing Discussion	48
Teaching and Learning through Dialogue	52
Features of the Mode	53
Summary	54
Key Reading	55
Useful Websites	55

Introduction

The main argument of this chapter calls into question much traditional practice and thinking about discussion in school settings and tries to reconcile two streams of thinking – about open discussion and about teaching through dialogue. These have tended to remain separate in research and theorizing but it is argued here that they should be viewed as a single mode of teaching: 'learning through dialogue and discussion'. The central feature of this mode is learning through the interaction of ideas among participants. Teachers need to be clear about the educational aims of this mode, its value and how to ensure a productive interaction. Dialogic teaching, as it is often referred to ('dialogic': 'in the form of a dialogue'), is more teacher-directed than open discussion and in unskilled hands can turn into 'question and answer'. We also need to consider dialogue (or 'exploratory talk') among learners. Dialogic teaching and learning have been extensively researched in recent years, practical recommendations from these studies have been well received and initial developments show very considerable promise (North Yorkshire County Council/Dialogos 2007; Alexander 2008a). However, the relationship of dialogic teaching to open discussion and the role of open discussion in school contexts needs much more careful consideration and further research.

What counts as a discussion in school settings?

Classroom interactions of various kinds are commonly labelled 'discussion' – casual conversations, question and answer sessions, dialogic interaction and fully open discussions. The teaching profession needs a clearer conception of discussion and needs in particular to clarify the distinction between three aspects: question and answer, dialogue and open discussion.

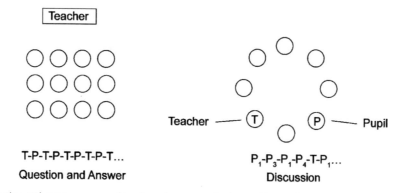

T-P-T-P-T-P-T-P-T...

Question and Answer

P_1-P_3-P_1-P_4-T-P_1...

Discussion

Figure 4.1 Question and answer compared to discussion – organisation and interaction

A key distinction in teaching is that between 'question and answer' and open discussion. These have quite different interaction patterns and work best in different organizational structures, as illustrated in Figure 4.1. Taking the time to set up the physical organization suited to discussion (ensuring eye contact among all participants and equality of status) can make a big difference, as work with 'circle time' and 'communities of philosophical enquiry' has shown.

Most of what goes by the name of discussion in schools and classrooms is better labelled 'question and answer' and is markedly different from discussion in other social and occupational contexts. Since at least the 1960s many class 'discussions' have been a way of driving home the points learners need to understand before undertaking the practice or application tasks typically associated with direct teaching. If, say, learners studying energy are about to make a model of a power station this is often preceded by a 'discussion' in which the teacher typically aims to ensure learners have grasped, say, three key points. Instead of directly telling learners, the points are elicited through a 'discussion'. However, this is not a genuinely open discussion but one guided towards the teacher's predetermined ends. This approach evolved in Britain in the Plowden era when 'teaching by telling' was frowned upon. What is arguably a much more educationally productive strategy – namely, establishing the three key points systematically by direct teaching, then proceeding to the model-making activity and then having a genuinely open discussion about, here, national energy issues – is rarely considered. The teacher, however, would have deployed both direct teaching and open discussion in effective ways.

Developing Discussion

Dillon (1994:7) defines discussion thus:

> Discussion is a form of group interaction, people talking back-and-forth with one another. What they talk about is an issue, some topic that is in question for them. Their talk consists in advancing and examining different proposals over the issue. The proposals may be various understandings, facts, suggestions, opinions, perspectives, experience and the like. These are examined for their contribution towards resolving the issue.

Dillon (1988a, 1994) also emphasizes the need for the issue to be open to discussion instead of having a pre-set answer towards which the teacher is working; and perhaps this should become the defining difference between open discussion and dialogue.

In using open discussion, teachers have two aims: to help learners learn through discussion and to help them learn how to discuss. Effective discussion is thus a means of learning and also an educational goal. It is perhaps helpful here to draw attention to the root of 'discursive' in 'running to and fro', highlighting the interactive nature of discussion, and the origin of 'discussion' in a verb meaning 'to dash to pieces', highlighting the analytic nature of the thinking involved (though synthesis is also important in discussion). Of course, the roots of a word are not necessarily the best guide to its most appropriate modern application. What needs to be considered along with word origins are the sorts of distinctions between ideas we want to make in the particular context – in the present case between testing knowledge, probing and developing understanding and exploring genuinely open or unresolved issues.

There is an important tradition of educational research and thinking in the work of Stenhouse (1975), Cowie and Ruddock (1998), Bridges (1979) and Dillon (1988a, 1994) that gives great importance to open discussion in school settings. Writers on dialogic teaching tend to neglect this and indeed seem sceptical of the educational value of open discussion. Alexander (2006: 48) wonders where even lively and extended discussions often lead, and suggests a need to pull such discussions (especially learner-led ones) together to synthesize understanding and prevent them just going round in circles. Good open discussion requires more than laissez-faire facilitation; and a discussion can be genuinely open without the teacher abandoning a positive role or failing to make use of expert subject and pedagogical knowledge.

Myhill (2006) is critical of the adversarial character of many school discussions in comparison to the collaborative development of thinking in dialogical exploratory talk of the sort researched by Mercer and Littleton (2007). Mercer also points up the supportive, collaborative ethos of exploratory talk and dialogue. However, a consideration of the various kinds of open discussion that might be undertaken in schools may help to show their educational value and potential. A non-adversarial open discussion is just as possible as a non-adversarial dialogue.

Types of open discussion

In the absence of any widely agreed classification, four main types of open discussion are tentatively suggested:

- discussion of controversial issues (e.g. fox hunting, abortion, eating meat – often perennial issues)
- decision-making discussions (e.g. planning the menu for a Burns supper, responding to a crisis or organizing a sporting event)
- critical, appreciative discussions (e.g. sharing perspectives on some cultural experience – a football match, concert, book, painting or artistic exhibition – in order to deepen understanding, critical appreciation and enjoyment)
- problem-solving discussions (e.g. in mathematics, management, history, design)

Teachers might usefully map the kinds of open discussion they can envisage in their classrooms. Perhaps no clear distinction can be sustained between decision-making and problem-solving discussions; and other useful groupings might emerge. Roby (1988) suggests just three main categories: informational; problematical; dialectic. 'Informational' are exchanges of knowledge, perspectives and experiences on an issue (like family upbringing); 'dialectical' involve resolving conflicting opinions on an issue and can easily become argumentative; 'problematical' are puzzles of various kinds including perennial ones such as 'What is art?'

Learning through discussion

Bridges (1988) argues that in discussion we learn through interaction with other discussants, which helps us to:

- enrich our understanding
- refine our understanding

We enrich our understanding by coming to understand diverse views or perspectives; by being reflective, which develops our self-awareness; and, by having to express our thoughts in discussion, coming to see more clearly what we know and think. We refine our understanding by being responsive, appreciative and attentive to other's views and being open-minded. Being open to diversity and variety of perspective is important. A group of very like-minded people may develop a rather weak discussion of a subject on which they probably have very similar views – though experts can agree in broad terms but still have a heated discussion on matters of detail and issues within a field. We also refine our understanding in discussion by having to be clear about what we are saying, providing evidence or reasons for our arguments, and being coherent and logically consistent. These processes also help learners to learn to discuss, along with appropriate training and feedback (for which systematic provision needs to be made and the crucial role of which should not be underestimated).

The outcomes of effective discussion are usually deeper understanding, wiser judgement, greater awareness of significant factors and better discussion skills. Learning to discuss is important for later learning and for social and occupational life. It is also, Dillon insists (1994: 112), a worthwhile pursuit in its own right. Dillon (1994: 113 ff.) argues that discussion is just a good way of life, a worthwhile pursuit in educational as in other contexts. Learning to discuss is an important educational accomplishment. Analogies can be made here with 'Philosophy for Children'. This seeks to develop in classrooms a community of philosophical enquiry that can be justified in instrumental and intrinsic terms (Davis 2007). Overall, therefore, discussion would appear to have very considerable educational potential.

Dillon's pedagogy of discussion

In terms of Dillon's research and analysis, the crucial difference from dialogic teaching, aside from the openness of discussion, is the role of questioning. Dillon (1985) argues strongly for a tactical avoidance of questions in leading a discussion. This comes as a major surprise to most, for it is the reverse of both traditional and standard current practice that assume that to lead discussion you need to be an excellent questioner. His contention is that teacher questioning foils genuine discussion, turning it into a question and answer session (or 'recitation') which is really a component of direct teaching, not genuine open discussion. Dillon has come to this view on the basis of systematic research on the effects of questions in education and other fields (Dillon 1982). He provides evidence that, far from making learners think, questions often do the opposite, and that learners respond at greater length and depth to statements than to questions (even high-level, probing ones). He also shows that in other fields (like therapy and the law courts), questions inhibit rather than encourage thought. Dillon's research has found support from Wood and Wood (1983) in relation to pre-school education. In contrast, Mercer and Littleton (2006) suggest that questions are a natural and necessary part of a teacher's linguistic toolbox, as they are for other professionals, including lawyers, police, journalists and research interviewers. He does not, however, refute Dillon's important survey.

But if as a teacher you are not to ask questions how else can you lead a discussion? Dillon offers a list of alternatives to questioning. First are statements. You can just offer your own view, or repeat what a learner has just said (Learner: 'It's a cube.' Teacher: 'It's a cube.' Learner: 'Oh no, it's a cuboid.') or note the contrast between two learners' contributions ('John said X but Mary is saying Y') or simply express how you feel about the situation ('Now I'm confused').

In addition to statements, you can use non-verbal means (such as passing the turn from one pupil to another with an open hand movement or eye contact), fillers such as 'uhuh' and 'mmhm', and expressions of feeling such as 'wow!' or 'nice!' Lastly, there is silence, not a sullen awkward silence but a deliberate, appreciative one of three to five seconds, giving learners time to think (teachers typically wait less than a second before asking another question if they get no response).

Dillon does acknowledge the role in open discussion of two kinds of question. The topic for discussion is usually in the form of a question, and if the teacher or another participant is genuinely perplexed it is natural to ask a question. What is crucial is not to use questions to conduct the general interaction. Questions from a teacher force a learner to stop thinking along their own train of thought (and in terms of which they may have been about to offer a contribution), and to attend instead to the teacher's train of thought. This often results in guessing what the teacher has in mind. This is not conducive to fruitful open discussion and may be a key difference between open discussion and dialogue.

Teachers also need to think of a way to get a discussion up and running without questioning because otherwise they will find themselves quickly resorting to questioning. It will become dialogue or much more likely question and answer and the interaction will be largely teacher-learner. A strategy to prevent this is simply to instruct someone to start by offering a view, then instruct another pupil to respond and so on. Don't join in until this learner-learner-learner pattern is well established; and then use Dillon's alternatives for your own contributions. Avoid asking questions to fuel the discussion. The success of this strategy depends of course on having a topic that is genuinely open for discussion and also aiding the discussion by summarizing from time to time. In learners-only discussions, learners can take various monitoring and summarizing roles to aid the process. It is also useful for teachers to map out beforehand for themselves various possible lines of discussion so long as this does not lead to guiding the discussion in a particular direction.

Teaching Development Activity 4.1 – Open Discussion

Select a topic for open discussion – one that is genuinely open. For example, it could be a controversial issue, a decision-making discussion such as planning a celebratory meal, or a discussion in which participants share their critical appreciation of some cultural or sporting event.

Follow the ideas outlined above for how to plan and start a discussion – just telling someone to start it, not contributing yourself until the discussion is well under way and using Dillon's alternatives to questions to facilitate the flow of the discussion.

You will need beforehand to try using Dillon's alternatives in conversation with small groups or pairs because you will, at first, find it very difficult not to slip into a questioning mode. Ask a colleague to observe or record the discussion. You can then compare the quality of contributions from learners with those in standard classroom 'discussions' which use questions to guide the debate. You may need to pilot this and ensure learners understand what is expected in order to give it a fair trial.

Teaching and Learning through Dialogue

We are here concerned with dialogic teaching (dialogue led by a teacher) and exploratory dialogue among learners without a teacher. Teaching through dialogue seems centrally concerned with handing over to learners a good grasp of key ideas, concepts, principles, evidence and processes. By teasing out understanding through probing questioning, learners are encouraged to articulate their perceptions and ideas. The process seeks to achieve this through structured, cumulative questioning and exploratory talk, a process in which scaffolding of the dialogue by the teacher can play an important role (Alexander 2008c).

Myhill (2006: 25) sees dialogue as a 'shared movement towards understanding' in contrast to typical classroom discussion that she claims is 'adversarial and preoccupied by promoting one's own standpoint'. But surely Myhill's picture of discussion is a distortion of what discussion can and should be, at least in Bridges' (1979) and Dillon's (1988a, 1994) accounts of the features of productive, well-conducted discussion. An equally negative picture of dialogic teaching could easily be painted, drawing on, say, the views of Brownhill (2002) of much 'Socratic teaching' as conducted now and in the past. Writers like Alexander (2008a) and Skidmore (2006), who favour dialogic interaction, seem rather optimistic about what equality can be achieved and not concerned about the inevitable dominance of the teacher's line of thinking.

Writers on dialogic teaching frequently refer to Bahktin (1981) who argued that dialogue and questioning allowed participants to create new meanings and new understandings; but these are also possible through discussion as envisaged by Dillon, Bridges and Stenhouse. Moreover, Wegerif (2008) has recently highlighted some further complexities of Bahktin's ideas in relation to the basis in Vygotsky and social constructivism of much writing on dialogic teaching. No doubt the debate between open discussion and dialogic teaching will continue.

Mercer (2006) has extensively researched exploratory dialogic talk – learning to conduct dialogue in groups – without a teacher. A key feature is the development of ground rules for pupils engaging in such talk and the establishment of a cooperative rather than adversarial ethos. The tentative, thoughtful trying out of ideas by thinking aloud and training in thinking together has produced impressive results. It is clear that very useful contexts for such exploratory dialogic talk occur in the course of planning and reviewing activities in enquiry and experiential learning contexts, exemplifying the use of one mode in the context of others.

In ordinary social contexts of discussion at home, at work, at leisure in a café or pub, participants do not normally interact through a typical teacher questioning approach. Why is it thought so important they do so in school discussions? Because it has been deeply ingrained since the time of Socrates. Yet questioning, which is only one of many linguistic forms, arguably has been expected to play too large a role in interactions between a teacher and learners.

School learners are able to operate according to different rules and expectations so long as these are clearly signalled. Philosophy for Children and communities of philosophical inquiry, generally Socratic in style, would also surely benefit from considering the ideas presented above about open discussion and alternatives to questioning.

It is a challenge for teacher-researchers and theorists to carve out a path through these various means of interaction. This chapter has tried to shed some light on the issues and suggest a way forward, including further research and practical approaches, which give an appropriate place to all three forms of interaction – question and answer, open discussion and dialogue, each of which in their appropriate contexts can contribute to effective learning.

Teaching Development Activity 4.2 – Classroom Dialogue

Try out some classroom dialogue (dialogic teaching) as discussed above. Take some aspect of a subject where you think learners need to deepen their understanding of some key ideas. Begin a dialogue on this using open-ended and probing questions and respond to answers so as to further deepen thinking. You aim is to develop a cooperative and supportive but probing exchange of ideas and understandings that hopefully will lead your learners to real progress in clarifying the ideas involved.

Reflect on your role, your learners' response and what progress they made.

Features of the Mode

As with enquiry, teachers usually have a double aim: to develop knowledge and understanding through dialogue and discussion, and to teach learners how to discuss and conduct dialogue effectively. The outcomes of effective dialogue and discussion are usually deeper understanding of concepts and appreciation of issues and reasoning in a discipline, greater awareness of significant factors, better judgement and improved discussion and dialogue skills.

Means of learning

Learners learn through interaction, by reasoning and argument. They both enrich and refine their understanding, enrichment coming from the diversity of views expressed and refinement from the need to be clear, to support views with evidence or argument and to be consistent.

Organization and resources

Since the aim is to promote interaction among all participants, eye contact is highly desirable, which implies a circle or semicircle, not rows. This is especially so in open discussion but is also valuable in dialogic teaching. In schools, some concrete props or recent experience as the stimulus or focus for discussion is helpful.

Teacher and learner roles

The teacher's role is to model discussion and dialogue skills, and to conduct or at least facilitate the flow of conversation, ensuring it proceeds according to basic values and ground rules. But while the teacher has a more directive role in dialogic teaching, in open discussion it is important not to dominate the interaction.

The learner's role is to participate, be a good listener, develop confidence in expressing a view and argue reasonably. In group discussion or exploratory dialogue without the teacher, it can be helpful for learners to share out various roles such as note-taker, summarizer, ground-rule monitor and so on.

Teaching skills

Central here is modelling appropriate participation. If following Dillon's model of open discussion, skill is required to support discussion using alternatives to questioning (statements, appreciative silence, 'fillers', non-verbal signals). If conducting a dialogue, skill is required in high-level and probing questioning and responding, aiming to develop cumulative, progressive understanding.

Assessment

This is usually through observation or recording of key features of the process, particularly the quality of thinking and reasoning but also of aspects like listening, turn-taking and confidence in expressing views. Evidence of learner understanding is often available through subsequent activities such as oral report-backs, written work and practical projects, as well through participants' contributions during the discussion or dialogue. Understanding and skills tend to build over time.

Issues

The main issues are developing the difficult pedagogical skills needed to support effective open discussion or dialogue, and to prevent the session reducing to a traditional 'question and answer' or into covert direct teaching.

Summary

Discussion is potentially a very valuable way of learning, in school and everyday life. But most of what is called discussion in schools is better described as question and answer and is either covert exposition, or a means of checking up on learner understanding, or an attempt to encourage learners to think, usually along predetermined lines. Genuine open discussion is at present relatively rare in schools (but has some excellent examples nevertheless) and in recent research and policy has been heavily overshadowed by 'dialogic teaching' approaches. It is important to be clear about the difference between question and answer, dialogue and open discussion. All have a role and at the boundaries merge into one another. A key issue is the role of questioning. Dialogic teaching, like question and answer, makes this central, emphasizing open, higher-level questions. Scaffolding learners' thinking can be critical and this requires considerable teaching skill. In contrast, theorists of open discussion like Dillon argue that questioning generally foils open discussion and suggest teachers use various alternatives. Dialogic teaching unlike open discussion often appears to have specific learning outcomes (not just process ones) in mind for the learners and the teacher takes a directive role in pursuing this agenda. For open discussion, Bridges advocates an equitable role for all participants. Dillon's and Bridges' positions are well theorized and researched but have generally been neglected with at most token acknowledgement and no sustained critique.

Teachers need to be able to handle all three kinds of interaction well in classrooms to meet the diverse learning goals of schools and to deploy different modes of teaching effectively. Advocates of dialogic teaching appear unnecessarily wary of open discussion which, properly conceived and conducted, has very considerable educational potential. So, too, has dialogic teaching – provided it is not compromised through classroom pressures.

Key Reading

Alexander, R. (2000) *Culture and Pedagogy*. Oxford: Blackwell.

Alexander, R. (2008) *Towards Dialogic Teaching*, 4th edn. Cambridge: Dialogos.

Bridges, D. (1979) *Education, Democracy and Discussion*. Windsor: NFER.

Dillon, J. T. (1982) 'The effect of questions in education and other enterprises', *Journal of Curriculum Studies*, 14(2): 127–52.

Dillon, J. T. (1985) 'Using questions to foil discussion', *Teaching and Teacher Education*, 1: 109–21.

Dillon, J. T. (1994) *Using Discussion in Classrooms*. Buckingham: Open University Press.

Hardman, F. (2008) 'Teachers' use of feedback in whole-class and group-based talk', in N. Mercer and S. Hodgkinson (eds) *Exploring Talk in School*. London: Sage pp. 131–150.

Mercer, N. and Littleton, K. (2007) *Dialogue and the Development of Children's Thinking*. London: Routledge.

Myhill, D. (2006) 'Talk talk talk: teaching and learning in whole-class discourse', *Research Papers in Education*, 21(1): 19–41.

Useful Websites

www.dialogos.com

Website associated with Robin Alexander. See below.

www.teachernet.gov.uk
This website carries information about teaching and learning strategies and psychology of learning. Many useful resources and links.

www.robinalexander.org.uk
Website of leading thinker and writer on primary education, dialogic teaching and the *Primary Review* in England. Links to Professor Alexander's publications and *Primary Review* papers.

www.literacytrust.org.
This website of the National Literacy Trust provides analysis of current policy and summaries of research and implications for practice.

Learning through Action and Experience 5

Chapter Outline

The Promotion of Active Learning	57
Learning Through Action and Experience	58
Knowing How and Knowing That	60
Active Learning Through Play	62
Cognitive Apprenticeship	63
Features of the Mode	64
Summary	66
Key Reading	66
Useful Websites	67

The Promotion of Active Learning

The mode which is the subject of this chapter – learning through action and experience – should have an important role in mainstream education at all stages, as it has had traditionally in pre-school, outdoor, further and adult education. In recent years, however, what has been most strongly promoted in educational theory and policy has been 'active learning'. Though currently very influential, there are continuing ambiguities and problems with its conception; and it will be important to address these first before examining in detail the mode of teaching we have called 'learning through action and experience'.

One modern conception of active learning is well captured in the Scottish Curriculum for Excellence documentation (Scottish Executive 2007: 5):

> Active learning is learning which engages and challenges children's thinking using real-life and imaginary situations. It takes full advantage of the opportunities for learning presented by:
>
> spontaneous play
> planned purposeful play
> investigation and exploring

events and real life experiences

focused learning and teaching

supported where necessary through sensitive intervention to support or extend learning.

In the context of (mainly) secondary teaching, Kyriacou (2007: 43) says that active learning refers to:

any activities where pupils are given a marked degree of autonomy and control over the organisation, conduct and direction of the learning activity. Most usually, such activities involve problem-solving and investigational work and may be individualised (such as an extended piece of work or project) or involve small group collaboration (such as small group discussion, games, a role-play simulation or collaborative project).

Similar conceptions are offered by Allen *et al.* (2007) and Watkins *et al.* (2007).

Several different kinds of teaching and learning seem involved here – play, experiential learning, enquiry, dialogue and direct teaching (for which 'focused learning and teaching' and 'sensitive intervention' appear to be code). The concept surely needs further clarification and appears to be attempting to include too many different aspects at once without any obvious unifying principle, except perhaps active engagement.

In such writings, active learning is typically contrasted with passive learning. As discussed in Chapter 3, while there remain significant issues with unengaged, passive learning in many direct (and indeed other) teaching contexts, there is an important role for active reception learning, and well-conceived 'seat work' linked to direct teaching. It is never clear how far those who advocate 'active learning' are denying a role for such direct teaching or just condemning unsatisfactory approaches to it. Neither is it clear how far physical activity, the manipulation of materials and social interaction are defining or common, but not necessary, features (see Watkins *et al.* 2007: 66–9; Stephen *et al.* 2008).

'Active learning' as currently conceived appears to be a mixture of the old-fashioned 'activity methods' of the English Hadow and Plowden reports, with roots in Dewey, and more recent ideas about 'constructivism' (critiqued in Chapter 6) as the basis for effective learning. As such, it attempts to combine ideas about being mentally active, personally engaged, physical activity, social interaction, choice, decision-making, investigation, exploration, play and active construction of knowledge. Together with ambivalent attitudes to direct teaching it is no wonder that practitioners as well as parents have difficulty interpreting the term (Stephen *et al.* 2008).

Learning Through Action and Experience

One argument of this chapter is that, in all deliberate learning, whatever the mode, the aim should be for learners to be active in the sense of mentally engaged. It should also be remembered, however, though this is too rarely acknowledged, that much important learning, in school and out, is tacit, implicit and unconscious, although it often occurs alongside conscious learning (Atkinson and Claxton 2000; James 2008). The main argument, however, is that a separate mode of teaching and learning can be identified, in which direct experience of a skill, activity or phenomenon is central. This is an important and distinctive mode of teaching, different from enquiry, dialogue and discussion, and direct teaching. This mode might best be labelled 'learning through action and experience' to distinguish it from the idea of active learning with its over-ambitious scope and ambiguities as discussed above. It is unfortunate that 'active learning' is so problematically related to 'learning through action and experience' but that is the reality that faces anyone trying to think through these issues today. Similar problems existed in the past, typified by the Scottish Primary Memorandum's assertion that 'thought itself is activity' (Scottish Education Department 1965) which, however valid, confused rather than clarified the debate at that time on 'activity methods'.

'Learning through action and experience' seeks to bring two related streams of thought about teaching approaches closer together – action learning (or learning by doing) and experiential learning (in some contexts a more diffuse and holistic idea). In both, direct experience (possibly simulated) is the fundamental basis for learning and this fact enables them to be considered as forming a unified mode.

The 'active learning' definitions cited above fail to identify direct experience as a central feature of such learning and generally also fail to recognize many standard curriculum activities as learning through action and experience (which they undoubtedly are; and they would benefit from being so conceived in teachers' planning and interaction). The essence of learning through action and experience is not decision-making, choice or mental engagement but the role of direct experience. Choice and decision-making have a role in enquiry and discussion as well as in action and experiential learning but are not in fact a central feature of some common forms of learning through action and experience – for example practising piano scales or a tennis stroke.

It may be useful to consider some examples of learning in this mode:

- Learning about measurement by making something which involves careful measurement, such as a Christmas cracker; the English Cockcroft Report (Cockcroft 1982) stated that developing 'a feeling for measurement' and a 'feeling for number' should be the prime aims of mathematical education in schools.
- Learning to write, enjoy and appreciate a poetic form such as a sonnet or haiku by attempting to write one.
- Learning about profit and loss in economics by being involved in managing the school tuckshop for a few weeks.
- Learning to think clearly by engaging in a discussion as part of a community of philosophical enquiry in the class.

The key points here are the central role of direct experience and the fact that learning through action and experience is not by any means confined to outdoor education, role-play or active play in early education, but applies to many regular learning activities of the standard curriculum. There is a strong case for more emphasis at the 14–19 stage where reports show that learners are often disaffected and would benefit from more sustained learning through action and experience, and 14–19-year-olds certainly say this when asked (Lumby and Fosket 2004). While there are undoubtedly problems in developing such learning regularly on a large scale at 14–19, successful examples are available and it is possible to combine such approaches with meaningful direct teaching to produce an effective and worthwhile curriculum experience at this stage.

Knowing How and Knowing That

It is important to ask what sort of knowledge and skills are being learned through this mode and how they are being learned. Here the distinction between knowing 'that' and knowing 'how' can be useful (Pring 1976: 18 ff., 2004; Schwab 1978). Schools have traditionally focused on both: on developing skills as well as factual knowledge and conceptual understanding. Learning how to express oneself clearly and concisely in English is 'know how' as is learning how to conduct an effective experiment, or design a teaspoon. Much schooling, however, seems based on the premise that theoretical knowledge is the main base for effective practical action; and mastering this 'theoretical' knowledge is often so divorced from practice that learners find difficulty applying it to novel contexts. However, theoretical knowledge is not all that is required. A practical 'know-how' is necessary and often this cannot be articulated or explicitly taught. It generally has to be learned through direct experience, perhaps involving guidance from an experienced practitioner and through careful reflection on experience. Admittedly, the distinction between 'knowing that' (propositional knowledge) and 'knowing how' (practical knowledge) has proved a controversial one among philosophers of knowledge (Winch 2009b). A key problem is that while the basis for 'know how' often can't easily be articulated and 'know how' can't be reduced simply to knowing that (Pring 1976: 31), some propositional knowledge certainly seems to underpin effective practical action. Thomas (2007: 32) quotes Fish's essay on the laconic dialogue between a baseball coach and a world-renowned player to point up the difference between playing a game and explaining it: 'He said, "Throw strikes and keep 'em off the bases" and I said "OK ...What else could I say."' Those who can explain well aren't necessarily better players.

McCormick (1999) points out, in a discussion of learning about snooker, that applying mathematics and physics abstracted from the realities of the snooker table makes it difficult to get accurate results and that there is a practical know-how which takes these realities into account and ensures the success of the snooker shot in a way that abstract mathematics and physics can't match. This is true of many areas of knowledge and experience. Pring (1976: 31) notes that 'learning that' is not necessarily the best way to learn how to make friends or ride a bicycle and that however important it is to know that certain statements are true, knowing how to do things (to play a piece of music, to enjoy a concert, to make a sketch, to appreciate a poem, to climb skilfully) is equally a cognitive achievement, a development of the mind which is not reducible to knowing that or to the kinds of knowledge that can be stated in propositions.

Planning and structuring action and experiential learning

These issues about knowledge have implications for managing and interacting when using this mode. Quay (2004) argues that outdoor education has traditionally dealt with sources of knowledge that originate within the experience itself and this sits uncomfortably with the general thrust of much school knowledge. He also emphasizes that experiential learning – doing combined with reflection – is a much more intricate process than schools often recognize. For Beard and Wilson (2006), experiential learning involves the whole person, not least the emotions and whole environment. Of course, the role of emotions in learning, now increasingly recognized, is not confined to any single mode.

Experience alone is not a sure route to learning. As Dewey (1938: 25) emphasized, some experiences can be mis-educative. Reflection on experience is widely considered necessary to develop understanding and generalization and hence the ability to apply the learning, or principles derived from it, to other contexts. Outdoor education (Higgins 2009) provides a very powerful learning process through which a learner constructs knowledge and develops skill and value from direct experience via a reflective process in which a teacher helps learners to process raw experience into useable knowledge.

Kolb's four-stage model (concrete experience, reflective observation, abstract conceptualization, active experimentation) aims to capture the nature of learning through action and experience (Kolb 1984) but critics see his model as too mechanistic and lacking in strong empirical validation. Beard and Wilson (2006) stress the interaction between stages and the holistic nature of experience-based thinking.

While teachers and schools often initially raise practical difficulties about curriculum constraints and organizational issues, there is now a sufficiently wide range of examples of successful practice in ordinary schools to validate the approach (see Chapter 8). Wurdinger (2005) cites the use by school pupils of oral history interviews with grandparents and so on to collect information and produce a book about local folkore in Georgia, USA (the well-known 'Foxfire' approach) as an influential example of learning through action and experience which involves learning how to interview people, and write and report accurately in a meaningful and motivating context.

At times it may be difficult to distinguish learning through action and experience from enquiry learning since the former is so often set in the context of an investigation or problem to be solved (but not all enquiry is through direct experience). It is possible to view such teaching as either one mode or the other, or possibly a combination – enquiry through action. Each choice will have particular implications for planning and interacting.

Active Learning Through Play

In the UK, recent concerns with transition from pre-school to primary education and with the effects of target-led transmission teaching induced by national curricula have led to a revival of active learning through play in the early primary years.

Developments in Scotland under the Curriculum for Excellence initiative have been widely praised and are generally agreed to be a decided improvement on recent practice under the 5–14 programme. Many useful exemplars are now available for teachers to build on (see websites below). There is much evidence of increased teacher confidence about learning through action and experience and improved attitudes to school and learning on the part of children. What is welcome is the extent to which these have included mathematical and literacy activities as well as other aspects of the curriculum. This promises a useful balance combining direct teaching for literacy and numeracy along with learning about these through action and experience.

It may be useful here to consider the High/Scope approach, an American development for pre-school and early elementary education which has had some influence in the UK and Australia and which can claim validation from a 40-year research study and other research (Muijs and Reynolds 2005: 186). The scheme is based on the idea that children should 'learn by doing', using a 'plan-do-review' sequence. In a nursery with children able to access facilities (say, for water play, reading, sand play, art, writing, dramatic play) independently, children first plan what materials they want to work with and what they want to do. Only once they have made a plan, however vague, can they go and do it. At the end the children discuss what they have been doing and whether it was successful. This cycle is central to the mode of learning through action and experience but need not be on such a large scale. Many shorter activities can be planned using an action learning cycle.

The theoretical dominance of the activity framework in early learning needs more consideration. One of the most famous and pedagogically influential statements about English primary education is that set out in the Hadow report of 1931 'the curriculum is to be thought of in terms of activity and experience rather than of knowledge to be acquired and facts to be stored' (pp. 92–3). It went on:

> Practical and physical activities should be paramount [. . .]as far as possible, the child should be put in the position to teach himself, and the knowledge that he is to acquire should come, not so much from an instructor, as from an instructive environment.

Alexander (2000) points out that, under pressure from the early educationists of the Froebel Institute, the original draft was changed. The original read 'activity and experience and knowledge to be acquired and facts to be stored'. This clearly would have implied a much more balanced view of teaching modes. The polarity set up between direct teaching and activity methods has not in the end proved helpful to educational development. In Scotland in 1950, a report advocating activity methods (Scottish Education Department 1950: 24–5) asserted that 'the infant acquires speech not from instruction but through his attempts to speak; the schoolboy learns football not by conning the rules but by playing the game'. This distorted and one-sided view fortunately had little impact on practice in Scotland.

Cognitive Apprenticeship

This is a teaching approach based on applying ideas from traditional learning in trade apprenticeships to the classroom which, like ordinary apprenticeships, can be viewed as an example of learning through action and experience (Collins *et al.* 1989). Learners are seen as apprentices of the teacher who models intellectual skills and guides the 'apprentices' in their active, cognitive learning. Using authentic contexts that mirror real-life problem-solving situations, the teacher aims to teach the processes experts use (how they make use of facts, concepts and skills and also tricks of the trade and monitoring their own actions) to solve problems and handle complex tasks. The teacher models, coaches and gradually withdraws support as the apprentices develop competence.

The analogy with trade apprenticeships is appropriate because much implicit learning is involved in learning to undertake complex cognitive tasks, just as it is in learning many crafts. The approach works best if it is based on authentic learning of whole tasks rather than contrived or piecemeal classroom exercises; and with individuals or small groups rather than the full class, which would require considerable organization. Cognitive apprenticeship insists on a positive role for the teacher (as expert), not a laissez-faire one.

Brown and Palinscar's (1989) 'reciprocal teaching' has many features of cognitive apprenticeship and has proved very effective in raising reading scores. The teacher models expert reading processes and coaches learners in four skills: formulating questions (e.g. how, what, and why questions – see Galton 2007: 76–7), summarizing, predicting and clarifying difficulties. It is reciprocal because the teacher and the learners (in a small group) take turns at acting as the 'teacher.' It is also worth noting Rogoff's (1990) discussion of 'apprenticeship in thinking' based on guided participation in culturally valued activities where much learning is tacit and implicit and where interaction is non-verbal.

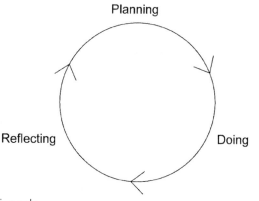

Figure 5.1 Action learning cycle

Learning through action and experience needs to be seen as more than hands-on activity. It is usually best conceived as involving a cycle of planning, acting and reflecting – with the learners having central involvement in the planning and reflecting phases as well as engaging in the action phase. Because of time and coverage pressures, teachers often fail to give learners adequate ownership of planning and reflecting and this can markedly reduce the effectiveness of learning in this mode.

Features of the Mode

Learning through action and experience covers a range of educational activities with varying degrees of structure and openness, yet all sharing the same essential means of learning.

Means of learning

The essence is learning through direct experience of a phenomenon or process and by reflection on this experience. The quality of learning through action can depend heavily on the quality of thinking about the action. Such thinking can be before, during and after the action. There can be a tension between thinking and acting and these aspects need to be effectively balanced, ensuring the action is properly planned for, sustained and reflected on. It can be useful to view learning through action and experience as a cycle of cycle of planning, doing and reflecting.

Organization and resources

These clearly depend on the activity – for example, if it is modelling with clay, learning to referee a game, practise the violin, conduct an experiment, undertake a piece of writing, organize a concert, participate in a citizenship or enterprise simulation. All will require facilities and material resources for the action phase and possibly for planning and reflecting. Activities and experiences can be planned for the whole class, groups or individuals; each context raises different issues of organization and safety (e.g. in the gym, science lab, outdoors, drama studio, art room).

Teacher and learner roles

The teacher's role is to involve learners fully in planning and reflecting, not to direct or push them through the activity. Learners need to be encouraged to sustain the action. These are thus support and challenge roles for the teacher. In some action and experiential learning contexts there is a tradition of more directive coaching, at least at certain stages of the activity. Some brief direct teaching may be necessary on safety procedures and other aspects. Roles from other performance contexts – such as sports coaching, directing a play, apprenticeship – can be adapted for this mode.

The learner's role is to become fully involved in the action or experience and to reflect intelligently on it at appropriate junctures.

Teaching skills

The main skills can be described as bringing out a performance from the learner or enabling the learners to get the most out of the experience. There are different ways of achieving these goals just as different theatre directors draw out good performances in different ways. But such nebulous interactive skills are just as much part of effective teaching in this mode as in the theatre or film studio, or on the sports field.

Assessment

Much of this will be through observation; but report-backs on experiences and activities can demonstrate learning (see Chapter 8 on 'performances of understanding'). Written reflections and reflections during group discussion are other valuable sources of evidence of knowledge and understanding for various activities involving learning through action and experience.

Issues

Helping learners sustain the action, developing the quality of thinking about action and, in many contexts, using interpersonal skills to draw out performances are important and challenging aspects of this mode. Modern curricula constrain the time available for such action and experiential learning, and can lead teachers to push learners through the activity too quickly. This is a challenge to teachers' organizational and curriculum management skills and commitment to the value of this mode.

The main issues which need to be considered are when to reflect in action learning (not just at the end, perhaps at interim stages), creating realistic or simulated contexts of action learning, practical management and the scale of the teaching unit, which can vary from small (within a lesson) to large (over a few days).

Teaching Development Activity 5.1 – Learning Through Action

Select some active learning situation (e.g. a measurement or model-making activity, a role activity such as manager of some event or process, some 'public speaking' activity) – one where a small group of learners are developing understanding and competence through direct experience of the activity or phenomenon. Plan to involve the learners as fully as possible in the planning and reflective phases as well as the doing phase. Help them develop ownership of all three phases. Encourage them to sustain the action phase effectively and consider how best to play your role in supporting and challenging your learners and offering feedback as you think appropriate. Reflect on the quality of learning, issues your learners' faced, how you played your role and the demands of organizing such action learning opportunities.

Summary

This mode has an established tradition in various stages and types of education and needs to be exploited more fully as a way of planning and managing many regular classroom activities which involve practice or application as well as learning from direct experience in school and out. Debate and policy development is currently focused on the idea of 'active learning' but this is an ambiguous and over-ambitious idea. Active engagement should be a feature of all deliberate teaching and learning, not of one particular mode. The 'active learning' conception based on constructivist thinking (itself inadequate as a comprehensive theory of learning) focuses on choice and decision-making as central criteria and includes enquiry learning which, it is argued here, would be better viewed as a separate mode.

Against the 'active learning' view it is suggested that a distinctive teaching mode, 'learning through action and experience', can be identified. Its essence is learning through direct experience of a process, activity or phenomenon. This is a separate mode from enquiry and builds on two related, well-established traditions of teaching – action learning and experiential learning – and links clearly to traditional activity methods in schools and recent developments in cognitive apprenticeship. It has an important role in the regular curriculum, as well as in outdoor education and early years educational play.

It is best seen as involving a cycle of planning, doing and reflecting. Learners need to be actively involved in all three phases, something that has been neglected in the past. Learners need both support and challenge and the teacher has a useful role in offering feedback during the reflective phase. The mode raises issues about the balance between knowing how and knowing that, and the role of reflection in helping learners express, process and consolidate learning resulting from action and experience. Much learning from action is implicit and tacit but crucial nevertheless.

Key Reading

Atkinson, T. and Claxton, G. (eds) (2003) *The Intuitive Practitioner*. Maidenhead: Open University Press.

Fox, R. (2005) *Teaching and Learning*. Oxford: Blackwell.

Jarvis, P. (2002) *The Theory and Practice of Teaching*. London: Kogan Page.

Pring, R. (1976) *Knowledge and Schooling*. London: Open Books.

Scottish Executive (2007) *A Curriculum for Excellence Building the Curriculum (2) Active Learning in the Early Years*. Edinburgh: Scottish Executive.

Watkins, C., Carnell, E. and Lodge, C. (2007) *Effective Learning in Classrooms*. London: Paul Chapman.

Wurdinger, S. D. (2005) *Using Experiential Learning in the Classroom*. Oxford: Scarecrow Education.

Useful Websites

http://www.geoffpetty.com/activelearning.html
Examples and ideas.

http://njaes.rutgers.edu/learnbydoing/weblinks.html
Many useful weblinks on this topic.

http://www.ltscotland.org.uk/earlyyears/sharingpractice/approachestolearning/learningthroughplay/
index.asp
Video and other examples of active play in the early years

www.education.ed.ac.uk/outdoored/
Ideas and developments in outdoor education

www.elschools.org
Website of Expeditionary Learning Schools Outward Bound. Information on its approach, which aims to combine rigorous academic content and real-world projects – learning expeditions – with active teaching and community service. Examples of expeditionary learning as implemented in schools in the USA.

Learning through Enquiry

Chapter Outline

Enquiry and Discovery Learning	68
Constructivism and Teaching	70
Enquiry Structures and Processes	71
Enquiry in Particular Subject Areas	73
Features of the Mode	75
Summary	77
Key Reading	78
Useful Websites	78

Enquiry and Discovery Learning

'Put the problems before him and let him solve them himself. Let him know nothing because you have told him but because he has learnt it for himself. Let him not be taught science. Let him discover it': so advised Rousseau (1911: 131) for the education of Emile. But those attempting to follow Rousseau's dictum have found it far from easy and have met with scepticism about the validity of the idea as a general strategy. The argument of this chapter is that enquiry learning is an important teaching mode for any subject; but it requires a conception of enquiry much wider than 'discovery learning' of set knowledge, and enquiry commonly needs to be balanced by other modes, including a fair amount of direct teaching.

Like discussion, enquiry learning in schools usually has two main aims: to develop subject knowledge and understanding through enquiry and to learn how to enquire. Thus learners might be expected to learn about magnetism through conducting experiments with iron filings, and in doing so learn how to conduct an effective experiment. Learners conducting a historical investigation into the Highland Clearances in Scotland, drawing on primary and secondary sources, would hopefully learn more about how to assess and draw conclusions from historical sources while also gaining insights into the Clearances.

The balance between learning through enquiry and learning to enquire needs to be judged in relation to the context. Sometimes learning to enquire might be the primary aim;

but it need not be taught solely through undertaking enquiry. Learning to conduct an effective experiment might better be introduced in some detail through direct teaching, followed by experience in planning, conducting and evaluating a series of experiments on different topics, enabling learners to develop a grasp of the range of issues that arise.

Under the influence of Dewey and Kilpatrick in the USA after the First World War, project work involving enquiry learning became a recognized part of primary curricula in North America and the UK. At secondary level, though, little progress was made against the dominant subject-based curriculum and national examinations. From the 1960s, however, 'guided discovery' in secondary teaching was promoted and important enquiry learning innovations like 'Man: a Course of Study' and the Humanities Curriculum Project developed (Bruner 1960; Stenhouse 1975: 38–9). In a classic essay, Bruner (1961: 21 ff.) asserted that 'the most personal of all that man knows is that which he has discovered for himself' and spoke of the powerful effects of 'permitting the student to put things together for himself, to be his own discoverer'. Bruner saw four key benefits of discovery learning: an increase in 'intellectual potency', a shift from extrinsic to intrinsic rewards and motivation, the opportunity to learn enquiry and problem-solving methods, and the advantage it gave for remembering facts and ideas.

In the 1960s and 70s discovery learning was widely debated. While research studies comparing direct teaching with 'discovery' methods were not encouraging for advocates of discovery (Child 2008), legitimate questions were raised as to whether they were or should be aiming at similar learning goals. In any case, many eventually concluded that the notion of discovery learning was too vague for credible research, it not being clear how far it was defined in terms of teaching, learning or outcomes (Noddings 2007).

Stenhouse (1967: 30, 1975: 38) argued strongly for enquiry learning (as opposed to guided discovery), claiming that 'the superficialities of the disciplines may be taught by pure instruction, but the capacity to think within the disciplines can only be taught by inquiry'. Stated baldly this view appears too extreme since many learners appear to have acquired an ability to think effectively about science and mathematics through traditional direct teaching. Perhaps, however, the key lies in the usually associated sustained practice in solving problems. Scott (2008: 33) argues that disciplines are more fluid and internally differentiated than Stenhouse implies and that school knowledge is a pedagogic translation of disciplined knowledge; and that at different times 'different pedagogic approaches, whether inquiry based or didactic, may be appropriate' (see also Chapter 10). Nevertheless, the general consensus now appears to be, at least in the West, that developing deep conceptual understanding and independent problem-solving ability require more than direct teaching on its own (Kyriacou 1995; Galton 2007).

Another of Stenhouse's arguments was that enquiry learning does not lend itself to pre-specified outcomes. Indeed, for Stenhouse (1975: 83), induction into the disciplines through enquiry was successful to the extent to which the learning outcomes were unpredictable. This is a central idea, but many teachers express concern about teaching in such open-ended contexts and the learning outcomes question led to a long-running debate in curriculum and lesson planning. While to some extent the issue turns on how broad the learning outcome specification is, genuine enquiry teaching does surely demand a willingness to be open about learning outcomes.

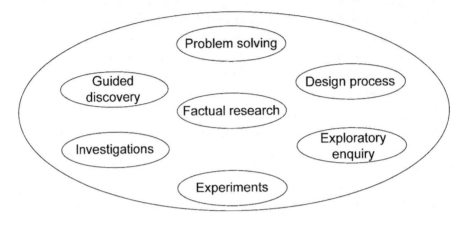

Figure 6.1 The variety of enquiry learning

Within the basic category of enquiry as a mode of teaching and learning there is a need to recognize a range of enquiry types and degrees of openness. Moreover, enquiry structures and processes can vary significantly among disciplines as well as having some common features.

Constructivism and Teaching

To understand the debate on enquiry learning we need to look further at the idea of constructivism – already briefly referred to in earlier chapters – for it now provides the main rationale for enquiry learning and for specific teaching approaches linked to an enquiry framework. Fox (2001) argues that constructivism, which has come to be the dominant view in education about how knowledge is acquired, is best regarded as a metaphor for learning, a guiding myth: the idea that knowledge needs to be actively constructed by the learner. Barnes (2008: 1–16) suggests that most important learning 'is a matter of constructing models of the world [...] finding out how they work by using them and adjusting them in the light of further experience'. For constructivists, learning basically involves making sense of our experiences. Piaget argued that we develop knowledge either by assimilating new experiences into our existing set of ideas, if they fit this set, or by 'accommodating' (modifying) our network of ideas to match the new experiences we are encountering. A key implication is that the teacher's role is to help learners, as Barnes (2008) puts it, to 'work on understanding' by setting up situations and challenges which enable learners to relate emerging ideas to their existing network of concepts.

Radical constructivism rejects the view of science as a solid, proven body of knowledge that can just be transmitted to learners. Instead, it contends that we build knowledge individually on the basis of our experiences. Social constructivism takes a social rather than individual perspective and emphasizes learners being inducted into cultural practices and ways of seeing the world by the social groups in which they live, work and learn. It implies that the best way to relate new ideas to existing ones is through exploratory talk in authentic activities with peers and more experienced adults. The roots of social constructivism lie in Vygotsky's ideas of the role of talk in learning and the 'zone of proximal development' (ZPD), commonly defined as the gap between what a learner can do unaided and what he or she can do with assistance from a more knowledgeable person; and also in the theory of situated cognition – the idea that knowledge is generated by the social context and social interaction (Lave and Wenger 1991). Constructivism in its various manifestations raises important questions about the nature of knowledge of the world. The debate on this does have implications for the role of enquiry in contrast to other modes in developing knowledge and understanding, despite the claims of some constructivists that teachers can put metaphysical questions about the nature of reality aside and focus on 'pedagogical constructivism' (see further Grandy 2007; Phillips 2007).

For Fox, constructivism rightly highlights the vital role of a learner's existing knowledge, the importance of understanding in learning, and the learner's active engagement and exploration. But, he argues, an uncritical acceptance of constructivism is a mistake: it cannot provide a comprehensive account of how we gain new knowledge, understanding and skills; it ignores a great deal of normal learning; it implies a negative attitude to direct teaching; and it does not match the realities of organizing learning in schools or how it is often achieved outside them. For example, practice of skills and routines is important and motivation remains a big issue in learning. Learners often find it hard to appreciate why they should do the hard work involved in learning which (though important) is not immediately rewarding or directly relevant. Fox's analysis implies a clear place for enquiry learning, dialogue and experiential learning but also for systematic direct teaching.

Reflective Exploration 6.1 – The Range of Enquiry Learning

Make a list of the various kinds of enquiry learning that learners experience in your teaching context. Compare with the range in Figure 6.1 and consider what sorts of enquiry it might be useful to develop, factors that have inhibited this and how you might give more scope to this mode.

Enquiry Structures and Processes

At first, in many school contexts, too little attention was given to the fact that learners would need to be trained in how to enquire effectively. This resulted in some very unsatisfactory learning experiences. The need for systematic teaching about enquiry is now fully recognized but there is often a danger of the teacher taking too much control of the enquiry process and failing to ensure that learners retain strong ownership. The balance here needs careful judgement. Dewey (see Pring 2007b) provided a possible model for enquiry through his general five-step problem-solving process that comprised: felt difficulty; clarification of the problem; identification of possible solutions; testing these solutions; and verification of the results. Bruner (1960) emphasized that the key concepts in any discipline were generally both simple and powerful, and Stenhouse (1975: 85–6) stressed that they also typically were problematic (see Chapter 2), a fact which learners conducting enquiries would need to come to terms with. As a general approach to reflective thinking, or a scientific process, or a design process, Dewey's model works reasonably but may not work so well for more open enquiries and investigations.

Many writers on enquiry learning stress the importance of questioning and they focus on teacher questioning of learners. Questioning is certainly important but in enquiry learning it is the learners who should be asking the questions – about the matter being researched, with the teacher modelling how to formulate questions about the focus of research (e.g. the behaviour of the snails being observed or the historical document being studied). Yet research shows pupils ask very few questions in class – about ten per week compared to the typical teacher's 1,000 per week (Dillon 1988a). The solution, Dillon argues, is for teachers to make deliberate room for pupil questions by stopping asking questions themselves and encouraging pupil questions – by formally inviting questions, waiting patiently (an attitude of 'contented expectancy'), welcoming questions when they come and 'sustaining the asking' (offering help to express questions effectively). Eventually a flood of questions may come. This is not a problem of course but the first stage of research – sorting questions into different types, reducing those that overlap, deciding on the most fruitful ones and how to seek answers.

Teaching Development Activity 6.1 – Supporting and Challenging Enquiry

Find a suitable focus for enquiry such as a group of snails, a range of fruits, some historical artefact or art object. Aim to generate questions from the learners about what they would like to investigate in relation to the object or topic of the enquiry. Support your learners as they refine and group the questions and decide which are open to practical enquiry in your context. Help them select one suitable question to explore and discuss with the learners how the enquiry might proceed. Help them organize the investigation, giving them as much ownership as is feasible, and then support and challenge them as they conduct it. Help them (without taking over) discuss their findings, what they think they have learned and their experience of undertaking the enquiry.

Enquiry in Particular Subject Areas

A comprehensive treatment is obviously not possible here but the discussion that follows many help to provide a sense of the ubiquity, range and diversity of enquiry learning and of teaching issues that arise.

Art education

Dobbs (1998) articulates a scheme for 'discipline-based art education' (adaptable for primary and secondary schools), centred on an enquiry process that can incorporate inter-disciplinary study. He identifies four art disciplines (recognized bodies of knowledge and skill with characteristic ways of working): art-making, art-criticism, art history and aesthetics. Each discipline provides a perspective from which to understand works of art and the context in which they are created. Artists, critics, aestheticians and philosophers of art conduct enquiries within these disciplines, bringing other relevant disciplines such as anthropology and communication studies into play as appropriate.

Learners develop broad, rich experiences and understanding by creating works of art (art-making), art criticism, enquiry into the historical, social and cultural context of art objects and by raising and exploring aesthetic questions about the nature, meaning and value of art. The four disciplines typically intermingle through relatively open enquiry-based experiences that can link with other subject disciplines. Thus the biology of plants can inform the creation of corn statues and ICT resources such as the internet can prove very useful.

This enquiry-based approach sits well with modern conceptions of art education with its emphasis on appreciating as well as creating art, and its links to citizenship education and the wider aims of education in general.

History

History teaching now generally adopts an optimistic view of young children's ability to understand the past and of the key role of enquiry in this. With teacher support, young learners can work in the same ways as historians, as historical investigators entering into the spirit of the past, hypothesizing and investigating sources, considering causes and consequences.

A central ability is to imagine what it was like to live in past times, to be present, for example, at a Viking burial. Active learning experiences can be very helpful here, for example in a working reproduction of a Tudor kitchen. Observation is very important and can build the historical enquiry skills of working with primary and secondary sources. Recording appropriately, classifying, cataloguing synthesizing and interpreting evidence also contribute to genuinely historical thinking.

A key issue concerns how far a body of knowledge is fundamental to becoming a good historian. Systematic knowledge of explanations of past events and established interpretations and facts are best taught using direct teaching. A balance between this, including a narrative approach for appropriate content, and more focused enquiry learning is likely to prove motivating.

History draws on and develops a network of concepts and learners need to grasp concepts like government, trade, battle, slavery, migration. The interdependence of English and history is very obvious to anyone teaching historical investigation using sources that, in classroom investigations, so often are based on written sources. But texts that are difficult to read can be of high interest and help develop the perseverance that needs to be brought to such tasks. ICT resources are increasingly important for such historical enquiries in schools. At a wider level, enquiry can help learners to understand how to locate, explore and link periods, people and events in time and place, just as in geographical enquiry they can learn how to find, explore and link features and places locally and further afield.

Science

For many writers on science education, enquiry means investigations. Various kinds can be distinguished such as 'fair testing', 'seeing what happens' and 'pattern-seeking'. These involve the understanding and skills required for observation, generating hypotheses, controlling variables and interpreting findings.

Various points of departure are possible. Topical media issues – for example, about brushing teeth or other aspects of healthy living, can provide a motivating stimulus for enquiry. Most science investigations raise considerations of resources, organization and safety. Explorations can begin in pre-school, for example exploring ice balloons (balloons filled with water, then frozen) using one's senses, especially sight and touch, and developing confidence in exploring physical objects, observing, and talking about what is found using appropriate vocabulary (Johnston 1996).

At secondary level, learners often find handling variables, analysing and evaluating difficult, and the teacher can play an important role in dialogue with learners to develop skills and confidence.

Enquiry may of course result in wrong ideas that then need to be questioned. Organizing a 'verification of outcomes' session is important so that learners are not just left to live with misconceptions. But recent research, from a constructivist perspective on learners' conceptions of scientific causes, suggests that learners cannot merely be told the correct answers. They often do not grasp these or absorb them but rather quickly revert to old, naive explanations (Driver 2004).

It is tempting to break scientific enquiry down into a host of separate 'skills' (though these involve understanding as much as skill) and steps. But a process with three or five stages is more helpful than one with nine, even if within some steps there are subdivisions; and while it is important to teach skills in a focused way it is also important, early on, to give learners experience of the enquiry process as a whole – if necessary in a simplified form.

Mathematics

Jones (2003) argues for a broad interpretation of problem-solving in mathematics. Investigations can develop confidence and independence in using and applying mathematics. They can be open-ended in the sense that in practical contexts there is not necessarily any one best way of measuring, calculating or exploring patterns, and so on. Jones recommends that teachers should explore investigations themselves before giving them to learners. There has been a tendency in recent years for problem-solving to become a separate component of the mathematics curriculum, but many now claim it is better to infuse explorations and investigations into the general course of mathematics teaching.

Other areas

Taking the recent Scottish Curriculum for Excellence documentation (Scottish Executive 2008) as an example it is clear that in all areas of the curriculum investigation and exploration are given an important role. Learners are expected to explore the richness and diversity of language; to explore religious beliefs and investigate various answers to questions about the meaning of life; they take opportunities to observe, explore, experiment and play, explore and evaluate different types and sources of evidence, discover ways to link actions and skills to create movement patterns and sequences. In all subjects enquiry in some form is given a significant role. The documentation aims to foster a general enquiring spirit, integrated into regular teaching, rather than just as a specific enquiry or problem-solving component of the subject curriculum. In social studies it is emphasized that terms such as investigating, exploring, discussing and presenting are used throughout all stages from 3–18 because at all stages learners are capable of exercising these skills. This principle can be applied to all curriculum subjects.

Teaching Development Activity 6.2 – Resourcing Enquiry Learning

Are there under-used, accessible resources that could be exploited for enquiry learning in your teaching context that would fit your current curriculum and expected key learning outcomes? Devise some way of making use of them and reflect on issues that arose in developing effective enquiry learning.

Features of the Mode

Enquiry teaching has a double purpose: to develop subject understanding through enquiry and to teach learners how to conduct an effective enquiry. Enquiry is best viewed as a broad term incorporating a range of investigative processes. Along with some common characteristics, enquiries in different disciplines tend to have distinctive features.

Means of learning

This is 'finding out for yourself,' through research, experiment, problem-solving and investigation.

Organization and resources

Enquiries are best conducted by individuals or small groups. Structure and organization vary with the discipline concerned. Resources (reference books, the internet, apparatus, art materials and so on) are usually a prime consideration. Different phases of an enquiry often require different organization –individuals, a group, the whole class. At times other modes (discussion or dialogue, or direct teaching) may be drawn on within the broad enquiry framework.

Teacher and learner roles

The teacher's role is not instructor but adviser on the process of effective enquiry and resources, giving the learners ownership of the direction of enquiry while supporting and challenging them. Modelling effective enquiry and investigation is also a key teaching role.

To learn effectively in this mode, learners should be prepared to try relevant investigative strategies, observe carefully, ask enquiry questions, experiment systematically and reflect critically on evidence.

Teaching skills

Modelling effective enquiry as an experienced researcher is central, along with interaction to support and challenge, helping enquirers to be disciplined but also open to ideas and evidence. At evaluation, the teacher should be a constructive critic, encouraging pupils to ask questions and evaluate reflectively. These are very different skills from those of direct teaching. Dialogic teaching may play an important role within a broad enquiry framework for a teaching unit.

Assessment

In open enquiry (as opposed to guided discovery), the specific outcomes are unpredictable, requiring a distinctive approach to assessment. Assessment often involves pupils reporting back on the results of investigations. Assessment typically involves observation and evaluation of process as well as consideration of outcome.

Issues

An important issue is how far enquiry is discipline-specific. A typical scientific enquiry process – observation, hypothesis, experiment, analysis and reporting of findings – may not be the best basis for historical, literary or religious enquiry, though all such enquiries may culminate in analysis, evaluation and reporting phases.

Another issue is the role of subject understanding. Can you learn to enquire in history, chemistry, literature without first knowing some basic history, chemistry or literature? If not, enquiry approaches need to be balanced by more structured learning using other modes, especially direct teaching. In several curricular schemes now, enquiry and systematic teaching run in parallel, with encouraging results.

Yet another issue concerns the degree of openness and ownership of the enquiry. Open enquiry, owned by the learner, may soon cross subject boundaries (Pring 1976). This poses a curricular challenge given National Curriculum prescriptions, and an organizational one with a whole class. More restricted enquiries, however, may not engender deep under-standing.

Summary

As with discussion, the aim in enquiry learning is twofold: to help learners learn through enquiry and to teach learners how to enquire. An issue is how far there is a general enquiry process as opposed to specific approaches for the different subjects. The teacher's role is to support and challenge, not laissez-faire, while enabling learners to retain ownership of the enquiry. This has proved to be a difficult balance to maintain. Other important roles are to advise or consult on the research being planned and in progress, and to manage resources for enquiry.

Most now accept that, while a systematic knowledge base is important for effective sustained enquiry, enquiries conducted in parallel with the development of systematic knowledge and skills can prove effective and motivating. ICT resources play an increasingly important role in enquiry learning in all subjects.

At first, Piaget and then radical constructivism provided the constructivist rationale for enquiry in science and mathematics education; but now social constructivist ideas have added an important dimension to enquiry learning through their emphasis on exploratory talk and collaborative group work.

For teaching set knowledge, 'guided discovery' is unlikely to prove very effective or efficient in comparison to direct teaching. Guided discovery is too narrow a conception of enquiry learning. More open enquiry has wider educational aims and uses. It helps make learners inro independent thinkers within a discipline; they become active thinkers and learn how to enquire as well as to learn through enquiry.

Enquiry involves a range of understanding and skills that may need to be taught discretely within a broader enquiry framework. Learners need early experience in the whole enquiry process to grasp the nature of being a scientist, historian, artist or whatever. There is a central role for discipline-based enquiry and also for cross-curricular enquiry. Learning through enquiry always needs to be balanced by systematic direct teaching.

Key Reading

Davis, D. and Howe, A. (2007) 'Exploration, investigation and enquiry', in J. Moyles (ed.) *Beginning Teaching Beginning Learning*, 2nd edn. Maidenhead: Open University Press, pp. 74–85.

Dobbs, S. M. (1998) *Learning in and through Art*. Los Angeles: The J. Paul Getty Museum.

Harlen, W. (ed.) (2006) *ASE Guide to Primary Science Education*. Hatfield: The Association for Science Education.

Haydn, T. and Counsell, C. (2003) *History, ICT and Learning in the Secondary School*. London: RoutledgeFalmer.

Jones, L. (2003) 'The problem with problem-solving', in D. Haylock (ed.) *Enhancing Primary Mathematics Teaching*. London: Routledge, pp. 86–97.

Pring, R. (1976) *Knowledge and Schooling*. London: Open Books.

Sang, D. and Wood-Robinson, V. (eds) (2002) *Teaching Secondary Scientific Enquiry*. London: John Murray.

Stenhouse, L. (1975) *An Introduction to Curriculum Research and Development*. London: Heinemann.

Useful Websites

www.teachernet.org.uk
Many ideas for enquiry teaching in different subjects.

www.ncetm.org.uk
Website of the National Centre for Excellence in the Teaching of Mathematics. Useful examples and ideas for investigations and problem-solving in mathematics.

www.ASE.org.uk
Website for the Association for Science Education. Good network links and useful ideas on enquiry in science.

www.kented.org.uk/ngfl/subjects/history/qca
Useful resources on teaching history, including enquiry learning.

www.LTScotland.org.uk
Recent documentation on the Scottish Curriculum for Excellence, setting out enquiry learning aspirations.

Part 3
Using the Modes in Practice – Further Considerations

Whole-class, Group and Individual Teaching

Chapter Outline

Teaching Modes and Class Organization	81
Whole-class Teaching	82
Collaborative Learning	83
Individualized, Independent and Personalized Learning	86
Classroom Environment and Layout	88
Summary	89
Key Reading	90
Useful Websites	90

Teaching Modes and Class Organization

Attempting to deploy the range of teaching modes effectively raises questions about the organization of teaching, a matter that has usually been discussed in terms of the balance between class, group and individual teaching. This in turn raises a host of other questions – about differentiation of learning, inclusion, resources and facilities for particular subjects and individuals, ICT developments, existing classroom layouts and the cost implications of any desirable changes. These are not merely technical matters: policies have often been determined by wider educational and political thinking, as we shall see regarding recent initiatives on personalizing learning.

Different teaching modes typically have differing implications for how learning is organized. Direct teaching works well with a traditional (desks in rows) classroom and can be used with large groups. Effective discussion normally requires smaller groups and a seating arrangement where all participants have eye contact. Learning through action and experience and enquiry learning often need specialized facilities and resources. Yet direct teaching can involve small groups and small group teaching can involve any mode. There is no simple correlation between teaching mode and class organization (which is but one feature, and not the most central one, in differentiating teaching modes). Moreover, since classroom facilities and arrangements typically reflect past (often one-sided) policies, resources and traditions, the organizational possibilities of any given classroom are rarely conducive to deploying the range of teaching modes in a flexible and balanced way. This chapter attempts to clarify all these various issues and so provide a basis for making decisions in diverse contexts about how to overcome organizational constraints and take advantage of organizational opportunities to exploit the full range of teaching modes.

'A judicious and flexible balance'

In terms of policy on class organization, Scottish primary education can prove instructive. Since the end of the Second World War, in report after report, the principle of a 'judicious and flexible balance of class, group and individual teaching' has been officially endorsed (Skinner 1994). But as Carr (2003a) points out, principles such as balance by themselves give teachers little direct help in deciding just what proportions of time to spend on each of these aspects. Besides, there are different conceptions of balance, reflecting different analogies – for example, a balanced diet, a physical balance, a judicial balance (each claim being given due consideration). Hence judgements about relative emphasis and specific time allocations need to be made on other grounds; all that the principle demands is that each has its appropriate role. There is a need, therefore, to consider what factors should inform particular judgements about balance.

Whole-class Teaching

Whole-class teaching has had varying fortunes in official educational policy thinking. To continue with the example of Scotland, in 1946, when education according to age, aptitude and ability was the official policy, and the idea of fixed intelligence prevailed, greater attention to group and individual work seemed logical. Whole-class teaching was dubbed 'hardly satisfactory' (Skinner 1994: 34) and while the judicious balance principle was officially acknowledged, after the 1965 Memorandum whole-class teaching was sidelined. One apologist claimed that class teaching was a relatively ineffective method and therefore should be seldom employed for the teaching of basic skills in primary schools; but there were occasions when it was the most appropriate unit – singing, physical education, religious education, art, geography lessons. It short it was fine for what in Scotland were then, scandalously, called 'the frills' but not for the 'basics'. Practice continued to stress whole-class teaching however, and a 1980 report (Scottish Education Department 1980: 44) lamented the fact that in many schools 'class teaching and class activities constituted the bulk of the programme'. This contrasts strongly with a report in 2000 (Scottish Consultative Council on the Curriculum 2000) that championed 'whole-class interactive teaching', especially for mathematics and literacy. Yet now, and especially in England, such 'whole-class interactive teaching' has come under mounting critique (Burns and Myhill 2004).

The reality of 'whole class' varies significantly from context to context. Classes of 50 and above can be found still in many countries but in the UK and Europe many secondary and some primary classes are smaller than 20. Besides, teaching units are now more fluid entities with team teaching arrangements using combined groups from different classes. Moreover, with assistants and auxiliaries and specialists there is now often more than one adult working in a class. Pressures to reduce class size continue but doing this is expensive and its educational effect remains a matter of debate.

Questions of streaming, setting and 'broad-banding' (setting into broader groups, for instance top and upper middle groups in one 'band') in upper primary and lower secondary stages continue to generate strong debate about aims, values and evidence (Gamoran 2002; Ireson 2008). In many countries teaching the class as a whole, emphasizing group solidarity and social cohesion, is considered very important. In some such contexts, however, differentiation exists in practice in that a fair proportion of learners repeat years (Skinner 1973).

Collaborative Learning

Although collaborative learning was strongly advocated in the Plowden era it was rarely effectively practised. Children sat in groups but tended to work as individuals (Galton and Simon 1980) and learners received little training in how to learn collaboratively. By the late 1980s the impetus of National Curriculum developments focused attention in the UK on raising standards through direct whole-class teaching and traditional seat work involving individualized learning (though not a few curriculum targets in Scotland actually implied collaborative skills – for instance, discussing together, cooperating to create a display or make a presentation, collaborating in a design task).

In North America at this period cooperative learning approaches were being developed (Johnson and Johnson 1993; Slavin 1995) and then, building partly on this, in the UK significant moves forward were made through the work educationists such as Bennett and Dunne (1992), Rogers and Kutnick (1990) and Galton and Williamson (1992). The influence of social constructivist ideas strengthened markedly and recent years have witnessed a remarkable growth of research and development in relation to collaborative learning. Most notable has been Mercer's work on exploratory talk, the collaborative group work research of Bennett and Dunne, of Kutnick, Blatchford and Baines and the adoption in the UK of North American approaches to collaborative group work (Martin 2007; Jollife, 2007). There are several important features of such developments that deserve attention and these are summarized below.

One outcome has been that collaborative group work is now well theorized, drawing on social constructivist thinking and theories of the role of talk in learning; it has been researched in realistic classroom contexts and evidence on its effectiveness provided; and teachers now have access to a range of practical models and advice on using collaborative group work. In some areas there has been widespread adoption of it by schools.

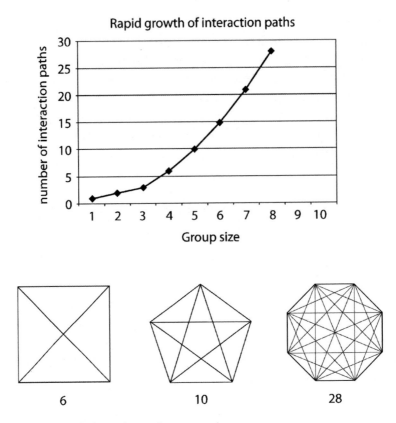

Figure 7.1 Large groups make interaction much more complex

> The fact that interaction paths increase so rapidly with group size implies that small groups (four or five) should be used for collaborative group work. Yet this appears awkward to organize in large, traditional classrooms. The benefits are so strong, however, that it seems important to make arrangements for small groups. Large groups tend to break down informally into smaller groups and in school this can affect group focus and lead to behaviour problems.

Bennett and Dunne highlighted the importance of teachers thinking out the social as well as the cognitive demands of any collaborative task, training learners to collaborate and offering feedback on collaboration during collaborative activities. They also showed that groups of about four worked well and that if the whole class could be involved in groups of four on the same collaborative task, this made things manageable for the teacher. Teachers in this study found themselves able to focus on observing learners and offering feedback to support and challenge.

Martin and Jollife both emphasize four key features of collaborative work as developed in North America:

- positive interdependence
- individual and group accountability
- explicit teaching of social skills
- face-to-face interaction

Martin reports benefits in higher attainment, greater learner productivity, more positive relationships and self-esteem.

Among a wealth of insights, a central emphasis in the research of Kutnick *et al.* (2003) has been the idea of developing what they call a 'social pedagogy' of the classroom – in contrast to the individualized pedagogy, based on teacher/individual learner interactions typical of the past. Social pedagogy in their sense aims to exploit the potential of collaborative learning for developing knowledge, skills and understanding. This implies thinking out carefully aims and principles for grouping learners, task design and teaching and learner roles in collaborative learning activities. Evidence of social as well as cognitive gains through collaborative learning is steadily accumulating and, in several cases at least, common fears that high attainers would be held back have been shown to be unwarranted (Kutnick *et al.* 2003). Collaboration can involve pairs and trios as well as small groups. Random pairs, for example, have been shown to be effective, not least if one is a higher attainer and the other a low attainer who will not feel left out (as they might in a larger group) and most likely will learn to collaborate better initially in a mixed-ability pair context. High attainers in such pairings can gain valuable practice in explaining, and consolidation of learning through rehearsal.

Teaching Development Activity 7.1 – Collaborative Group Work

Organize a class into groups of four or five for a collaborative task that each group can tackle. Each group is to undertake the same task, the members of the group collaborating to accomplish it. It can be a discussion or some production activity, or some enquiry or investigation that can be completed by a small group in a limited time.

Think through your role in supporting and challenging their collaboration. This requires considering both the social and thinking aspects of the task and offering feedback and discussion as the task proceeds. It is important to pilot this with one group first to get a feel for the process and possible issues you will meet when the whole class is working in groups. Establish a rule that the group can only ask you for help if no one in the group can suggest a way forward.

Interact following your role guidelines and observe the quality of the work, the end results and issues that arose for learners. Reflect on how effectively you played your role as a teacher managing, supporting and challenging this collaborative activity.

Individualized, Independent and Personalized Learning

Three distinct, yet often related, aspects need to be included under the heading of individualized teaching today: one-to-one, independent and personalized learning. Let us consider each of these in turn.

One-to-one

Many teachers' and educationists' first thoughts on organizing learning appear to be based on the assumption that the ideal teaching situation is one teacher to one learner, thus enabling the teacher to focus fully on that learner's particular needs. As Hastings (1998: 106) points out, this was certainly the avowed position of the English Plowden report of 1967 that sought to introduce 'progressive' methods to primary schools:

> One-to-one- teaching was seen by the Plowden committee as the ideal teaching and learning situation. The committee's advocacy of small group teaching was a compromise adopted in recognition that with 30 or more children a regime of one-to-one teaching was not possible.

Hastings notes that the attitude widely persisted:

> Thirty years on concern about increased class sizes is often expressed in terms of adverse effects on one-to-one teaching, still reflecting the view that it is in this kind of teaching that the best quality learning takes place in the classroom.

Even in the era of mega universities, influential educational writers like Luarillard (1993: 148) argue that 'the ideal teaching and learning process is a one-to-one discussion'. Such attitudes die hard, even if they are now only very tenuously connected with Rousseau's account of individualized education in *Emile* or Plato's equally famous account in the *Meno* of Socrates teaching Pythagoras' theorem about the square on the hypotenuse to a slave boy. The issue is important because of the current strong advocacy of personalized learning and because advances in ICT appear to make individualization more practicable.

The premise that one-to-one learning is the ideal needs to be questioned. On economic grounds it is not practicable now or in the forseeable future, even with advances in ICT. The Plowden report pointed out that in a class of 30, using fully individualized instruction, each child would receive only seven minutes teaching per day.

Moreover, important developments since Plowden in understanding human learning emphasize the crucial role of social interaction and the value, for example, of peer tutoring, peer assessment and collaborative group work. In some school systems – for example, Soviet Russia under the influence of Makarenko (Grant 1969) – group processes have been viewed as central to effective learning based on a system of mutual support. Pacific Rim nations, like those of the former Soviet Union and Eastern Europe, typically place a strong emphasis, on grounds of equity, on the whole class moving together and supporting weaker learners. The class as a unit has traditionally played a significant role in education, offering a sense of identity and solidarity.

Independent

Some countries inculcate a strong sense of individual responsibility for learning. In Scotland the 'arm round the jotter' approach was long regarded as a virtue, ensuring independent working and developing resilience, perseverance and self-sufficiency. Someone raising their hand in past decades to say 'Please Sir, I'm stuck' might easily be told (I myself was) 'Well unstick yourself, laddie!' Modern teaching principles rightly emphasize consultation and support for learning and the value of collaborative work; but how is independence (vital for learning how to learn – see Chapter 8) to be fostered?

In many British schools, 'group work' has meant children working individually but on identical tasks, making learning individualized only in a trivial sense. Differential support from the teacher is, however, a possibility. In earlier decades individual teaching was stressed because children were considered to have differing powers of concentration and work rate; and following the Plowden report a general, individualistic philosophy of learning prevailed with encouragement, especially in open-plan primary schools, to make personal decisions about managing one's learning workload – for example, deciding when to do one's allotted mathematics tasks (Sharples 1990). The practical results, however, were generally regarded as very unsatisfactory (Galton and Simon 1980).

Personalized

When introduced in England (DfES 2004), personalizing learning was said to involve taking a highly structured and responsive approach to each child's and young person's learning to enable them to progress, achieve and participate; and to achieve their full potential, whatever their talent or background. Another main feature was the aim of engaging pupils, and their parents, as partners in learning decisions.

Many, however, found the idea far from clear when it first appeared. It seemed more like a policy slogan than a clear concept, the validity and premises of which had been critically considered. For example, it seems important to think deeply about how much choice is possible and desirable, to balance individualization with other valued goals such as social solidarity and community development, and to consider the significant cost implications and opportunity costs.

The Department for Education and Skills (DfES) policy aims to enable learners to participate in the design of their learning in school, family and community and to provide support for learners having difficulties, to help them succeed. Teachers are expected to have high expectations of learners and parents and carers are to be given regular information and advice.

It soon becomes clear that individualization is to be managed using attainment evidence. However, Doddington and Hilton (2007:111) point out that under this approach to personalizing learning the emphasis on measurement of abilities means that knowledge of the child is reduced to knowing only his or her levels of performance on set tests. But, they note, what can be measured may not be the most important thing children can learn; and some of the richest experiences in learning may defy measurement. Moreover, personalization in many cases amounts to differentiation into sets, which, as we have seen, is not unproblematic. It is also true, however, that many teachers consider that in practice individualization is most effectively undertaken within group work, through appropriate support and differentiation rather than full scale individualised teaching.

Critics like Hartley (2007, 2008) and Burton (2007) note that the aim of increasingly personalized services goes along with national delivery and a culture of consumerism and enjoyment of learning. Commentators like Fielding (2007) have welcomed the policy of learners being given a voice in pedagogy and the emphasis on their general well-being in school. But, like others he expresses concern about a performative, technicist approach and the neglect of community and social solidarity in the push for individuality. Fielding, drawing on the philosophy of John MacMurray, advocates the development of person-centred learning communities. A review of individualization in Nordic countries (Carlgren *et al.* 2006: 301) sees a desirable trend from individual teaching to a recognition of the 'teaching of individuals'. No doubt developments and controversies on this matter will continue.

Classroom Environment and Layout

Classroom layout practices have naturally tended to reflect official thinking about desired teaching methods. But teaching policies have tended to change more quickly than classroom facilities can be altered, and so there is often a lag between the new policy, classroom facilities and practices, and rarely the flexible organization required for a balance of class, group and individual work. There have been major swings in policy here, for example, in regard to inclusion, collaborative group work and individualized learning. Other policies such as inclusion and ICT developments have further implications for classroom design (Becta 2006).

Traditional classrooms with fixed desks (sometimes tiered) proved unsuitable in the 1970s when active learning using flexible groupings and integrated days were officially endorsed. While many question how far progressive teaching practices spread following Plowden, there is little doubt that the report led to marked changes in the physical organization of classrooms and resources. Some schools even ensured that in open plan classrooms there were not enough chairs for each child in order to force group work, the 'integrated day' and active methods on teachers (Hamilton 1982; Sharples 1990). But, eventually, research suggested (Croll and Hastings 1996) that it might be better for pupils to sit in rows of separate desks rather than in groups around tables, both for individual work and for whole-class teaching, for which groups of tables often proved rather awkward.

A teacher attempting to deploy various teaching modes to good effect will soon become aware of organizational issues but it is important to focus on opportunities as well as constraints in the particular context. Modern teaching and learning requires the most flexible arrangements and it will be easier to develop these in some contexts than in others. Different arrangements naturally suit different learning patterns, for example, tables for small group work, rows for whole-class direct teaching, a circular or horseshoe arrangement for frequent whole-class discussions, learning stations for individualized teaching, and, for younger children, cosy reading corners. A classroom physical environment that informs and engages, and enables easy movement and resource access has been thought important in some traditions (Moyles 2007), though resources, curriculum and teaching policies continue to develop apace and one can see large changes in primary classrooms within a short space of time. A U-shaped pattern means everyone has a front seat and eye contact with all learners.

Many (e.g. Prashnig 2006) now emphasize the quality of the physical environment and conditions for learning (including issues of noise, harsh lighting, colours and classroom displays) but wider conceptions of the classroom learning environment or climate in relation to learning and teaching expectations and learning culture are probably much more important (Entwistle and Peterson 2004: 541; Cohen *et al.* 2009), and we have already seen (Chapter 2) that questions have been raised about much of the learning styles research.

Hastings and Wood (2002) note that in the UK (and this doubtless applies elsewhere), primary classes usually have four to six children at a table; but they challenge the rationale of group tables and argue that seating should reflect the actual mix of learning activities children experience. They note that collaboration can be in pairs or trios as well as small groups and say it is not necessary to have basic seating in attainment groups since, say, a reading group can be formed quickly from different seating locations. Their argument is that, since most time in class is spent working alone, individual or paired desks in rows will help attention in whole-class teaching and work rate in individual or pair work; and small groups can quickly form for collaborative group work. The aim, they suggest, should be balance and flexibility and remaining alert to the effects of layout and seating on focus, concentration and time on task.

Summary

Each of the four modes has different requirements for the organization of learning but these do not equate simply to traditional categories of class organization that have been the focus of so many official teaching policy swings – such as whole-class, group or individual teaching, or questions of differentiating learning through streaming and setting. It is important to keep these issues conceptually distinct from questions of teaching mode, while recognizing that they affect each other. For policy-makers and teachers they raise questions of teaching ideology, often conflicting or contested research evidence, and have practical repercussions on learner attitudes and motivation, and on the quantity and quality of teaching interactions. There is also a need to consider how far groups are collaborative, the physical layout of classrooms and the role of resources.

The principle of a judicious and flexible balance of class, group and individual teaching has been long established in educational systems like that of Scotland, and remains the most promising operative principle for the future. However, it has tended always to be compromised from time to time by policy initiatives emphasizing one aspect such as individualized teaching or whole-class teaching, and other considerations are necessary to make a specific judgement about what exact balance is desirable in a given context.

Collaborative group work, long commended, was not properly researched and developed before the 1990s. Now it is increasingly promoted and is being supported by a number of factors: realistic research in classrooms; evidence on effectiveness and manuals to train learners (very necessary for effective collaborative learning); and detailed theorization drawing on social constructivist thinking and research on the role of talk, enquiry and experiential learning.

Classroom layouts and resourcing are also intricately involved in these matters. It is now obvious to most that modern teaching and learning would be helped by the most flexible and adaptable classroom layouts; but in the past, layouts tended to reflect one dominant teaching mode or teaching ideology. Some recent research argues convincingly for basic seating in pairs with flexibility to move to whole-class, collaborative group or other arrangements. Developing an engaging environment with ready access to resources and easy movement is considered important in the younger classes. Some argue for attention to the quality of the physical environment but the teaching and learning culture of the classroom is even more important.

Key Reading

Baines, E., Blatchford, P. and Kutnick. P. (2009) *Promoting Effective Group Work in the Primary Classroom.* Abingdon: Routledge.

Dunne, E. and Bennett, N. (1990) *Talking and Learning in Groups.* Basingstoke: Macmillan.

Martin, M. (2007) *Building a Learning Community in the Primary Classroom.* Edinburgh: Dunedin Academic Press.

Mercer, N. and Hodgkinson, S. (2008) *Exploring Talk in School.* London: Sage.

Petty, G. (2004) *Teaching Today.* Cheltenham: Nelson Thornes.

Useful Websites

http://www.tlrp.org

Website relating to the ESRC's Teaching and Learning Research Programme. Excellent papers and links on current key issues in teaching and learning, particularly collaborative group work, neuroscience, and personalized learning

www.casel.org

Website of The Collaborative for Academic, Social and Emotional Learning. A useful site on social and emotional aspects of learning.

Inter-disciplinary Learning, Thinking Skills, Learning How to Learn

Chapter Outline

The Resurgence of Interdisciplinary Studies	91
Teaching for Understanding	95
Rich Tasks	96
Learning to Think	97
Learning to Learn	98
Summary	100
Key Reading	101
Useful Websites	101

The Resurgence of Inter-disciplinary Studies

In the UK, the development of effective subject teaching dominated the period following the introduction of National Curriculum policies in the late 1980s. More recently and worldwide, however, there has been a revival of interest in inter-disciplinary (also called cross-curricular) learning. This stems from concerns about the fragmented nature of learning in a subject-based curriculum, from a greater emphasis on relevance and meaningfulness to learners and the influence of wider developments in knowledge integration in society. It also stems from an interest in more generic, cross-curricular aims (e.g. enterprise education, sustainability and the four capacities – confident individuals, effective contributors, successful learners and informed citizens – pursued by the Scottish Curriculum for Excellence) and in thinking skills and learning how to learn. Such general and inter-disciplinary learning is now viewed as a key to raising standards further and countering disaffection from school.

The changing status of integrated studies

Project work and thematic teaching, under the influence of Dewey and of ideas about the desirability and naturalness of curriculum integration, had become a regular component of primary teaching in the UK by the 1970s. However, there had been some important criticisms. Kirk (1973) argued that advocates of inter-disciplinary or thematic teaching tended to contrast an idealistic account of cross-curricular teaching with a long discredited version of subject teaching. He examined five supposed justifications for integrated studies and found them all wanting. These were that thematic teaching:

- was less academic and abstract
- used more enlightened teaching approaches (active, discursive and enquiry learning)
- was more motivating since it is more geared to pupil needs and interests
- was more relevant
- was better for developing general qualities such as critical thinking and problem-solving

Kirk suggested that these features were in no way logically entailed by thematic work as opposed to subject-based teaching; in practice they could equally be found in good subject study, while the opposite features could be found in poor thematic teaching, of which there was no shortage of examples.

The discussion of subject-based teaching has now moved on, however. Banks *et al.* (1999) suggest that whatever the case for integrated studies, subject teaching needs deeper scrutiny. Subjects are not stable entities and there are significant differences between academic disciplines, the discipline (history, say) as it is presented as a school subject, and teachers' personal experience and construction of the discipline. Moreover, Carr (2007) has recently questioned the long unchallenged rationale for a largely subject-based curriculum at secondary level, a rationale based essentially on ideas about the fundamental structure of knowledge.

Pring (1971, 1976) had looked closely at curriculum integration and identified three acceptable bases for it:

- relating different disciplines or subjects to a particular issue (such as health, global warming or war)
- in practical thinking (where decisions of various kinds, from different disciplines, need somehow to be brought together to provide an overall decision – e.g. in choosing curtains, considerations of cost, suitability of fabric, effectiveness of the colour scheme, warmth)
- through learners following their own developing lines of enquiry, where interest might naturally move across various aspects of a topic as understanding develops and thereby involve different disciplines (an interest in horses might naturally move from principles of horse care to riding skills, to the zoology of horses and then to the history of employment of horses)

A seminal Scottish paper on thematic teaching argued that while, in principle, a thematic approach provided the best opportunity for rigorous learning, in practice it was regularly 'guilty of wallowing in extremes of superficiality' (Scottish Committee on Primary Education 1987: 28). One of the paper's targets was the then dominant topic web approach (see Figure 8.1), characterized by a very loose conception of integration and rarely involving any sustained enquiry learning. The paper argued that project work required more effective structuring and proposed two possible mechanisms: the process of enquiry and collaborative story-making. Let us consider each in turn.

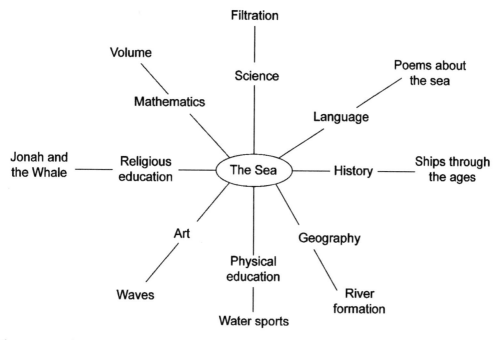

Figure 8.1 A traditional topic web

Traditional topic webs often misguidedly aimed to incorporate as many different subject areas as possible. Moreover, there was often no clear line of enquiry to structure learning. The result was often an unsatisfactory mix of didactic teaching, weakly integrated activities and poor quality 'research' from book resources.

A general model of enquiry was offered. Unfortunately it looked very much like a scientific enquiry process (observation, hypothesis, experiment etc.) and this might not suit enquiry in all disciplines (though, of course, hypothesis and evidence would suit many historical enquiries perfectly well). A more general problem-solving procedure such as outlined by Dewey (see Chapter 6) might be better but might not work well with open, exploratory investigations. On the other hand, a primary teacher cannot be expected to master the details of enquiry in a range of disciplines, and in practice enquiry might be reduced to scientific investigations (into which geography would usually fit), historical and more general problem-solving or open investigations and explorations. Through these, learners might gradually get a feel for the kinds of process and thinking involved in mathematical, humanities and science enquiries and learn to seek appropriate evidence and explanations for the particular subject matter. There is a case at secondary level for arranging for learners to look at enquiry across a range of disciplines to appreciate similarities and differences.

Storyline

The main development of the second suggested way of structuring thematic study, 'collaborative story-making,' has been 'storyline'. This is an approach to integrated, thematic learning, very well received by teachers in an increasing range of countries, which resonates well with recent developments in teaching, learning and curriculum. Storyline (Bell and Harkness 2006; Bell *et al.* 2008) has an established pedigree in Scotland where it originated in the late 1960s in the wake of the Scottish Primary Memorandum (Scottish Education Department 1965), which encouraged curriculum integration and group work based on child-centred learning principles.

Developed initially for primary schools, it has been shown to be adaptable to all stages of education, not least upper secondary, and has been used in simulation exercises in business contexts and nurse education. Storyline uses a story structure to provide a supportive and engaging context for meaningful learning geared to learners' interests and concerns as well as the curriculum goals of the teacher and school; and to pose questions to which learners can respond with imagination and creativity by undertaking a range of enquiry work including problem-solving and factual research. Ideas developed are presented in various ways such as through writing, drama and art.

The typical procedure in a primary school is as follows. First a context is created in the classroom – for example, a family home, a street, a business, a castle. Then the learners create characters and develop a frieze or other display that gives tangible representation to, and acts as a constant reminder of, the context and characters and motivates learners' thinking and activity. The story's setting and characters being established, the teacher introduces an incident that sets the story in motion. A related key question (e.g. 'How can you advertise your market stall?') poses problems which pupils then respond to by research enquiry and activities such as writing, model-making and drama. Subsequent story episodes centred on incidents in the story trigger further key questions and learner activities. The story moves through the incidents or episodes (with key questions and activities) and is finally brought to closure, usually by some culminating event such as an opening ceremony (if, say, a business is being set up), a festival or a visit to an actual flower shop, castle or whatever. This culminating event provides a natural occasion for learners to review all their varied learning.

As in the case of other forms of curricular integration and thematic or project work, formal research studies are sparse but there is now growing documentation reporting teachers' views of the high quality of thinking and learning which results and the eager engagement of learners. In view of its popularity among teachers who have tried it, and its relationship to current trends in curriculum thinking, storyline deserves the serious attention of educational researchers of the kind recently given to learning through collaborative group work (see Chapter 7). It embodies clear planning principles and structures, a bank of detailed examples is available, and successful development experience in school settings has been achieved in several countries around the globe.

Learners can explore sensitive personal and social issues in a non-threatening context. Storyline lends itself to a blend of class, group and individual working, use of ICT and all four modes of teaching and learning. A typical storyline might extend over several weeks taking up a significant amount of the teaching week during its operation, momentum being maintained through regular slots alongside standard subject teaching (but not replacing it entirely).

Storyline is thus a clear improvement on the weaknesses of traditional topic web approaches. There is a natural, organic move from one subject to another as answers to key questions are researched and as the storyline unfolds. It resembles in many ways Pring's account of a learners' own enquiry, conducted as a collaborative group enquiry, based on an imaginary but educationally potent context, broadly structured by the teacher. Learning is essentially within an enquiry framework but will involve all four modes.

Teaching for Understanding

Developing understanding should clearly be a central goal of education. From the1970s a major project at Harvard University (Project Zero) sought to develop, in close collaboration with teachers, an approach to teaching and active learning which makes knowledge come alive for learners through a focus on teaching for understanding (Blythe 1998; Wiske 1998). Central here was the development of a performance view of understanding. If someone understands something they can think about it flexibly and apply it flexibly; and their understanding can be assessed by observing them deploying their understanding. Applicable to any stage or subject, the approach aimed to make sense to working teachers, deepen and sharpen typical practice and provide a language to discuss teaching ideas. Teaching for understanding has four interacting elements:

- generative topics
- understanding goals
- performances of understanding
- ongoing assessment

The project was motivated by accumulating evidence that even high-achieving under-graduate students in the USA showed only surface learning at entry to university and often lacked the capacity to take knowledge learned in one context and apply it to another. Considerable evidence for effectiveness of the teaching for understanding approach is available (see Wiske 1998) but not in the form of a typical research evaluation.

Initially, teaching for understanding focused on subject discipline understanding and seemed wary of an integrated, cross-curricular approach. The project emphasized building cognitive strategies through direct instruction or modelling, and learners interacting constructively with each other, which meant ensuring time for significant discussion or dialogue. Tasks were based on what were labelled 'generative topics' – topics such as global warming, coming of age themes in literature, revolution in history, forensics in science, and migration. Understanding goals are goals such as 'how biologists distinguish plants from animals' and 'the basis of measurement units'. The core is in-depth learning covering a broad range of material and applying knowledge to real-world problems, learning to think with, rather than just about, an idea or concept.

Recently, the issue of inter-disciplinary study has been taken up by Project Zero, teasing out issues about the nature of such inter-disciplinarity (Nikitina 2006; see also Harvard website below) in a way which can be expected soon to influence thinking about cross-curricular approaches in schools.

Teaching Development Activity 8.1 – Inter-disciplinary Learning

Develop and undertake a short unit of teaching based on some form of integrated or inter-disciplinary study (see discussion above) involving two or three subject areas. In planning, note down how you think this integration can be accomplished and what benefits you expect it to have for your learners. Afterwards, reflect on the effectiveness of pupil learning and consider how teaching using this approach might be improved.

Rich Tasks

The curriculum of the Queensland New Basics Project (Education Queensland 2001) is built around a series of 'rich tasks'. These are large-scale, holistic tasks that have obvious relevance in everyday life, including work, education, citizenship and other activities. The tasks are systematically completed and assessed at three-yearly intervals (Years 3, 6, and 9). In between, students are developing prerequisite understanding, knowledge and skills. Half of weekly curriculum time is given to completing rich tasks and developing prerequisite skills and the new basics. Teachers are free to structure the rest of programme for the other half of the time.

A feature which contrasts with Project Zero's 'teaching for understanding' approach, where the emphasis initially was on disciplined-centred topics, is that the rich tasks are viewed as inevitably trans-disciplinary, modelling a life role and presenting significant problem, engaging learners in forms of relevant social action. Examples of rich tasks are 'when things go wrong' (coping with tragedies and disasters) and 'pictures at an exhibition' (representations of historical or contemporary situations).

The rich tasks are not traditional holistic, integrated learning, and not short projects. Rather they are the culmination of three years' work in a performance of learning which is rigorous and relevant and which aims to overcome the problems of an otherwise crowded and fragmented curriculum. This development was influenced by American research evidence (Newman *et al.* 1996) on 'authentic tasks' which suggested these features were vital for improved outcomes with low-achieving learners in urban America. The tasks aim to have developmental, cognitive and intellectual depth and breadth so as to guide curriculum planning across a significant span of schooling.

Overall, there is much to ponder and to research in this area of inter-disciplinary learning. The mistakes of the past have shown the need for an effective structure for thematic teaching and learning, clear thinking about inter-disciplinarity and the role of enquiry processes. There are now many useful models to explore, some on a large scale, some able to start from small beginnings. Deploying various teaching modes within an overall enquiry framework can contribute significantly to their success.

Learning to Think

The teaching of 'thinking skills' has been strongly promoted in recent years. It is widely claimed that thinking skills are vital for effective learning, for later education and modern living. Some suggest ICT is changing the way people handle information and engage in thinking (see Chapter 9). Moreover, metacognition – becoming aware of and thinking about one's own thinking – is considered crucial for general progress. But what is thinking, how can one make sense of the numerous programmes, packages and lists of thinking skills, and what evidence is there that 'teaching thinking' is effective?

Thinking is actively using one's mind to develop connected ideas – to reason logically and critically, solve problems, understand phenomena and aspects of the world. Thinking has always been an avowed broad aim of education (though not always of schooling: some, but not all, working-class education and colonial education was specifically designed to close learners' minds rather than to open them – Gordon 1963: 30). But in practice schools have often appeared to emphasize learning facts and content in a reproductive way rather than advocating learning to think independently or creatively.

Traditionally, it was assumed that children learned to think within each subject. Research on creativity introduced ideas about divergent and convergent thinking and divergent thinking was said to be important, though no strong programmes were developed. However, in the 1970s writers like de Bono (1976), who had promoted his idea of 'lateral thinking' (thinking 'outside the box'), argued for introducing thinking as a separate subject, a set of general skills. A debate arose about whether there were general thinking skills and whether therefore thinking should become a separate subject or whether thinking was subject- or discipline-specific and should remain in the disciplines (Johnson 2001). By 'discipline-specific' is meant thinking based on understanding of the concepts, nature and principles in each subject discipline (mathematics, history, science, literature or whatever) and on the basis of observation, experience and reflection; and applying this thinking to activities such as appreciating a poem or solving a mathematical, social or practical problem. Thinking is said by some to involve 'skills' like analysing, comparing, interpreting, evaluating and many others. Johnson raises the question of how far these are best conceived as 'skills'.

A number of separate thinking skills programmes were developed (Kirkwood 2005) and, dauntingly, over 35 different frameworks of thinking skills became available (Mosely *et al.* 2005). There is now greater recognition of the existence and value of both generic and subject- or context-specific thinking skills and therefore of the value of within-discipline study and also separate thinking programmes (Smith 2002). However, with many of the general thinking skills schemes there is a tendency to focus on thinking procedures and problem-solving performances and to neglect to teach learners how to think critically about ends as well as means (Papastephanou and Angeli 2007).

Teaching Development Activity 8.2 – Developing Thinking

Select some aspect of thinking you wish to develop. Consider what needs to be learned, and make some appropriate assessment of your learners' present level of performance and what you would count as improved performance in this aspect of thinking. Work to develop such thinking in your learners over a series of activities, and then test your learners appropriately once more. Compare the results with the first test.

Infusion of thinking skills into regular teaching (McGuiness 2005) has been developed as a third way between thinking as a separate subject and traditional thinking taught informally as part of regular subject teaching. One specific strategy for teachers here is to be explicit to learners about the subject learning goals and also the goals of the particular thinking process or 'skill' being developed. Recent research suggests teachers are happy to infuse thinking into some subjects more than others (Burke *et al.* 2007), but thinking needs attention in all areas of the curriculum, not just the core.

The need to intervene in children's thinking processes and to help them become aware of themselves as thinkers has also been increasingly recognized and the idea of a 'thinking classroom' where concern for thinking is explicit has been promoted. Frame (2008) provides an extended example involving outdoor education that illustrates how well suited a storyline approach is to developing the features of a thinking classroom. Applying thinking is now being recognized as being a matter of disposition and character as well as of skills and knowledge. But effective transfer of learning remains an unsolved issue despite many debates and initiatives over the years (McCormick 1999; Kirkwood 2005; Papastephanou and Angeli 2007).

Learning to Learn

The need constantly to update learning and skills in modern, rapidly changing knowledge economies and a context of lifelong learning has led to an emphasis on pupils being able to learn independently and 'learn how to learn'. Recent research and theorizing suggest that these in fact amount to the same thing.

What seems to be sought is awareness of one's own understanding about learning in general, and about one's own learning and needs – being able to make informed decisions about the course and direction of learning and to devise strategies to overcome problems in learning: in short, autonomy, or independence, in learning (see Fredriksson and Hoskins 2007). More traditional accounts emphasize study skills, reasoning, learning strategies and metacognition (Moreno and Martin 2007). Newer thinking discussed below goes significantly beyond such a conception.

However, current teaching does not promote such autonomy. Recent research (Bullock and Muschamp 2006; James 2008) has shown that while primary children and secondary-school learners see their responsibility to work hard to learn, teachers tend not to incorporate learners' views or evaluations of teaching and learning. Metacognitive abilities are often not recognized by pupils or teachers and work planned for pupils too rarely involves them in making decisions. Pupils are often unaware of where they have independence.

Much educational talk about learning how to learn treats it as a general skill that can be learned and then applied to various contexts. The TLRP research casts doubt on this (James 2008: 8). Instead, the researchers suggest, teachers should develop a set of classroom practices to help learners learn independently in new settings.

Dearden (1984) suggested three criteria for autonomy (independence) in learning: making independent judgements; being disposed to critically reflect on these judgements; and integrating beliefs and conduct around them. Winch (2009a: 278) puts the emphasis just on effective learning and questions the idea of a general ability ('If I can learn I must be able to learn how to learn') while highlighting literacy and numeracy as achievements with wide application to a range of learning contexts.

Confidence and independence come from successful learning. Cultivating virtues such as patience, perseverance and self-discipline is important and these are considered best learned through practice in diverse contexts. Independence can be promoted by many of the strategies discussed throughout this book such as formative assessment, exploratory talk and teaching thinking. Learning how to learn, viewed as a collection of good learning practices which will promote independence in learning in individual and collaborative contexts, can provide a firm foundation for lifelong learning.

Developing learning how to learn in this sense of cultivating independence in learning appears to be one of the most challenging issues facing teachers. Traditional classroom processes and curriculum pressures typically tend to work against it in practice. It requires developing a different focus in teaching and communicating this to learners and parents. Pedder's research (2006) suggests it requires teachers learning how to do all this in practical classroom contexts, rather than on staff development courses, which will in turn require support from colleagues and school management to re-orientate teaching and learning towards this goal. But it does get to the heart of effective learning.

Teaching Development Activity 8.3 – Learning How to Learn

Select a piece of teaching and consider carefully how it might develop the kinds of learning conditions that further independence and confidence in learning (see discussion above). After undertaking this teaching, reflect on pupil motivation, the quality of learning and the practical issues you faced, particularly in terms of encouraging independence in learning. How might these issues be better resolved?

Summary

In the UK, the development of effective subject teaching has dominated recent decades following the introduction of National Curriculum policies in the late 1980s. More recently, however, there has been a revival of interest in inter-disciplinary (or cross-curricular) learning. This stems from concerns about the fragmented nature of learning in a wholly subject-based curriculum; from a greater emphasis on relevance and mean-ingfulness to learners and in terms of wider, cross-curricular aims (e.g. the four capacities pursued by the Scottish Curriculum for Excellence); and from increasing policy development and research on curriculum-wide issues such as thinking skills and learning to learn, often now viewed as key to raising standards further and countering school disaffection.

Before the introduction of national curricula in the 1980s, project work and thematic teaching had been coming under severe criticism for producing shallow learning, and moves were afoot to strengthen them with more rigorous strategies and approaches. These were, however, abruptly cut short as the strongly subject-oriented National Curriculum policies took root.

Now, however, three important developments offer ideas for a modern approach to cross-curricular teaching. 'Storyline' from Scotland builds on earlier work offering a structure for cross-curricular enquiry and is increasingly influential in Europe and to some extent North America. From the USA has come a new emphasis on 'teaching for understanding' (Harvard's Project Zero) though this at first downplayed the cross-curricular element in favour of deep disciplined understanding based on life-relevant tasks. Queensland's New Basics reform has introduced as a key element trans-disciplinary learning called 'rich tasks'. These developments have renewed study of the theoretical basis of curriculum integration and inter-disciplinary learning.

Teaching thinking skills has become very popular but there is a vast range of programmes and theoretical positions; a continuing debate about classifications of skills and teaching approaches, the existence of generic thinking skills and how far infusion into regular teaching as opposed to separate programmes is desirable. Evidence of effectiveness of teaching thinking as a set of generic skills remains equivocal.

Learning to learn is also now much discussed, researched and promoted. Recent research and analysis suggests it is not a separate skill which can be developed but rather that efforts should focus on developing successful independent learning.

Key Reading

Barnes, J. (2007) *Cross-Curricular Learning 3–14.* London: Paul Chapman.

Bell, S., Harkness, S. and White, G. (2008) *Storyline.* Glasgow: University of Strathclyde.

Kirkwood, M. (2005) *Learning to Think: Thinking to Learn.* Paisley: Hodder Gibson.

Pring, R. (1976) *Knowledge and Schooling.* London: Open Books.

Wiske, M. S. (ed) (1998) *Teaching for Understanding. San Francisco: Jossey-Bass.*

Useful Websites

www.storyline-scotland.com

The website which provides information, news and links to schools around the world but particularly in northern Europe which have used or are developing a storyline approach to cross-disciplinary learning.

www.pz.harvard.edu/

Website of Project Zero, Harvard university's well known project (involving Howard Gardner and David Perkins) for developing ideas on teaching for understanding.

www.sapere.net

A website for philosophy for children.

www.takeonepicture.org

'Take One Picture' is the UK National Gallery's country-wide scheme for primary schools. The site includes ideas for using painting from the collection to inspire cross-curricular work in primary classrooms. Examples of children's work and art resources are also available.

www.21learn.org

Website with ideas on learning how to learn.

www.thinkingtogether.org.uk

A useful site on exploratory talk and other aspects.

Part 4
Background Theory

Learning and Teaching with Information Technologies

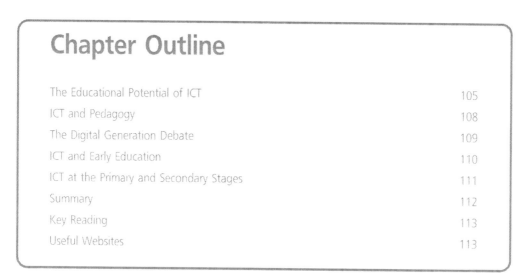

Chapter Outline

The Educational Potential of ICT	105
ICT and Pedagogy	108
The Digital Generation Debate	109
ICT and Early Education	110
ICT at the Primary and Secondary Stages	111
Summary	112
Key Reading	113
Useful Websites	113

The Educational Potential of ICT

ICT has enormous potential for improving learning and teaching. To begin with, the range of such technologies is now developing at a remarkable rate – computers, the internet, digital cameras, mobile technologies, virtual learning environments, interactive whiteboards, electronic games and so on. This potential of ICT is usually described using the idea of 'affordances': the perceived and actual fundamental properties of an object that determine how it might possibly be used. Kirschner *et al.* (2004) highlight the fact that affordances can be technological (for instance, pencil and paper or laptop), social (individual or group, say) or educational (e.g. a competitive or collaborative context).

Allen *et al.* (2007), drawing on DfES papers, list the following properties or affordances of ICT:

- interactivity
- provisionality
- capacity and range
- speed and automatic function

Leach and Moon (2008), in a wider discussion of material and symbolic tools that enable cultural action, identify six ways in which ICT tools can help teaching and learning:

- easier access to a wide range of information
- easier links with other teachers and other learners
- more effective teaching of key concepts and disciplined understanding
- making calculations, writing, presentation and storage, easier and quicker
- pedagogic (helping teachers support learners and aiding collaboration)
- easier research (better access to sources, evidence, experts)

Pritchard (2007) suggests four purposes of ICT use:

- Finding things out
- Developing ideas and making things happen
- Enhancing and sharing information
- Reviewing, modifying and evaluating work in progress

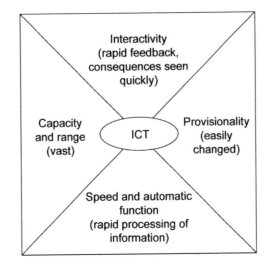

Figure 9.1 Features of ICT that can transform teaching and learning

Experts agree that ICT has enormous potential for transforming learning and teaching. Schools and teachers, however, still face many challenges in exploiting its key features and so realizing this potential.

Can ICT Radically Transform Teaching and Learning?

The educational world continues to hear claims that ICT will radically transform learning and that computers will shortly take over as the main source of learning. Unfortunately, there is a long history of such claims about educational technology, including ICT. And a recent prominent claim (Prensky 2001a) has been that the digital generation (those growing up in the age of digital technology, say the last 20 years) has particular skills, attitudes and approaches to learning that require radical changes in the way education is organized and conducted. It is even claimed that the digital generation is developing different thinking processes and learning styles.

Yet past claims have always proved to be grossly exaggerated, from those relating to 'teaching machines' and television in the 1960s through microfiches in the 1970s to claims at the millennium that e-learning would replace classrooms within a few years. The reality has always been far short of the rhetoric however; hence new claims need to be looked at cautiously. A balanced approach to learning and teaching will surely always be appropriate.

Several aspects of resource access and use currently stand out: variations in provision among schools; gaps between school and home; the digital divide in access among various groups such as rich and poor, rural and urban homes; and a divide among those with access between skilled, enthusiastic users and unskilled, unconfident ones. Gaps can be large, they raise equity issues, and contexts change rapidly. But inequalities are difficult to address and need to be carefully considered in planning teaching using ICT.

Teaching Development Activity 9.1 – ICT and Teaching

Select one ICT resource you are familiar with and have confidence in using. Select one feature from Figure 9.1 that you think clearly applies to it. Prepare your role and the learner's role so as to exploit this feature as effectively as possible. Reflect on the results and how these differ from your normal approach to using ICT. What difficulties lie in your path in terms of exploiting this feature of ICT to enhance teaching and learning and how might they be overcome?

Resourcing schools with ICT

From the 1990s there were large investments in ICT resources in schools in the UK, as in many other industrialized countries. But there were many variations in how such investments were deployed in local authorities and schools and at present there are still significant differences in the resourcing of individual schools. There are also wide differences in teacher confidence regarding the use of ICT and in teachers' knowledge and skills in using it to enhance teaching and learning.

The situation continues to change rapidly in relation to resource provision and of course information technologies themselves are developing rapidly. Teachers are likely to continue to find varied resourcing and competence contexts as they move from school to school or between training contexts and schools. The question is how best to respond to whatever context one finds oneself in. Some writers (e.g. Allen *et al.* 2007) have suggested it is helpful to think in terms of a broad grouping into high, medium and low resourcing as an initial guide to action in the next few years. Even though actual levels of resourcing will almost certainly improve, significant differentials are likely to continue.

They consider a 'high level' of provision at present to include ready technical support, portable computers, good software for all ages and a range of equipment such as interactive whiteboards and programmable toys, along with policies for safely using, teaching and learning with ICT. A 'medium level' suggests resourcing is less impressive in these ways; and a 'low level' will be poor in most or all of these aspects. The pace of change is very fast, however, and this account already seems very dated.

Wider questions about technology

An influential evaluation of ICT developments in the USA (Cuban 2001) suggested that there was little substance behind the rhetoric of much of the supposed progress and that many teachers were far from confident and found many obstacles to using ICT in the classroom. Whichever way future policy evolves, it will need to take seriously the multiple obstacles to technology that teachers report. Reynolds *et al.* (2003) claimed there had been excessive optimism about ICT and its potential for improving educational standards, and advocated more detailed research to examine exactly how ICT can really improve such standards. Conlon and Simpson (2003) argued that for too long the questions which dominated educational discussion of ICT were mostly at the technical and craft levels; visionary questions about educational aims and the proper place of technology were not much discussed – but urgently needed to be. In Scotland for instance there has recently been a £40 million investment (GLOW) giving access to online learning resources and transforming the way school learners experience education. Conlon (2008) notes that officially only its supposed positive benefits have been emphasized. He raises issues about opportunity costs and concerns about the lack of critical thinking regarding the project. He wonders if it will prove as successful as its promoters have promised. He voices concerns about the culture of such large-scale ICT investments in schools and the lack of critical attention to the downsides of technology. Drawing on writers like Postman, Edgerton, Hartley and other critics of technology he notes the dangers of the trivialization of culture, data safety, managerialism and a neglect of ordinary relationships in schools as communities, along with the very possible result of only surface changes in pedagogy.

ICT and Pedagogy

A full discussion of the concept of pedagogy is provided in Chapter 10. At present we need only note that in ICT contexts pedagogy is generally used as jargon for teaching and learning strategies, though sometimes with a wider recognition of theories such as constructivism. The main debate in ICT contexts has been around the suggestion that, while ICT has enormous potential for enabling constructivist learning, in practice in schools it still mainly serves transmission teaching.

Conlon and Simpson (2003) draw attention to research by Becker which suggested that constructivist-oriented teachers are much more likely to be innovative technology users and wondered if staff development might not do better to focus on the case for constructivist classrooms than on ICT alone. Unless more traditional teaching ideas are challenged, Conlon and Simpson argue, any technology adoption is likely to be limited to applications (such as PowerPoint presentations) that are consistent with those beliefs.

Teaching Development Activity 9.2 – ICT and Teaching Modes

Consider how you could use ICT in relation to an example for each of the four teaching and learning modes discussed in earlier chapters. Try your ideas out and reflect on the role of ICT in helping you use these modes effectively

However, we surely need a wide conception of changes in teaching and learning in discussing ICT and pedagogy. There is a danger is assuming, as many writings do, a one-way move from transmission teaching to constructivist teaching and of ICT as the central mover. We need to consider other change forces in trying to understand pedagogic change and hold a wider conception of teaching and learning than is apparent in the instruction/construction debate. Derry (2009) draws attention to the need to aid learners to think about knowledge rather than information in working with ICT.

The Digital Generation Debate

Prensky (2001a, 2001b) calls those growing up with digital technology 'digital natives', culturally at home with ICT, unlike 'digital immigrants' – the older generation who need to learn the new 'language' of ICT cultural norms and expectations. Digital immigrants, he states, have less confidence and facility and more negative attitudes. Prensky's terminology is unfortunate but the debate has now been joined in these terms. Critics consider the contrast too starkly drawn and provide evidence that some 'natives' are not as confident, skilled or positive to ICT as Prensky suggests while at least some 'immigrants' are highly skilled, creative and make full use of ICT in their lives (Bennett *et al.* 2008). The debate has stimulated a closer look at ICT attitudes and skills among the digital generation and the way in which these relate to home and school (e.g. Livingstone and Helsper 2007; Plowman *et al.* 2008).

Prensky views the ICT revolution as a matter of exponential change, a rapid explosion of opportunities, facilities and effects on education. He argues that television significantly changed education outside school and that ICT is transforming learning in and out of school – in its locus, nature (with online digital lifelong learning emerging in society) and the distribution of expertise between teachers and learners. He is at pains to stress that learners are adopting and using ICT much more rapidly than their teachers, that many teachers are becoming fearful of their lack of expertise and the changed relationships implied, and that ICT learning outside school is markedly different from traditional transmission teaching inside school.

Prensky (2007) advocates a new approach to teaching, exploiting emerging information technologies which learners find useful, have learned to use outside school and want to use to learn in school. Prensky suggests most teachers should abandon trying to keep up to date with new technologies and develop a different role, one concerned with helping learners to understand key learning gaols and criteria and to use the expertise they do have (e.g. their ability to aid learners to think critically about the information they are finding online).

Somekh (2006b) argues that digital technolgies are not suited to a curriculum fixed by adults, with short learning bursts and a set body of knowledge to master, and that schools need different forms of pedagogy and curriculum structure. She suggests that the teacher's role should change from manager and controller to co-constructor of learning activities and enabler of genuinely constructive learning while still retaining a key role in selecting and presenting knowledge and activities designed to educate learners. Learners' roles also need to change of course, and in a less dependent direction.

Her argument is that ICT changes teaching: immediately it draws attention away from the teacher to the screen. She says it is vital that this does not become a learner-ICT resource interaction only (distance learning has shown the problems this raises) but should develop as a three-way interaction. She also points out that the flow and sustained engagement in ICT activities is often inhibited by sudden changes of timetable and so on (see GTCE 2006 for an extended example from the PELRS research project).

ICT and Early Education

When computers first started to appear in nursery schools, a debate ensued about their value and possible dangers at the pre-school stage (Yelland 2005; Riley 2007). There was concern about ICT being too complex for young children, being 'unnatural' compared to three-dimensional wood blocks and 'real life' experiences, possible ergonomic problems of young children sitting at computer desks, and distraction from traditional activities which were considered the core of childhood. But these fears have largely vanished and the very positive effects of ICT are now widely acknowledged and embraced within a modernized conception of early childhood education.

A basic principle for Yelland (2005) is that children need to be able to use technology (real digital cameras and mobile phones, not just toy ones) for activities in the nursery when they want and need to. Children are early adopters of new technology and interactive whiteboards are increasingly common in nurseries. Riley (2007) cites research suggesting that pre-school children learning with ICT resources show enhanced learning and enjoyment.

Initially, ICT tended to be grafted onto existing nursery learning which had been designed without ICT in mind. Now ICT is being treated like other resources, affording opportunities that can be exploited naturally to meet aims and principles and support various investigation possibilities, adding a new dimension to traditional play, with nursery staff helping children learn skills and exploit ICT resources. ICT use is in a wide educational context where teachers are trying to balance support and non- intervention. Writers such as Riley (2007) favour ICT packages which support integration, are transparent, intuitive, support health and safety awareness, involve parents, leave the child in control, support play, encourage collaboration and avoid violence and stereotyping. Traditional 'drill and practice' resources are not considered very useful and, say some, are undesirable.

Writers suggest ICT in the nursery may help mitigate some of the effects of the digital divide and that it can play a very useful role in communication, collaboration, creativity, socio-dramatic play and developing metacognition. Policies on ergonomic issues are now generally well developed. Recent thinking recommends policies that involve children working away from computers part of the time and children being taught self-responsibility in relation to ergonomics and health and safety. ICT is regarded as encouraging language, motivating children's initiatives and collaboration.

Young learners, it is said (Yelland 2005; Siraj-Blatchford and Siraj-Blatchford 2006) should be developing the ability to access and retrieve information, and learning to use technology in authentic activities such as creating a schedule for a visitor to the nursery. Ambitious yet defensible claims are made about, for example, development through ICT in early education of the ability to thrive on fluency, to make quick decisions with incomplete data, develop collaborative skills, and navigate and select relevant information. This is to be achieved by encouraging children to apply ICT playfully for a range of different purposes which implies an investment in generic software such as a floor turtles, movie-makers and paint tools that can be used for a range of purposes (as opposed to dedicated application software typical of commercially-inspired children's ICT toys). Children should be finding out about and identifying uses of technology in their everyday lives and using computer toys to support their learning, becoming aware on curriculum walks of traffic lights, bar code scanners and so on. Technology thus requires thoughtful integration into the early education curriculum.

ICT at the Primary and Secondary Stages

We shall focus here on interactive whiteboards as a useful case study of the potential of ICT and the issues it is now facing in primary and secondary schools. Teachers and learners express positive attitudes towards electronic whiteboards but there is little evidence as yet of clear effects on attainment or on the teaching and learning process (Smith *et al.* 2005). Interactive whiteboards have many potential advantages – they are flexible and versatile, offer multi-media efficiently, facilitate participation and interaction and enable the teacher (or learner!) to model ICT skills. Their advantages for interaction and participation are frequently mentioned, and it is certainly easy to share information more easily than with traditional resources. Moreover, the teacher can either retain a dominant role or adopt a much less dominant one as seems appropriate. But learner participation often slows down the pace of teaching without always proving beneficial. Two main senses of interactivity need to be considered: feedback to learners on their responses, and interactivity in the sense of increased dialogue among learners and between teacher and learners.

To date there is little evidence of any significant development in the quality of teacher-learner or leaner-learner dialogue through the use of interactive whiteboards and there is clearly a need to research further how the interactive potential of interactive whiteboards might be exploited educationally. Initially most use of interactive whiteboards was to enhance whole-class teaching (Smith *et al.* 2005). It should be noted that interactive whiteboards are of course excellent for presentations. While typical PowerPoint presenting in schools and elsewhere leaves a great deal to be desired, skilled and intelligent use of interactive whiteboards as presentation resources could enhance direct teaching considerably, as part of a balanced approach to the use of teaching modes. Development here has tended to be sidelined by the instruction/construction polarization in discussions of how pedagogy might be transformed by ICT. There is also a need for further research on the effects of visual information on learning (see Reedy 2008).

Hammond *et al.* (2009) suggest that teacher confidence, access to support and modelling of ICT use, a hands-on approach, a willingness to try things out, teacher beliefs in the potential of ICT, and a supportive school culture for this, are keys to developing effective use of ICT in teaching.

Orlando (2009) provides evidence that because teachers do not appear generally to have become constructivist in their pedagogy, this does not mean that they have not been changing at all as a result of involvement with ICT resources. This study suggests ICT gives teachers new ways of reflecting on their teaching and enthusiasm for trying different strategies. In short, it offers a more bottom-up route to developing teaching. The potential and actual changes as a result of ICT resources are complex and it is important to develop a wide perspective on all the possibilities.

Summary

Resourcing schools with ICT has remained problematic, despite several waves of investment and policy rhetoric. Considerable variety in the quantity and quality of provision is likely to remain, and not least in the range of skill and confidence among teachers. Increasing clarity is developing about the potential of ICT for transforming teaching and learning, but studies continue to show that there is a long way to go in this respect in relation to classroom practice. The debate has tended to centre on moving from instruction to construction but there is a need to look critically at some aspects of constructivism, and a wider perspective – such as that provided by the four modes of teaching – is likely to take the debate further including a positive, though balanced, role for direct teaching with ICT.

The idea that the post-digital generation of learners is significantly different in approaches to learning, confidence and knowledge about ICT and its use has generated a strong debate. Most commentators adopt a cautious approach and call for more research evidence. Nevertheless, the debate has stimulated research and development in innovative teaching and learning approaches using ICT.

ICT use has been very effectively developed in many early education contexts when naturally integrated into the curriculum and can be shown to contribute to many central aims of early education. Generally in schools, features such as interactive whiteboards do have considerable potential for developing both motivating and effective teaching. It is here, and in other developments such as the use of mobile technologies and game-based learning, and the role and safety of the internet, that the focus is now directed, rather than on the drill and practice techniques and facilities of earlier times.

Wider questions about technology need to be raised and debated and a critical approach to large-scale policy developments should be given a hearing; for there is a danger of large-scale changes being far less successful than their advocates envisage and a danger also in embracing technology uncritically – of losing sight of important educational aims, values and principles.

Key Reading

Allen, J., Potter, J., Sharp, J. and Turvey, K. (2007) *Primary ICT*, 3rd edn. Exeter: Learning Matters.

Austin, R. and Anderson, J. (2008) *e-Schooling*. London: David Fulton.

Conlon, T. (2008) 'The dark side of glow: balancing the discourse', *Scottish Educational Review*, 40(2): 64–75.

Gage, J. (2006) *How to use an Interactive Whiteboard Really Effectively in Your Secondary Classroom.* London: Fulton.

Siraj-Blatchford, I. and Siraj-Blatchford, J. (2006) *A Guide to Developing the ICT Curriculum for Early Childhood Education.* Stoke-on-Trent: Trentham.

Useful Websites

www.ltscotland.org.uk/ictineducation

www.nextgenerationlearning.org.uk

www.unescobkk.org/education/ict

www.terry-freedman.org.uk

All these sites contain a host of ideas and examples relating to ICT and learning.

www.marcprenzky.com

Articles on ICT and innovative teaching approaches using ICT by Marc Prensky.

www.becta.org.uk

Reviews and reports on national developments in ICT and teaching.

10 Understanding and Developing Pedagogy

Chapter Outline

What is Pedagogy and why is it Important?   114

Pedagogy and Early Education   118

Educational Message Systems and Critical Pedagogy   119

Pedagogy, Andragogy and Heutagogy   120

Pedagogical Content Knowledge   122

Summary   123

Key Reading   124

Useful Websites   124

What is Pedagogy and why is it Important?

In their recent book on pedagogy, Leach and Moon (2008: 165) boldly assert: 'Pedagogy can change people's lives, it has a power to transform'. Pedagogy has undoubtedly become a central concept in the educational debate and anyone seriously attempting to improve teaching and learning needs to understand the ideas now associated with the term. Three problems need to be faced, however. Many teachers in Britain (but not generally elsewhere) are put off by what they see as unpalatable jargon and the traditionally negative connotations of the word; in the past, the systematic study of pedagogy has been neglected in the UK, or at least in England; and in recent years pedagogy has spawned many offshoots – critical pedagogy, productive pedagogies, pedagogical content knowledge and many other related terms which now also need to be understood. This chapter addresses these issues and explains the origins and development of the concept and related ideas, and their application in a range of educational contexts. The main argument is that, despite its awkward past, 'pedagogy' has become a crucial idea in educational debate and there is now no good reason why it cannot be an acceptable term in educational discussion in Britain, as elsewhere. Modern conceptions of 'pedagogy' direct attention to vital ideas without which teachers will miss out on some of the most important recent educational thinking and discussion about teaching and learning.

Yet unlike in most continental European countries, where it has long been a familiar term with a positive connotation, to many UK teachers pedagogy remains awkward, ugly jargon. Ask around a group of British teachers (as I did) and you'll soon be told: 'a ghastly word'; 'I hate it, I don't want to think of myself as a pedagogue'; 'I never know how to pronounce it'; 'Nobody explains exactly what it means'. In Britain pedagogy is often used just as an erudite word for teaching methodology, so reinforcing the suspicion of academic jargon for the sake of status.

But for all its academic pretensions in the English-speaking world, pedagogy has the lowliest of origins. In ancient Greece 'pedagogue' meant a slave who accompanied a school pupil – '*pais*' (boy, and also slave, genitive '*paid-*') combining with '*agogos*' (leader) to produce '*paidagogos*'. Over time it came to mean 'teacher'. Through Latin it became pedagogue in English, but had developed connotations of dogmatism, severity and, by the time Shakespeare depicted Holofernes in *Love's Labours Lost*, pedantry. Through the continental tradition and 'scientific' American educational research, pedagogy came to refer to 'the art and science of teaching' (many forgetting that teaching is also centrally a moral practice). Alexander (2008b: 50) notes that the continental view of pedagogy as a science of teaching entailed the wide sense of a systematic body of knowledge, not necessarily an experimental science in the positivist tradition.

Alexander (2008b: 43–50, 173–5) rejects the idea of pedagogy as just an alternative word for teaching technique, though he notes a tendency, even in policy-making circles, to use it thus. He suggests it should be used in a way that includes the bigger picture of teaching – why teachers do what they do, justifications, values, theories, evidence and relationships with the wider world – so that teaching is viewed as a broadly educative process and not a merely technical one.

Writers such as Leach and Moon (1999, 2008) and McCormick and Murphy (2000) offer a way of structuring such a conception. Pedagogy is seen as having a number of dimensions that need integrated consideration: views of the nature of knowledge, of learners, assessment tasks and discourse patterns (the forms of language generated by a group with shared interests and aims), and of teacher and learner roles and relationships. Clarifying and critically examining such assumptions should lead to following through the implications for curriculum, for specific teaching and learning strategies, and for assessment; and then the development of a particular pedagogical 'setting' (or context) that embodies these articulated assumptions. This is very different from trying to think about teaching methods in isolation or in an unreflective manner.

When operating in the classroom, teachers, though guided by internalized principles, are not usually explicitly thinking critically about the wider aspects of teaching; their focus naturally is on immediate teaching actions and handling the complex social situation of maintaining class order and engagement in learning. Reflection on wider issues – such as aims, values, assumptions about knowledge and learning – needs time and support at the planning and reviewing stages and in continuing professional development sessions (see Chapter 12). There is a danger of time for reflection being crowded out in schools under the

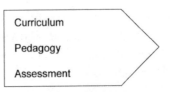

Education's three message systems

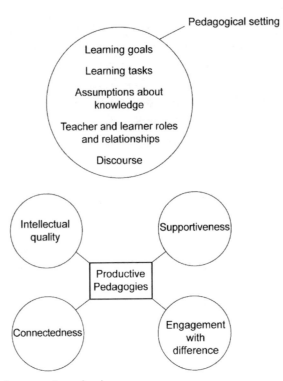

Figure 10.1 Developing conceptions of pedagogy

In recent decades the idea of pedagogy has developed in important ways – as understanding has developed about teaching and learning, operative factors and their educational and social repercussions. Modern, still evolving, conceptions are far removed from their origin in Ancient Greece where *paidagogos* denoted a slave who accompanied a child to school.

pressure for other initiatives and developments. The old assumptions that reflection can be achieved during normal teaching or in regular lesson planning, or that a once-for-all preparation in thinking about teaching strategies will suffice, can no longer hold. The debate on ICT and pedagogy (discussed in Chapter 9) shows clearly the difficulties of changing pedagogical practice and of addressing assumptions about learning, knowledge and so on. Establishing this wider conception of pedagogy throughout the profession is a major step towards securing conditions in which teachers can adequately address such issues.

Sociological studies of pedagogy unsurprisingly place a distinct emphasis on social justice considerations and not a few such studies only seem interested in what might be called instructional pedagogy in so far as it affects issues of social justice. Yet sociology also has a potential contribution to make to mainstream instructional pedagogy. The French sociologist, Durkheim, was in fact Professor of Pedagogy in Paris, and British sociologists influenced by him (e.g. Bernstein – see below) made pedagogy significant in British writings on educational sociology. The continental line of thought also influenced the Brazilian educator, Freire (see below).

Dewey in Chicago was also Professor of Pedagogy and provided one route for the development of instructional pedagogy in the USA and UK. These two streams of writing on pedagogy, sociological and instructional, are coming together through the writings of those such as Leach and Moon, Alexander, Murphy and McCormick, and the Queensland developments on 'productive pedagogies'. Together they provide a deeper theorization and wider role for pedagogy as a central idea in educational thinking. Different emphases can still be detected, however, as well as common threads. For example, much of the existing literature on the Queensland pedagogical framework focuses on social justice issues (though to be fair, some writers do discuss instructional pedagogy where this has social justice repercussions), while Alexander places the emphasis on classroom talk and wider thinking about teaching interactions. Leach and Moon put more emphasis on assumptions about knowledge and about learning (debates on forms of constructivism versus 'symbol processing' approaches). McCormick and Murphy, however, also deal with gender issues and all three discuss questions of discourse. Teachers somehow need to take account of all these perspectives for they are all highly relevant to good teaching.

Official policy discussions in the UK have eagerly adopted the term but seem mainly concerned to point up government policy concerns – which so far have focused on changing teaching strategies, perhaps too narrowly conceived. Leach and Moon (2008) stress the potential power that teachers have, when they deploy pedagogic strategies and skills, to transform learners' perceptions and horizons and make clear that it is not just teaching techniques that are in question. They encourage teachers to be intellectually curious about all aspects of pedagogy, learning and teaching, including new ideas in brain science (see Chapter 11).

Teaching Development Activity 10.1 – Pedagogical Assumptions

Select a standard, even a routine learning task you think important for your learners. Consider carefully, in the light of the discussion of pedagogical dimensions above, the assumptions you are making about the:

- educational aims of the activity
- the nature of learning
- the nature of the knowledge involved
- your teaching role and the learner's role
- expected classroom interaction

In response to these reflections, revise the task, then undertake the teaching and consider the outcomes.

Pedagogy and Early Education

In 2006 the Scottish Executive somewhat surprisingly sponsored a document, *Let's Talk about Pedagogy* (Learning and Teaching Scotland 2005), urging early years practitioners to 'embrace pedagogy' and make it the focus of professional debate. The British nursery school tradition has developed a marked reluctance to discuss 'teaching' which unfortunately persists. But a wealth of recent research studies on learning through play (Anning 2006; Wood 2007) now suggests the need for interactive support for children's play while also valuing children's perspectives and reconciling those of child development theory and the sociology of childhood. 'Talking pedagogy' in the wide sense and developing a pedagogy of play, experts suggest, could do the trick and galvanize evidence-based reflection on interactive roles. The Scottish early years paper suggests that pedagogy is about learning, teaching and development, 'influenced by the cultural, social and political values and principles we have for children in Scotland, and underpinned by a strong theoretical and practical base' (Learning and Teaching Scotland 2005: 9).

On the European continent, with its longstanding tradition of systematic study of teaching, pedagogy and pedagogues are common, positive terms. If British practitioners became reconciled to talking pedagogy, early education and care here might benefit more readily from the globalization of research and comparative studies. Fumoto *et al.* (2004) argue for a wider conception of teaching in early education, drawing on the ecological perspective of Bronfenbrenner and adults' abilities to capture children's momentum towards learning. A useful question concerns how this differs from pedagogy. Variety in terms used may have arisen from education, care and social development coming closer together in the early years.

Developments in the integration of services for young children have raised the suggestion that some of those who work with young children should be called 'social pedagogues'. In Europe, moves to integrate the early years workforce are developing two basic categories – teachers and pedagogues (David 2006). Both have educational roles, require social awareness and need to take pedagogy seriously in its emerging wider sense. Some advocate this terminology for Britain, despite strong misgivings in various quarters. Social pedagogues and pedagogy may become increasingly accepted since other possible terms are also problematic and Europe-wide communication is increasingly important.

The term social pedagogy in this context (along the lines of European social pedagogues who have a training in personal development and take a holistic approach in working with children and youth) should be clearly distinguished from social pedagogy as advocated in recent writings on collaborative group work to refer to principles of grouping and theories, and strategies of collaborative learning (see Chapter 7).

Educational Message Systems and Critical Pedagogy

Bernstein (1973) viewed education as a social institution having three message systems (curriculum, pedagogy and assessment) that conveyed messages about what was to count as proper knowledge, proper ways of gaining knowledge and proper ways of assessing learners' knowledge. These messages, he argued, were based on power differences. A society's particular educational values and message systems typically worked to the disadvantage of already disadvantaged groups and served to reproduce social and cultural inequalities.

Bernstein aimed to understand and counter the wastage of working-class educational potential. He claimed standard educational arrangements had unfortunate consequences for lower social groups. Though schools might officially espouse equality, the message systems typically served to reproduce social inequalities. For example, Bernstein (1977) suggested that progressive primary educational contexts involved an 'invisible pedagogy' (implicit not explicit learning through play). Middle-class children found it easier to recognize, access and conform to this hidden pedagogy. Bernstein further argued that different pedagogies have different 'framing', by which he meant the extent to which control over the selection, organization and pacing of knowledge is in the hands of the teacher or learner and involves different links between school knowledge and everyday knowledge.

Bernstein's work is complex and abstract. While his theories have been critiqued by various writers, such as Pring (2004), they have, recently, informed thinking about 'productive pedagogies' in the influential Queensland reforms, and examples of how educational practice can be changed have been reported on (Keddie and Mills 2007). Hayes *et al.* (2006: 154) exemplify how such message systems operate in modern school systems, inhibit learner initiatives and restrict achievements to low performance. In relation to the new reforms, they argue:

> We believe the message should convey to the students that the tasks they are asked to perform have meaning and value beyond school, that the criteria by which they are judged are worthwhile and explicitly articulated and that their performances will be enhanced through feedback and practice.

They also emphasize the need for effective alignment of the three message systems if productive pedagogies are to be successful, since some approaches to curriculum and assessment thin out pedagogies and narrow the purposes of schooling. Thus higher-order thinking will require appropriate assessment tasks as well as effective interactive pedagogy.

In this context it is worth also drawing attention to Freire's (1970) famous banking metaphor of education. This views learners as an empty bank account into which the teacher, like a bank clerk, deposits knowledge by direct transmission, knowledge being viewed as a commodity like money. Teachers as authority figures decide what and how much knowledge to transfer and this, Freire claims, results in oppression and dehumanization. Freire proposed, by contrast, a view of education as problem-posing and the teacher as a contributor to dialogue with learners in which critical thinking takes place about issues meaningful to learners.

This critical pedagogy of Freire is linked to the Frankfurt School of 'critical theory' (critical of societal power relationships and their effect on social equality). For Freire, thinking critically about their context help learners see links between their problems, experience and the social context in which they live – a first step towards taking action against oppression. Educationists like Apple (Apple and Beane 2007) and Giroux (2006) have sought to apply Freire's ideas, along with other thinking, to education in the USA, particularly in relation to the education of disadvantaged urban youth.

Pedagogy, Andragogy and Heutagogy

While pedagogy remained an academic term for teaching approaches in education generally, the American adult education theorist Knowles (1970) introduced the term 'andragogy' (drawing on some American and East European adult education sources) to capture the specific approaches to teaching he argued were suited to adult education. For Knowles, pedagogy was associated with didactic, teacher-controlled knowledge transmission and so failed to reflect the adult learner's capacity for greater self-direction. Hence pedagogy, the teaching of children, was to be replaced by andragogy (from '*andros*' – man, hence leading or teaching adults).

It was unfortunate that in adult educators' minds pedagogy has been associated with didactic teacher-controlled learning. This association certainly sounds strange to anyone familiar with British or American early and primary education, since the 1970s dominated, in theory at least, by progressive ideas including open classrooms, child-centred teaching and self-directed learning, even if practice did not always match theory. Self-chosen enquiry is, moreover, a core feature of pre-school practice.

It was equally unfortunate, as Elias (1979) noted, to assume that adult education should focus exclusively on self-directed learning. There should be room in adult education, as elsewhere, for each of the four modes of learning, for a mix and overall balance of methods. This has long been the norm in university education (see Chapter 2) and so why not in adult education? Elias regarded pedagogy and andragogy merely as two different ways of approaching the education of adults and children and agued that andragogy on its own was not an adequate way to enhance the professionalization of adult education. There is in fact no sound basis for the distinction between andragogy and pedagogy as Knowles (1979) eventually recognized. All four modes of teaching are valuable at all stages of education. Unfortunately, there has been a tendency in some educational contexts to assume a progression from direct teaching to open enquiry and self-directed learning as one matures – for example, in some university course designs and in Mosston's influential analysis of physical education teaching styles (from 'command to discovery' – Mosston and Ashworth 1990). This assumption is too rarely challenged. Yet the youngest children in pre-school are capable of successfully engaging in enquiry and are also capable of elementary discussion (Dillon 1994; see Chapter 4 of this volume), and the introduction of a problem-based learning approach in the first years of university courses has proved at least as successful as traditional lecture/tutorial diets (Savin-Baden and Wilkie 2004).

In the last few years andragogy has been further refined through the idea of 'heutagogy'. This emerged in relation to vocational education involving distance learning and ICT (Hase and Kenyon 2007). The basic idea is that of self-determined learning, not just self-directed or traditional independent learning. Heutagogy was coined from a Greek root similar to 'auto'; 'auto' was thought too misleading and so was adjusted to produce 'heut' which was added to the '-agogy' suffix, meaning therefore 'self-leading' or 'self-directing' (Hase, personal communication 2008). Heutagogy is the process of allowing learners to decide what they want to learn, how they want to learn it and when they want to learn it. This enables students to become very responsible for their own learning. In the field of vocational education a need was perceived to move from andragogy to truly self-determined learning, seen as appropriate to workplace learning in the twenty-first century, particularly in relation to developing 'capability'.

A key aim in vocational education is to develop capability, not just transmitted knowledge and skills; and this implies learners having much more control of their learning. That this could be applied to the development of flying safety procedures shows the problems of top-down, centrally transmitted knowledge and skills and a faith in the self-determined learning of involved professionals. It was felt that andragogy still had connotations of a directive teacher-learner relationship. It remains to note here that self-determined learning has long been the basis of nursery education philosophy.

Emphasizing the modern role of self-determined learning is valuable but of course a balance needs to be struck with other kinds of learning. A 'blended heutagogy' (Ashton and Elliot 2007), combining an element of self-determination with more directed aspects, is one possibility. Heutagogy is now appearing in the literature beyond that of vocational education and the idea, along, unfortunately, with the awkward terminology, will no doubt become more common.

Reflective Exploration 10.1 – Developing Pedagogy

Take some time to make notes on the various wider considerations surrounding an aspect of learning in your context. What aspects of your current pedagogy appear to need development and what resource issues and other obstacles do you face? What positive opportunities are there for change?

Pedagogical Content Knowledge

Shulman's idea of 'pedagogical content knowledge' (1987: 9) refers to the kind of knowledge needed to teach subject content effectively. This includes knowing:

> the most regularly taught topics in one's subject area, the most useful forms of representation of those ideas, the most powerful analogies, illustrations, examples, explanations, and demonstrations – in a word, the ways of representing the subject that make it comprehensible to others [...] an understanding of what makes the learning of specific topics easy or difficult: the conceptions and preconceptions that students of different ages and backgrounds bring with them to learning.

Such knowledge is central to teachers' work but would not typically be held by non-teaching subject experts or by teachers who know little of that particular subject. When first developed by Shulman, this conception seemed tied to a view of subject knowledge as rather static and to a teacher-centred transmission pedagogy, linked to ideas about fixed ability; but Shulman later modified his stance to incorporate a more situated view of learning and give more emphasis to student agency as opposed to dependence on the teacher (Leach and Moon 2008: 157–9). Banks *et al.* (1999) have stressed the dynamic nature of teacher understanding in this area and the interacting roles of subject discipline knowledge (each teacher having a unique personal history in relation to acquiring this), school subject teaching expertise and general pedagogical knowledge. The combination of these results in a unique personal understanding and perspective for each teacher. Developing pedagogy partly involves developing a reflective approach to understanding one's own perspective and identity as a teacher in relation to these three aspects. Such thinking about pedagogical subject knowledge links up with a long-established European tradition of the study of 'didactics' and pedagogy, where these terms to some extent cover aspects usually considered under 'curriculum' in the UK and USA (Alexander 2000: 542–7; Alexander 2010: 412).

The survey in this chapter of the origins, development and wide range of meanings and application of 'pedagogy' hopefully shows the way in which educational thinking is continuing to develop. Words and concepts evolve to meet changing understanding, aims and contexts. For all its earlier negative connotations in the UK, the term pedagogy should now prove no more difficult to use than terms like dyslexia, autism, dyspraxia – or other words from Greek roots (like television). But the ideas pedagogy signals of course require careful thought.

Summary

The terms 'pedagogy' and 'pedagogue' have long had off-putting connotations to most serving teachers in the UK, if not elsewhere. But pedagogy is an evolving concept, increasingly prominent in educational debate and policy discussions and beginning to influence educational practice. Pedagogy is an increasingly influential idea internationally and the time is ripe for teachers to overcome past inhibitions and address the issues this signals in educational policy and practice.

In some educational writings, pedagogy is still used just as an erudite term for teaching methods or approaches. But writers like Alexander have argued for a broader and more powerful conception – as teaching and its accompanying wider theory and justification, seeing this as a way of generating sustained and deep thinking about educational interaction, aims and values. Writers like Leach, Moon and Murphy have argued similarly; and, drawing to some extent on discussion of pedagogy in educational sociology, a conception has been evolving which focuses on the assumptions about knowledge, learning, teacher-learner relationships and other dimensions of educational transactions, including wider ideological power structures and relationships. This serves to bring discussions of teaching into the modern debate on knowledge and learning, including aspects of educational sociology and ideology. Much of the discussion of pedagogy has come from sociological writings on education and acknowledges that teaching strategies are never ideologically neutral, but build in assumptions about knowledge, learning, and educational aims and values that need to be critically examined.

In early education, pedagogy has now been promoted as an alternative to teaching strategies, because teaching has, regrettably, never been a happy term in the pre-school tradition, being associated with didactic transmission of knowledge and with not taking account of young children's developmental processes. And, even though a wide conception of teaching has been argued for here and elsewhere, the close integration of teaching with other aspects of childcare and development has made pedagogy an attractive idea. Following widespread European practice, the role of some childcare and youth workers is now being conceived as that of 'social pedagogues' combining educational, social development and welfare aims.

Policy moves as typified in the Queensland reforms involve productive pedagogies (well theorized, principled strategies which aim to realize in classroom practice the values and principles of social justice combined with effective learning). Such writings draw partly on work by Bernstein on pedagogy as a 'message system' that determines or reflects educational norms and practice and helps to reproduce educational inequalities, and partly on Freire's work on critical pedagogy.

In adult education, pedagogy has been seen as equated to traditional teacher-dominated direct teaching and the term 'andragogy' has been coined to reflect more self-directed learning, though still facilitated and led by adult educators. Now, especially with ICT developments, yet another term, 'heutagogy', has appeared, especially in vocational and adult education, meaning self-determined learning and focusing on exploitation of electronic and other learning resources. Discussion of pedagogy in relation to subject knowledge has opened up thinking about the relationships of school subjects, parent disciplines and teacher's personal subject perspectives.

All these are part of the expansion of the meaning of pedagogy. They result in teaching strategy decisions being considered in a wider perspective and in an integrated way, taking into account new ideas about knowledge, learning, teacher roles and educational contexts and work in the sociology of education.

Key Reading

Bernstein, B. (1996) *Pedagogy, Symbolic Control and Identity: Theory, Research, Critique.* London: Taylor & Francis.

Freire, P. (1970) *Pedagogy of the Oppressed.* London: Penguin.

Leach, J. and Moon, B. (2008) *The Power of Pedagogy.* London: Sage.

Learning and Teaching Scotland (2005) *Let's Talk About Pedagogy.* Glasgow: LTScotland.

Mortimore, J. (1999) *Understanding Pedagogy.* London: Paul Chapman.

Useful Websites

www.education.qld.gov.au/curriculum
Information on 'productive pedagogies' in Queensland.

www.standards.dcsf.gov.uk/research/themes/early_years/Researchingpedagogy/
Report on research on early years pedagogy.

Brain Science, Cognitive Psychology and Teaching 11

Chapter Outline

How can Neuroscience Help Teachers?   125

Common Neuromyths in Education   129

Numeracy, Literacy and the Brain   131

Insights on Early Education, Adolescence and Lifelong Learning   134

Summary   136

Key Reading   137

Useful Websites   137

How can Neuroscience Help Teachers?

Until recently, evidence about how the brain worked made little apparent impact on teachers' thinking about classroom practice. Ideas about teaching strategies were based on a mix of traditional professional craft knowledge, psychological studies of learning, and educational philosophy and sociology. Research on teaching strategies aimed to develop a science of teaching based on observational and experimental research on learning and teaching in schools. Behind these ideas, however, were inevitably assumptions about the nature and development of memory, intelligence, attention and so on. Thus, deeply ingrained ideas about general ability and the value of ability groups can be traced back to theories of fixed intelligence that held sway in the 1940s and 1950s. Howard-Jones (2008) points out that many such assumptions may now be questioned on the basis of new neuroscientific research. Yet there is a very big jump from brain studies to teaching strategies.

Neuroscience (the chemical, biological, physiological study of the brain and nervous system, how it operates, develops and changes) and cognitive neuroscience (the study of neuroscientific aspects of perception, memory, learning and so on) have emerged as potentially important sources of evidence that might eventually lead to recommendations for classroom practice. Cognitive neuroscience adds to cognitive psychology by getting inside the workings of the 'black box' of the brain.

The main reason for the recent impact of neuroscience on education is that new techniques (brain imaging studies and ways of monitoring the electrical activity of the brain such as MRI, FMRI, PET and EEG) have become available for studying the brain in action. This has led to a range of new information about how the brain is structured and how it functions – for example, studies of how people with dyslexia process information when reading or which parts of the brain are activated when doing algebra.

But how far does this research add anything new or contrary to what traditional educational thinking and research suggest? What role is left for traditional research and thinking about teaching, and how much do teachers need to know about brain science to become effective in their work? This chapter tries to answer these questions.

Recent surveys (Howard-Jones and Pickering 2005; TLRP 2006) demonstrate that teachers generally express a keen interest in ideas from neuroscience that might apply to teaching, that they think knowledge of the brain is important for designing curricular programmes and that they are attracted to brain science explanations of learning. This is natural given the many enduring teaching problems teachers face and the appeal of science, seen as providing reliable knowledge.

Anyone committed to education can be expected to be curious about the brain and its functioning. The prospect of accelerated and enhanced learning from research on the brain is an enticing one. To many, brain science promises to offer new explanations and diagnoses of learning difficulties and teaching issues, and to suggest more effective remedial strategies. Books and staff development opportunities on accelerated learning which claim to be 'brain-based' are eagerly taken up, in the process usually sidelining cognitive psychology, the craft knowledge of teachers and wider educational theory. Some writers argue that even if brain science just confirms teachers' craft knowledge, this is valuable, while others (like Blakemore and Frith 2005) argue that efforts should focus on findings that may be counter-intuitive (e.g. that mathematical abilities are not all of one piece – see below).

Applying neuroscience to teaching presents several problems, however. We are still at an early stage of neuroscientific research and neuroscientists themselves are generally very cautious about applicability; they stress the importance of basic research and the build up of theory as a basis for longer-term applications. Unfortunately others, keen to popularize brain science for teachers, have been less careful, resulting in a distortion of findings and theories and misguided recommendations based on 'neuromyths'. However, the very big jump involved in applying neuroscientific findings to classrooms is being increasingly recognized. Few teachers understand neuroscience and can't be expected to develop expert knowledge. The argument of this chapter is that it should however be perfectly possible, and is very desirable, to gain a clearer understanding of how neuroscience works, what sort of evidence is found and how theories are gradually developed and tested. Clear communication about findings and their implications is required. And close collaboration between neuroscientists, cognitive psychologists, educationists and teachers is needed to ensure research is well focused and applications valid. Decisions about teaching cannot just be based on facts about the brain. No one group has a monopoly of wisdom or insight into teaching; all have a role to play.

Some, like Davis (2004), point up important conceptual and value issues and argue that neuroscience cannot, in principle, tell us much about the nature of learning and understanding. Cognitive psychologists like Bruer (1997) suggest that trying to move from neuroscience directly to the classroom is too ambitious and that ideas and research in cognitive psychology provide a very necessary stepping stone in thinking about learning, memory and teaching strategies. Besides, it is a mistake to think of there being a one-to-one correspondence between mental processes and educational phenomena. Ideas like understanding cannot be reduced to mental processes whatever the neural concomitants of understanding might be in particular contexts. Davis (2004), for example, criticizes a writer who argues that the implication of recent neuroscientific studies is that learners should be taught to think for themselves. This, Davis insists, assumes certain educational aims and values that are not universally accepted. There are longstanding debates about autonomy, communitarianism and the liberal tradition of thinking for oneself. Neuroscientific facts alone cannot tell us what matters in human flourishing. Some discussions of neuroscience, emotions and morality raise similar difficulties, as does the idea of lifelong learning as a goal.

Many popular texts and some neuroscientists talk about how the brain learns, thinks, understands and so on. For Harre (2002), however, it is people, not brains, who think and understand, and he argues that we need to retain the ordinary language of knowledge, actions, motivations, feelings and intentions, and not succumb to a reductionist view of learning. We cannot study learning directly by looking at how the brain operates. Imaging studies show where activity is occurring but they do not show us directly, as it were, learning, thinking or memorizing. Cultural aspects also need to be brought into play – Davis (2004) argues for example that playing the violin in an orchestra is not purely an individual matter but involves participation in a larger cultural environment. Davis links such observations to his claim that because of the intentional nature of learning, which can't be confined to processes inside individuals, neuroscience is limited in how far it can explain learning. This is not obviously convincing, however, and others (e.g. Howard-Jones 2009) argue for a halfway house in this matter.

Reflective Exploration 11.1 – The Brain and Learning

How do you react to the idea that neuroscience appears likely to provide deeper insights into certain aspects of human learning and eventually, in some way, may inform approaches to teaching and learning? What do you and your current learners know about the brain and its development and working? What neuromyths have you encountered in reading and discussion among friends and colleagues? How far have these influenced your own approach to learning and teaching?

A recent review of neuroscience and education by the Organization for Economic Cooperation and Development (OECD/CERI 2007) makes a case for 'transdisciplinary study' (bringing together the thinking of neuroscientists, psychologists and educators) as the way forward, but others (see Cigman and Davis 2009) think this hard to achieve given the very different basic perspectives of the various disciplines. Clearly, however, communication and working at the boundaries between disciplines is likely to help.

Figure 11.1 Image courtesy of Dr Mark Bastin, SFC Brain Imaging Research Centre, University of Edinburgh.

Figure 11.1 shows a section of the hippocampus (from the Greek for a sea horse, which the shape of the hippocampus resembles) of a mouse, showing brain cells (neurons) and dendrites (from the Greek for 'tree-like'), the branching formations which extend out from the cell bodies, aiding connections with other cells. In the last 20 years, new research technologies and investigative techniques have enabled neuroscientists to explore the workings of the brain in much more detail and to link findings with insights from psychological research on memory, learning and thinking. These new techniques have provided much more detailed information about the working of neurons (brain cells) and their connections; and about their role in learning and thinking. The human brain has some 100 billion neurons.

It is also important to remain alert to the danger of teachers becoming over-dependent on neuroscience for educational decisions and progress, and not working at solving teaching issues from within the classroom. Teachers do, however, have a very positive contribution to make to discussions about neuroscience and education in helping to raise and sharpen the issues that need to be addressed by researchers; and teachers also require help in interpreting the implications of neuroscientific findings for teaching. This chapter, hopefully, is a small contribution to this.

At present, many studies merely indicate correlations – what is linked with what – but the direction and nature of causation and development of deeper understanding await further, more complex investigations. Despite these caveats, recent research, as we shall see, is providing revised ideas about the operation of the brain that do cast light on educational issues and can inform decisions about teaching strategies. The point to be grasped is that, like other disciplines, neuroscience develops by findings and theories that later require revision, sometimes radical revision. It is not all a steady march forward. We can expect current ideas to be far from the final word on how the brain operates or how humans learn. Brain plasticity, for example, is a key idea – the idea that the structure and functional organization of the brain can change through the lifespan as a result of experience, whether by deliberate learning, environmental influences and exposure, or in response to brain damage. This idea has now replaced older ideas about little plasticity after childhood. But it is important not to oversell the idea of plasticity. There are some limits; and there is much more to be researched.

Common Neuromyths in Education

By 'neuromyth' is meant an idea that has now been shown by recent neuroscientific research to be misguided or which stems from a distortion or exaggeration of earlier research. Neuromyths often emerge in popularized accounts of brain-based learning. The main ideas now identified as neuromyths by neuroscientists (OECD/CERI 2007; Geake 2008) are:

- we only use 10 per cent of our brain
- the effects of 'brain gym'
- the need to drink copious amounts of water to prevent brain dehydration
- critical periods in human development
- left- and right-brain thinking
- the value of 'hot-housing' in infancy and an early start to school
- some aspects of multiple intelligences
- VAK (visual, auditory, kinaesthetic) learning styles
- sleep learning
- the need to learn just one language at a time
- the extent of male and female brain differences
- how vital the first three years of life are for later development

While commercialized self-help texts have helped to spread such myths it should also be noted that some have their roots in earlier neuroscientific research findings, now being revised through more sophisticated studies. The notion of critical periods for example, was not a distortion by unscrupulous consultants or poorly informed teachers. Some ideas now regarded as myths about early learning were once taught as reliable research in standard educational and psychological texts.

'We only use 10 per cent of our brain'

This well-known saying gives a very misleading impression of how the brain operates. Neuroscientists now point out that the idea is contradicted by 'virtually every datum of modern brain research' (Della Sala and Beyerstein 2007: xix), though some early brain studies did suggest a few brain regions had no function (OECD/CERI 2007: 113). The myth appears to have arisen by the distortion of a remark (in a foreword to an influential book by Dale Carnegie) by the psychologist William James that he doubted most people used more than 10 per cent of their potential, and was repeated by Einstein in a radio interview. Current evidence suggests that the brain as a whole is very active all the times, as we would expect from the evolution of so vital an organ.

Left- and right-brained thinkers

Neuroscientists tend to see this as among the most damaging myths in educational thinking. The claim is that thinking is either by the (supposedly creative) left hemisphere of the brain or the (rational, logical) right; that these are different types of thinking; that people have a strong preference for one kind; and that western education favours one kind of thinking (logical rationalistic as opposed to creative, holistic). Like many neuromyths, this is the result of taking some early research on the brain and going far beyond the information available from the research, while at the same time not taking into account more recent studies which provide a very different picture.

Split brain experiments in the1960s on subjects whose corpus callosum had been severed to treat dangerous cases of epilepsy suggested that higher mental functions in brain-damaged subjects could be separated and studied independently. Popular writings fuelled the now widespread belief that the two different sides of the brain control different modes of thinking and that everyone has a preference for one mode. However, while the different hemispheres are specialized to some extent, both sides of the brain work together in almost all situations, tasks and processes. We all use both sides of our brain and higher-level thinking is not strictly divided into roles that occur independently in different halves of the brain. (It may be of interest that many neurons have their nucleus in one hemisphere and extensions in the other.)

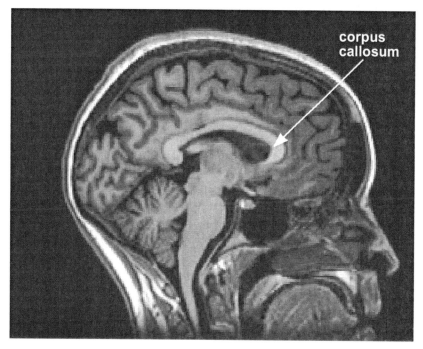

corpus
callosum

Figure 11.2 Image courtesy of Dr Mark Bastin, SFC Brain Imaging Research Centre, University of Edinburgh

The 'corpus callosum' (literally, 'tough body' – compare 'callous') is a dense mass of fibres that joins the two hemispheres of the brain. The two halves of the brain are far from independent, contrary to some ideas surrounding the 'neuromyth' of right- and left-brained thinking.

Numeracy, Literacy and the Brain

The aim of this and the following section is to provide an overview of recent findings relating to key aspects of learning that should be of interest to teachers generally, to give an idea of the range of research studies and the kinds of light they are beginning to throw on issues in teaching and learning. In many writings now, it should be noted, ideas from neuroscience research are closely interwoven with ideas from cognitive psychology, and this is reflected in the discussions below.

Mathematics

Recent research (OECD/CERI 2007: 99) has shown that infants have a quantitative sense in relation to 1, 2 and 3. They can discriminate these quantities from each other and also from larger quantities. They also have some ability to approximate for larger numbers with reasonable gaps. For example, they can distinguish 8 and 16 but not 8 and 9, and seem to be aware that 1 + 1 is 2 and that 5 + 5 are *about* 10. Experts consider that infants have an evolutionary endowed number sense that is used as a perceptual tool to understand the world and that they build on this in early childhood.

Neuroscientists argue that mathematics teaching should build closely on children's informal and intuitive understanding, that traditional approaches underestimated young children's mathematical capabilities and that teachers have an important role in 'scaffolding' deeper understanding and mapping mathematical symbols to the real world. This helps link procedural and conceptual knowledge, which is so critical for success in mathematics.

Imaging studies suggest that *learning* mathematics builds neural networks for *handling* mathematics. The parietal cortex plays an important role but mathematical processing is by no means restricted to one side or part of the brain. Even simple mathematical operations activate several areas of the brain. Areas used for algebra appear to be independent of those for number, which itself involves a highly dispersed network of brain structures (Varma and Schwartz 2008). Teaching can help to bring different aspects of mathematics together for the learner. Teaching methods using number lines and linking number and space work well and this may be related to 'a biological disposition to associate number with space' (OECD/CERI 2007: 102).

Neuroscientific evidence is consistent with the finding that ability in one area of mathematics (spatial, say) does not necessarily predict ability in another (numerical, say). Hence care needs to be taken in testing and grouping for mathematical learning, and individual strengths and weaknesses should be looked at more closely. Learners with dyslexia may have difficulty reading mathematical problems (and so need, say, software support for this) but otherwise show strong mathematical abilities.

An important recent finding (OECD/CERI 2007) is that new mathematical knowledge can dramatically change brain activity patterns and these changes depend on methods of teaching (methods based on understanding as opposed to learning by drill). Here again there are implications for assessment – which should involve testing of understanding, not just checking correct answers.

Language, reading and dyslexia

While the brain has evolved certain structures and areas for spoken language – Wernicke's area (important for understanding language and meaning) and Broca's area (important for the production of speech) have been known of since the nineteenth century – there is no specific brain area for *literacy*. Appropriate experiences help children establish neural pathways to support reading, and vocabulary development and pre-reading skills are significant here. Limited exposure to these, it is well known, considerably disadvantages children learning to read.

Discussing learning to read is complex. There are different kinds of script: character-based scripts like Chinese and alphabetical scripts like Italian, English and so on. Alphabetical languages can be divided into two main groups: those that are highly phonetic – one letter, one consistent sound, like Greek or Italian, which are said to have shallow orthographies (spelling systems); and those with deep orthographies, such as English and French, where there are more complex and irregular relationships of sounds to letters. These factors affect the reading process.

It was once thought that character-based writing like Chinese and Japanese required visual memory skills while to read highly phonetic languages like Italian or Greek (one sound being represented by only one letter) required good phonological skills (ability to distinguish phonemes) once the symbol-sound links had been learned. But Goswami (2009) considers that brain imaging studies suggest that reading any language depends on a well-functioning phonological system (the system related to hearing sounds and their various components) and that it is oral language skills that underpin the acquisition of reading – which begins primarily as a phonological process. In the early stages of learning to read, she reports, it is the neural structures for spoken language that are particularly active.

Some theorists favour a dual-route theory of learning to read (i.e. phonological processing and the direct processing of meanings) and this naturally supports a balanced (both top-down and bottom-up) approach to teaching reading. However, Goswami (2008) argues that, overall, current evidence from imaging studies supports a single-route model of reading development based on developing connections between symbols and sounds.

Dyslexia

Dyslexia remains a complex and controversial subject, some questioning its existence, others seeing it as a remarkable gift. There are various theories about its cause and possible remediation. For our present purposes we can define it as a reading difficulty that is not the result of general or local intellectual deficit or motivational problems. It is prevalent and widespread across various social, economic, cultural and linguistic groupings.

Goswami (2008) explains that children with developmental dyslexia show under-activation in key phonological areas of the brain, but this can be compensated for by targeted phonologically-based training. They find it difficult to detect and manipulate component sounds in words, to count the number of syllables and to recognize rhymes and shared phonemes. The development of phoneme awareness is slow and hard. Goswami argues that neuroscience is changing the ways in which dyslexia is being conceptualized. It can be viewed more as involving an alternative development pathway to reading than as an insurmountable learning difficulty. The most efficient of the various approaches to helping dyslexics to read seem to be those offering intensive phonological exercises. But while recent studies may help to identify those at risk of dyslexia, neuroscience is a long way from understanding just what goes wrong in the processing of reading in the case of dyslexia.

Insights on Early Education, Adolescence and Lifelong Learning

The extent of evidence, theorizing and drawing of implications for teaching on these topics is growing rapidly and will repay further exploration than there is scope for here (see e.g. Blakemore and Frith 2005; OECD/CERI 2007). A brief overview follows below.

Early education

Current understanding (David and Powell 2007) is that babies come into the world 'intentional' from the start – eager to interact with others and explore their world's properties, peoples and objects by making use of their senses, and all this leads to learning. They experiment more as they develop physically, engage in proto-conversations and are 'mind readers' by age 2. The brain develops through a complex interaction of nature and nurture, with experiences affecting the particular neural paths that develop. It is also accepted that young children learn best through relaxed, happy play and interaction with those who love them and show them affection.

It is now considered that most of what were formerly dubbed 'critical periods' in development are better regarded as 'sensitive periods', for language acquisition for example. Some experiences like language exposure and learning have their most powerful effects during specific sensitive periods in the maturation of the child's brain while others can affect the brain over a longer time. There appears to be an optimal time in childhood for consolidating the ability to discriminate sounds; and if a second language is learned as a child, it seems easier to acquire a good accent and the grammar than in later life (OECD/CERI 2007).

In the 1970s it was argued that the first five years of life were crucial for brain development and this led to suggestions that an early start to formal education was desirable. This was reinforced by the belief that there were critical periods for learning certain things, and that development might be accelerated by providing a highly enriched environment. Neuroscientific and other studies have now undermined each of these ideas, however (OECD/CERI 2007). It is clear that the brain continues to develop through adolescence, and the evidence is that while strong deprivation has a negative effect on development it does not now appear that a highly enriched early development adds much benefit.

Adolescence

Neuroscience is now showing the perhaps surprising extent to which adolescent brains are still developing, particularly in the frontal lobe and parietal cortex where 'synaptic pruning' does not begin until after puberty. Myelinization also increases here (myelin is a fatty substance which insulates neurones and improves the speed and efficiency of communication

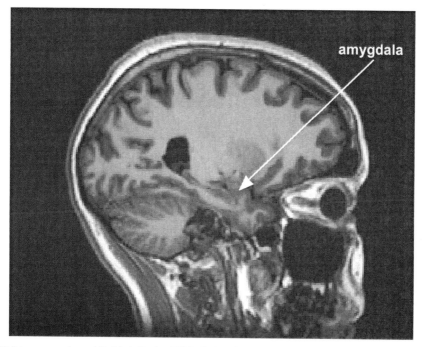

Figure 11.3 Image courtesy of Dr Mark Bastin, SFC Brain Imaging Research Centre, University of Edinburgh

The amygdalae (from the Greek for almond) are small almond-shaped structures deep inside each hemisphere of the brain. They have been shown to play a key role in emotions. Neuroscientists hope that further research will aid deeper understanding of the role of emotions in learning and that this will lead to developments in teaching.

within the brain). Evidence suggests that the adolescent brain finds it harder than the fully adult brain to direct attention on future tasks, to multi-task and to take others' perspectives. It is also suggested that teenagers tend to activate different areas of the brain than adults when learning algebraic equations. This is possibly related to more robust memorizing processes. These established findings are beginning to be linked to the fact that the adolescent brain is still developing and this implies that secondary and tertiary education can have an important influence on brain development.

'Plasticity' means that humans are well organized for lifelong education. Perhaps, with age, adapting to change is harder but older adults may show greater strategic abilities, building on experience and skills. One reported study (TLRP 2006) showed that juggling practice in older persons led to increases in the size of the brain areas activated by this activity, returning, after three months' rest, almost to the original size. Other studies of adults reinforce the notion that the brain adapts to new learning late in life. There is, no doubt, much yet to be discovered about learning and the adult brain.

Teaching Development Activity 11.1 – Exploring Learning Styles

Use some standard way of assessing your learners in terms of their apparently preferred learning styles. Check the results in terms of your own knowledge of the learners. Now offer each group a task in which they use an alternative learning approach: for example, those with a supposedly 'verbal' preference have to use a kinaesthetic approach, and so on. Plan out what each approach would involve. Observe the learners' ability to learn in the new way and their reaction to the approach. How far does this lead you to question the accuracy of the initial assessment and perhaps suggest that learners are able to be flexible in learning? See also Chapter 2.

Summary

Many teachers express a keen interest in the findings of brain research that purport to have implications for teaching. This is understandable given the intractability and continuing challenge of many aspects of teaching; and faith that science provides reliable evidence about causes and effects and eventually remedial strategies. The possibility of optimizing learning and developing accelerated learning has also motivated interest in brain science among teachers and educators. However, few teachers appear to have a detailed or accurate knowledge of how the brain works and obviously few can be expected to develop neuroscientific expertise. It is probably more important to understand broadly how neuroscience research works, how theories develop and are applied, how these relate to the psychology and philosophy of learning, and to understand the main findings and implications, than to have extensive mastery of details about brain areas and functioning. Teachers are likely to remain reliant on expert advice in this rapidly changing area of research and understanding.

Yet so far this has proved a dangerous strategy. Many 'neuromyths' have been propounded in commercially inspired texts for teachers and the research evidence for popular practices like 'brain gym' and some aspects of 'accelerated learning' have been questioned by neuroscientists. The exposure of 'neuromyths' and distorted ideas about learning and the brain poses the danger of promoting cynicism about neuroscience and education.

There is now a widespread recognition among interested parties of the need for caution in moving from brain research to educational recommendations, the need for interdisciplinary studies and the important roles of teachers in helping to set the agenda for brain research related to teaching and education. Some argue that traditional cognitive psychology is a necessary bridge between neuroscience and everyday teaching, and has a continuing important role. But, unfortunately, so far there has been much less recognition of the need to consider values and aims and the philosophical aspects of learning and teaching as an intentional human activity. It is not clear what brain research can itself contribute to teaching and learning understood from this crucial perspective. It is, however, important to give a greater role to philosophical discussion of the nature of learning in debates about neuroscience and education, to prevent a reductionist approach to teaching and learning.

In short, there is something new and important for teachers to explore and understand, but the traditional roles of other disciplines and perspectives and cautions against reductionism need to be maintained in order to draw effectively with expert support on the insights from the rapidly growing findings of neuroscience. This is an area requiring communication between relevant experts – psychologists, teachers and educationists – not just between neuroscientists and teachers. Commercialized educational ventures in this area need to be carefully monitored. That said, some real insights and a neuroscientific perspective are now contributing to the thinking and practice of teachers in relation to areas such as dyslexia, early education, adolescent behaviour, memory, music and many others.

Key Reading

Blakemore, S-J. and Frith, U. (2005) *The Learning Brain*. Oxford: Blackwell.

Cignan, R. and Davis, A. (2009) *New Philosophies of Learning*. Chichester: Wiley/Blackwell.

Geake, J. (2008) 'Neuromythologies in education', *Educational Research*, 50(2): 123–33.

Goswami, U. (2008) 'Reading, dyslexia and the brain', *Educational Research*, 50(2): 135–48.

OECD/CERI (2007) *Understanding the Brain: The Birth of a Learning Science*. Paris: OECD.

TLRP (2006) *Neuroscience and Education: Issues and Opportunities*. London: Institute of Education, University of London.

Useful Websites

www.icn.ucl.ac.uk/sblakemore

Website of neuroscientist Sarah Jane Blakemore. Contains recent articles on the adolescent brain.

www.teach-the-brain.org

A commercial brain-based education site.

www.educ.cam.ac.uk/neuroscience

Cambridge University website on research focusing on how the brain functions, how it changes during the development of reading and mathematics and related aspects of language number, memory and attention. Links to articles by Goswami and others.

www.tlrp.org/pub/commentaries

Useful extended commentary on issues in relating brain science to education.

www.oecd.org/edu/brain

Very useful collection of brain maps, glossary of neuroscience terms and articles on the brain and education.

Part 5

How to be Reflective

Developing Teaching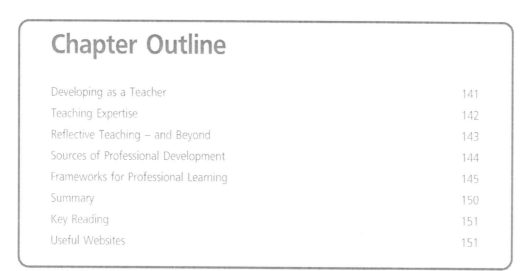

Chapter Outline

Developing as a Teacher	141
Teaching Expertise	142
Reflective Teaching – and Beyond	143
Sources of Professional Development	144
Frameworks for Professional Learning	145
Summary	150
Key Reading	151
Useful Websites	151

Developing as a Teacher

Earlier chapters have emphasized the variety and complexity of teaching, the ongoing debates and mounting research evidence about teaching and learning, the spate of policy initiatives, increasing use of ICT and ever-stronger worldwide influences in education. Together these point to one clear conclusion: teachers need to continually develop their approaches to teaching and learning and other aspects of professionalism. The traditional assumption about teacher education (surprisingly, still evident recently – see Boyd 2005: 1) was that a once-for-all preparation would basically suffice. But such a view is now unsustainable and it is appropriate, therefore, in this final chapter to consider the ideas, structures and resources that teachers can exploit in the task of continually developing professional understanding, knowledge and skill.

It will be useful, first, to consider the nature and development of teaching expertise and stages of professional growth; and then to examine the concept of reflective teaching, which has long been highly influential but needs critical scrutiny. The range of emerging sources, opportunities and structures for professional development can then be assessed in the light of the ideas about improving teaching and learning identified throughout this volume. Finally, teachers' involvement with, and use of, research on teaching requires discussion – taking account of research findings in planning and conducting teaching, undertaking action research as an individual or as a group of interested teachers, and participating in larger research projects in collaboration with educational researchers and policy-makers.

Teaching Expertise

It is natural to expect that having a clear idea of the nature of teaching expertise and the way in which it builds will provide a good base for understanding how to develop more effective teaching and learning. There are, however, several theories and effective teaching, as we have seen, is not just a matter of technical expertise (see further, Carr and Skinner 2009 and Alexander: 2010: 404–436). Let us look, then, at relevant studies of teachers as experts and consider what might be the learned about teacher development.

One well-known approach is in terms of changes in teacher concerns as experience grows (Fuller 1969). Fuller proposed a three-stage model of teacher development in which teachers, as they gained experience and expertise, moved from concerns about self, to concerns about tasks, to concerns about students and the effect of teaching. In another study, Conway and Clark (2003: 465) confirmed that 'concerns appeared to shift, as Fuller predicted, from self to tasks to students – a journey outward'. However, as the teachers' understanding of teaching changed, their concerns and aspirations also shifted from their ability to manage their classrooms to 'concerns about their personal capacity to grow as a teacher and a person' – a journey outward certainly, but, Conway and Clark suggest, also inward, with heightened reflexivity and attention to their identity as a teacher. While it is not clear that these are stages everyone has to go through, or how long such a progression takes, the stages do provide some sense of direction for professional development. A shift in concern from one's own performance to clients' needs is also common in other, related areas such as public speaking.

Berliner (1994) offers a five-stage model of professional growth from novice to expert:

- novice
- advanced beginner
- competent
- proficient
- expert

His central point is that there are differences in how teachers at different levels of expertise interpret classroom events. Experts are more likely than novices and those at other stages to discern what is important; and naturally they rely more on experience and show more fluent performance. They exhibit more effective use of well-practised classroom routines than novices, and can maintain a brisk pace without losing control of lessons. They also tend to have more sense of responsibility for performance, to be more critical of their own performance and have a greater emotional investment in teaching. Rollett (2001) emphasizes the ability of experts to call quickly on proven strategies, which frees them to handle unexpected events, quickly grasping the issue and drawing imaginatively on resources to resolve the situation. They develop caring, powerful learning environments for their learners as individuals, focusing on positives.

Glaser (1999) suggests experts generally have very specific proficiency, highly procedural and goal-oriented, and tend to perceive large meaningful patterns. In solving problems they search their memory or, for novel problems, use general problem-solving tactics, and monitor their own problem-solving processes skilfully.

It can undoubtedly be daunting to encounter a long ladder of development at the start of initial teacher education and to realize that on completing initial training one is only likely to have reached the degree of expertise associated with an 'advanced beginner'. But while the choice of labels may be unfortunate (what newly-qualified doctor or lawyer would be described as an advanced beginner?) the sequence of stages is probably typical in any profession or challenging occupational role. Many who now emerge from initial teacher education into schools are impressive in their qualities, commitments, ideas and skills and are recognized as such by children, experienced colleagues and parents; and professional growth thereafter can be rapid.

Ericsson (1996), another prominent writer in the area of expertise, argues that for high expertise one generally needs ten years from starting in areas such as sport and music (though impressive, promising performances are usually evident early on). There is no reason to assume that highly skilled performance in teaching will require less.

Unfortunately, what is not so clear from research is what helps teachers to move through the various stages from novice to expert. Ericsson draws attention to the evident roles of motivation, support from mentors and deliberate effortful practice with focused feedback from coaches. The aim for teachers should surely be deep, critical understanding of realistic teaching experience. Unreflective experience may just ingrain survival skills. It is this combination of awareness of classroom realities with a well-developed understanding of teaching and learning that recent research suggests is the key (Blatchford *et al.* 2003; James 2008). These aspects have tended to be kept far too separate in the past.

Reflective Teaching – and Beyond

Brooks (2004: 13) points out that reflection is regarded as a very important means of professional development because learning comes from reflecting on experience, not just from experience itself (see also Chapter 5). Schön (1983), in his influential discussion of reflective practitioners, emphasizes that teachers do not just apply knowledge and professional skills developed in training but continue to develop their thinking through reflecting on experience, reflecting in-action and on-action. Commentators like Eraut (1994) have noted, however, that teaching gives little scope for deliberative reflection (as opposed to rapid, barely conscious 'reflection' in the heat of classroom activity), though possibilities increase as teaching expertise develops.

The central point here is that teaching is not reducible to established, set skills that can just be applied. Skills need to be refined and new ones developed by critical reflection on practice and by applying them in teaching. Many commentators (e.g. Moon 2004) suggest teachers keep diaries and journals. But while questions need to be asked about time and motivation for this by hard-pressed teachers, Moon claims they have a popular appeal to teachers and various studies report evidence of their usefulness (i.e. Hatch *et al.* 2005).

Once dominant ideas such as the 'competent teacher' and 'reflective practitioner', while still basically viable, have come under increasing scrutiny. Writers like Moore (2000, 2004) and Carr (2003a) are critical of the common assumption underlying both conceptions of an applied science view of teaching, and possibly unhealthy introspection and invalid speculation about causes and cures during reflection. Moore argues for 'reflexive' teaching, by which he means looking closely at one's own developmental history as a teacher and life outside school and before entering teaching. He also suggests directing attention to factors in the wider societal context, and power issues.

At first sight the idea of the competent teacher is attractive for professional development. But it tends to incorporate a narrowly technicist, skills-based view of teaching and competence lists usually fail to capture the complex interpersonal relationships and skills that are hard to itemize. Moreover, in practice competences rarely encourage theorizing; and one can formally acquire the competences but still fail in classroom.

Sources of Professional Development

Alexandrou *et al.* (2005) identify three models of continuing professional development (CPD) which together provide a comprehensive view of possibilities.

Systems-led CPD

This is top-down, focused on central or local government priorities and aims at developing consistent, coherent teaching aligned with policy developments, standards and competences. It is often linked to a ladder of promotions, further qualifications and enhancement. There is the danger of developing a compliant culture (MacDonald 2004) and not encouraging teachers to be creative or to challenge and critique the status quo. Teachers are provided with changing practices but have no significant role in shaping these. The risk is that many teachers become demotivated as they become aware of contradictions between the performativity culture and their traditional educational values and career perceptions.

Individual-led CPD

Rooted in principles of lifelong learning and liberal education, traditional individual CPD often turned out to be too spasmodic to be really effective. Officials often criticized it as lacking accountability and policy relevance. But it fits recent initiatives on personalizing learning and can usually also help teachers meet official standards.

Profession-led CPD

This is based on the argument that the profession itself (through its various professional associations) should maintain and enhance professional development to raise the status and quality of the profession and should aim to shape rather than just respond to government changes. There may, however, be significant overlaps in places with systems-led CPD.

Hoban (2002) points out that teachers potentially have access to a wide network of resources for developing teaching (colleagues, courses, online resources and so on) and need to learn to exploit these. The issue is how to combine these fruitfully and find time to exploit them. The answer appears to lie in collaboration and securing official recognition of the need for time for such tasks.

The old distinction (Hoyle 1972) between 'restricted' and 'extended' professionals needs to be re-examined. 'Restricted professionals' (the term was initially not pejorative but identified the scope of professional priorities and interests) were conscientious practitioners who worked hard, planned lessons carefully and cared about their pupils. Their focus was on their classroom (where they saw their careers continuing) and their learners. They felt ready for a long career in teaching without much further training, assuming a basically unchanging set of teaching skills and stable government policies and priorities. 'Extended professionals', by contrast, were interested in the broader context and purposes of education and sought to constantly improve their professional skills by reflecting on their own teaching, discussing with other teachers and attending in-service courses.

There has been greater recognition recently of the importance of encouraging a significant number of teachers to seek sustained professional development while remaining focused on a continuing career as a classroom teacher, instead of assuming career progression implies moving into teacher management roles. Scotland's Chartered Teacher scheme exemplifies this possibility.

Stenhouse (1975: 143–4) argued that since teaching needed continuing development all teachers should become extended professionals in the sense of systematically questioning their own teaching and conducting classroom action research on it (he was critical of traditional 'scientific' educational research as unable to cope with the realities of classroom conditions). It is now common for teachers to be expected to take account of educational research findings in their teaching (e.g. Glasgow and Hicks 2003; Taber 2007) but research often cannot be directly applied to classroom teaching in the sense of specific strategies (though some has obvious implications as earlier chapters have indicated at various points). More often it is a matter of changed understanding and perspectives that inform practice in a more complex and general, but eventually perhaps radical, way (Hammersley 2002).

Frameworks for Professional Learning

Professional bodies such as the General Teaching Councils in England and Scotland have recently developed frameworks for CPD, in consultation with teachers and education authorities. The English council (GTCE 2007) acknowledges that, while teachers learn professionally every day in the course of teaching, in the past many teachers' experiences have proved rather static or amounted largely to acquiring survival skills that have often ingrained what is far from the best practice. The GTCE's framework of professional development experiences aims to help teachers plan their professional development to meet identified needs in the light of official teaching standards expectations. Professional development is regarded as an entitlement, a responsibility, a way of supporting and recognizing teachers' expertise and an important basis for professional and personal satisfaction in a teaching career.

Chapter 2 referred to evidence (James and Pollard 2006) that promoting more effective pupil learning depended to a considerable extent on further learning on the part of teachers. The GTCE and other bodies argue that teacher learning needs to be in a context of wider school improvement and that sustained school improvement and raised standards depend not on individual teachers learning alone but on the collective work of teachers and a shared professional knowledge (GTCE 2007). However, the GTCE does not make clear what scope should remain for individual teacher development and it also fails to acknowledge how much such professional knowledge is contested because of differences in aims and values among teachers, policy-makers and theorists. See further Alexander 2010: 404–436.

The framework is intended to encourage diversity and differentiated programmes and to ensure that professional learning is recognized for accreditation and career advancement as well as professional development in its own right. Teachers, it recognizes, need time for sustained reflection, structured learning, and time and support to identify professional development needs and plan for them.

The demands on professional development are formidable. Teachers need to learn to work with evidence, adopt new practices, learn from observing and discussing with other teachers, work within a learning team using mentors and coaches, engage in classroom collaborative enquiry and problem-solving, network with professional and other associations, design courses and conduct classroom-based research activities. This is quite a challenge and very different from past expectations and opportunities. A major question is where adequate time is to be found (Galton and Macbeath 2008) and, since time involves costs, this is obviously likely to remain an issue.

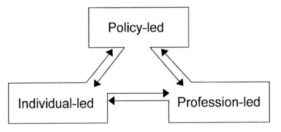

Figure 12.1 Action research patterns

Action research typically involves a tension between developing a sustained focus on one issue and being open to development into other related problems. This is a dilemma that often has to be resolved as an action research project develops.

The Researching Teacher

Over recent decades action research has become a recognized activity for practising teachers and networks of teachers exist to support teachers undertaking such research. There has been an impressive grass-roots evolution of collaborative support among teachers and researchers (see websites below). In teaching contexts, an action research project typically involves selecting a teaching issue to investigate, trying out some promising change in teaching, monitoring its effects, looking carefully at the evidence obtained and writing up a reflective discussion of the findings to inform further development and to share with interested colleagues.

The main idea to grasp in classroom action research is that of a cycle of planning, acting and reflecting. It is a form of learning through action (see Chapter 5). An action research project can have one main cycle or several shorter cycles leading to a spiral of reflective action (see McNiff 1988).

Three typical problems arise for teacher action researchers. Many find it hard to focus down to a small enough aspect to research, for a small topic appears trivial and unimportant. Psychologically this is understandable, but focus is vital for developing solid evidence and deep understanding, and for the action to make a significant difference. While breadth can dissipate effort, a small study well conducted can lead to real change in teaching and paradoxically often helps illuminate other issues and influences colleagues.

Another common problem is that many teachers express a strong desire to replicate other researchers' studies in their own classrooms. Instead of beginning from what has already been established, for example about collaborative group work, many teachers feel compelled to find this out for themselves in their classrooms, to reinvent the educational wheel as it were. The importance of context in teaching and inexperience of research makes this again perfectly understandable; and there is certainly a place for replication studies in research. But it is not necessarily the best or only strategy for advancing professional knowledge for the practising teacher. Support is now available to design effective action research and to provide ongoing support to ensure effective professional learning from it (see websites below).

Some teachers beginning action research find it hard to settle on a problem. They opt for a project on questioning but, as they start to explore, they decide the real problem is how children are grouped. Then they conclude the issue is not grouping after all but class discipline. Once more this is understandable: problems in classrooms tend to be related. But, as already emphasized, after a brief survey of the area and related issues, fixing on a clear focus is crucial.

Having decided on a suitable topic for action research, the next step is a reconnaissance – scouting out the selected issue, finding out what the problems are in the area being investigated, getting the lie of the land. Observing typical current practice can help; for example, a teacher keen to develop the ability to handle discussion may reflect and come up with observations such as 'It always comes back to me. I just can't get the pupils to participate.' If the focus is teacher questioning, a teacher might record and transcribe a short interchange to see how it differs from what had been hoped would happen. Who does most of the talking? What is the quality of pupil response? Who controls the discussion?

Some researchers prefer to do a full reconnaissance and try one well thought out change. Others prefer a series of shorter cycles, making small changes each time as insights emerge and so evolve a better practice. Each approach has its strengths.

Identifying a possible change can come from thinking about the evidence from a reconnaissance and looking at other writings about the issue and appropriate teacher websites. As in research generally, experiments that fail are often at least as illuminating and eventually contribute as much to improved teaching as those where things go right. The important thing is to reflect intelligently on the evidence and its implications for taking teaching forward.

Teaching Development Activity 12.1 – Action Research

Undertake one cycle of small-scale action research (see the discussion above). Go through the cycle and evaluate the results and where your action research might now further develop. Try to involve a critical friend to observe and discuss with you and, if possible, collaborate with another teacher.

Combining teaching and research

Researching one's own teaching raises an important question: how feasible is it to be at the same time a teacher and researcher? There certainly are tensions – between analysis and action and between detachment and engagement, as well as in relation to the use of time. Researchers are concerned with analysis, with observing and exploring a situation or practice with a view to understanding it. Teachers are committed primarily to action. To be sure, they are, or should be, interested in understanding educational practices and contexts and in rational, evidence-based discussion of educational issues, aims, values and policies. But they are constrained by the need to act – for example, to teach Primary 5 on Monday morning. A researching teacher inevitably faces this dilemma and the imperative for action will inevitably win, which means that discussion and enquiry are cut short as practical decisions need to be taken about how to act.

The other main tension affects the nature and quality of any research that is undertaken and confidence in carrying it out. From a research perspective one needs to be detached, neutral and objective. But as a teacher one is engaged, involved, alert to individual needs and issues. And in their teaching roles teachers need to engage fully with their class, which is a very different relationship from the detachment needed for a proper research stance. With careful organization, however, being a researching teacher is viable, worthwhile and rewarding. The key to all these dilemmas is to recognize the tensions and separate out the roles, not trying to be both a teacher and researcher at the same instant. With increasing recognition of the importance of teacher action research this is now much more possible than in the past. (See Smith and Easton 2009).

Somekh (2006b) points out that earlier assumptions about relatively simple cause-effect relations have been replaced by an awareness of the complexity of teaching contexts and development, and that action research soon leads to raising issues of educational policies, aims and values, not just of teaching strategies alone. She argues for integrating research and action in a series of flexible cycles framed within a holistic, fluid and flexible approach; for collaborative partnerships of teachers and researchers; and for recognition that action research is not value neutral. She suggests that action research should begin with 'a vision of social transformation and aspirations for greater social justice' (Somekh 2006b: 7), and should not be naive about power relationships. Reflectivity, including reflecting on one's developing identity as a teacher, is vital here, as is engagement with a wide range of existing knowledge. It is here that collaboration with outside academics and researchers can help.

There is surely a need, however, to encourage various entry points to action research and not to insist that teachers beginning action research adopt experienced researchers' interests, commitments and agendas rather than work through their own, initially usually very practically focused, problems. Hatch *et al.* (2005) provide a valuable example of the role informal enquiries by a class teacher can play in developing key teaching insights, and how collaboration overcomes common feelings of isolation through realizing that other teachers experience similar teaching problems. The teacher in this case found written reflections helped significantly and developed a change (against standard policy), allowing her learners to speak Spanish in the English class – which enabled them to articulate and share problems in learning English and make better progress. And here again, initial teaching strategy concerns soon led to wider policy interests.

Sachs (2002) argues for activist, collaboratively engaged teachers (rather than individually focused ones, compliant to external performance measures) who aim to mobilize professional action in the best interests (as they see it) of learners on a basis of democratic empowerment. Paterson (1998) provides evidence of the diverse civic activism of teachers and the positive effects of this on their professionalism.

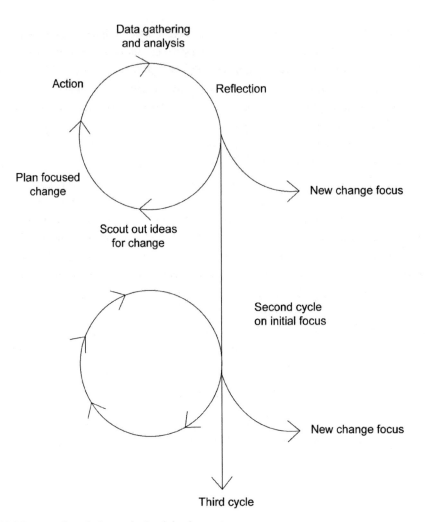

Figure 12.2 Sources of continuing professional development

In planning their own professional development teachers can draw on three interacting systems as indicated in Figure 12.2. It is increasingly recognized that each source has a valuable role to play. Developing one's own particular professional development path involves working around issues of choice and initiative values, accountability and resourcing.

Summary

The explosion of ideas about effective teaching and learning and developments in technology and policy aimed at raising standards mean that teachers need to continually develop teaching. There are now various structures, resources and ideas that teachers can explore to continue their professional development. Ideas about teacher expertise and studies of professional growth provide useful insights. Networks of action research and collaborative electronic networks, as well as communities of educational enquiry, have developed well in recent years.

Professional development can be seen as a triangle of system-led, profession-led and individual-led development. Teachers now have access to a wide network of learning resources, including colleagues and others, in developing teaching. Tensions in action research can best be addressed through collaboration and action research networks without destroying individuality. Generally, however, it is likely that some tension between the three systems of professional development will remain, even as teachers develop an increasing voice in professional and educational development. Successfully negotiating this challenge is one route to effective and personally satisfying development as a teacher.

It is hoped that the ideas in this chapter will provide a stimulus for CPD and that the ideas in earlier chapters, including the broad framework and detailed discussion of modes of teaching, will prove a firm foundation for the balanced development of effective teaching and learning and for the professional and personal satisfaction this can bring. I believe the time is ripe for such a broad and balanced conception of teaching and for developing varied, positive teaching roles for promoting effective learning.

Key Reading

Berliner, D.C. (1994) 'Teacher expertise', in B. Moon and A. S. Mayes (eds) *Teaching and Learning in the Secondary School*. London: Routledge, pp. 107–13.

Burton, D. and Bartlett, S. (2005) *Practitioner Research for Teachers*. London: Paul Chapman.

Day, C. (2005) *A Passion for Teaching*. London: RoutledgeFalmer.

Hopkins D. (2002) *A Teacher's Guide to Classroom Research*, 3rd edn. Buckingham: Open University Press.

Moon, J. (2004) *A Handbook of Reflective and Experiential Learning*. London: RoutledgeFalmer.

Moore, A. (2004) *The Good Teacher*. London: RoutledgeFalmer.

Pickering, J., Daly, C. and Pachler, N. (2007) *New Designs for Teachers' Professional Learning*. London: Institute of Education, University of London.

Somekh, B. (2006) *Action Research*. Maidenhead: Open University Press.

Useful Websites

www.bera.org

Website of the British Educational Research Association. Many useful links and ideas about the role of research in education.

www.ncaction.org.uk/

This website uses pupils' work and case study materials to show what the National Curriculum looks like in practice.

www.teachers.org.uk/cpd
Many useful ideas and links on CPD.

www.gtce.org.uk
Website of the GTCE. Good for frameworks of professional development and courses, ideas and useful links.

www.gtcs.org.uk
Website of the GTCS. Useful papers and research reports on professional issues and development available to download.

www.ase.org.uk
Website of the (UK) Association for Science Education. Links to resources, ideas and policy issues.

www.did.stu.mmu.ac.uk/carnnew
The current website of CARN, the Collaborative Action Research Network. Useful links to a range of support services for action research in education, including a journal, bulletin and teacher researcher conferences.

Glossary

accelerated learning

Learning using **'brain-based'** approaches that, it is claimed, result in faster learning.

action learning

Can refer simply to learning by doing or to a specific form of collaborative action research and development (devised by the industrialist Reginald Revans in the1940s), found in some business and vocational education contexts.

action research

In education this typically involves making a change (the action) to educational practice and assessing its effectiveness by systematically collecting evidence and interpreting the results. It now often draws on support from teacher/researcher networks and sometimes collaboration with experienced educational researchers. This often leads to action researchers exploring wider educational and value issues thrown up by the research as cumulative understanding, practical change and policy developments are sought.

active learning

This term now tends to conflate three meanings – active engagement with learning (not necessarily implying physical activity), learning through direct experience, and (under the influence of constructivist thinking) the provision of choice and initiative in learning tasks. Learners should be mentally engaged in all explicit learning, including direct teaching contexts.

affordance

In discussion of ICT in education, it refers to the action or cultural possibilities of an object or resource. An affordance of computer word processing is the facility with which writing can be revised and of a digital camera the ability to transmit pictures promptly.

alignment

The principle of ensuring that assessment tasks test the intended learning of the curriculum and that they are consistent with the teaching approaches used. Failure to align curriculum, teaching and assessment can distort learning – for example, if pupils focus on conventions of written English at the expense of learning to write creatively and with imagination, or on reproducing factual knowledge as opposed to developing deeper conceptual understanding. Congruence rather than tight alignment (which might restrict development of open, complex learning) is now advocated.

amygdala/ae

The amygdalae are small, almond-shaped sections of each hemisphere of the brain with a key role in emotions and memory. Often referred to as a unit – the amygdala.

andragogy

A term (from the Greek for man – *andros*) used to characterize the learner-focused approach and especially the reflective, self-directed learning claimed to be appropriate for adults, as opposed to the didactic transmission supposedly typical and appropriate for children and youth – **pedagogy** (from Greek for child – *paidos*). See also **heutagogy**.

assessment for learning
An initiative centred on developing effective **formative assessment** involving significant changes in traditional oral assessment practices (increasing wait time after questions, 'no hands up', groups working towards a best answer) and more helpful written comments on learning.

authentic assessment
Assessment based on, or relating closely to, the real-life application of the knowledge, skills and understanding being developed.

axon
A long fibrous extension of a neuron through which the neuron sends information (electrical impulses) to other cells.

behaviourism
A school of psychology focusing on relations between stimulus and response in individuals and aiming to build an experimental science of behaviour. Strongly criticized as an inadequate basis for school learning which, it is argued, should aim at genuine understanding. Behaviourism informs many modern school discipline ('behaviour management') policies.

blended learning
Learning where traditional approaches are combined with learning using ICT, including online learning.

brain-based learning
A fashionable term for strategies and approaches claimed to derive from brain research – but often showing a misunderstanding or exaggerated interpretation of findings (see **neuromyth**).

brain gym
A set of 'brain-based' exercises (typically involving arm and leg crossing) intended to help children focus on learning. Though neuroscientists have questioned the basis for these exercises, many teachers claim children enjoy them and afterwards show improved attention and effort (but all this might be explained by novelty, physical activity, a change in routine and other factors.)

Broca's area
A section of the left hemisphere's frontal lobe with a role in the production of speech and understanding of language.

classroom climate
Relationships, ethos and the physical environment of the classroom. It is argued that these can affect the quality of learning. The Hay McBer report identified classroom climate as a major factor in its model of effective teaching.

co-construction
Learning where the teacher and learner, or a pair or group of learners, share ideas (e.g. in brainstorming) to produce learning which would not occur to one person alone. 'Sustained shared thinking' about some experience or problem between an adult and a child in early education is an example. Status is given to the contributions of both child and adult and the teacher is seen as a co-learner or co-investigator.

cognition

Cognition refers to operations of the mind – such as perceiving, thinking, learning, remembering.

cognitive apprenticeship

An approach to teaching based on an apprentice model. Learners are seen as apprentices of the teacher who models intellectual skills and guides the 'apprentices' in their active cognitive learning. Considered important because much implicit learning is involved in learning to undertake complex cognitive tasks.

cognitive neuroscience

A combination of cognitive psychology and neuroscience that explores the neural basis of learning, memory and other aspects of **cognition** and their behavioural manifestations.

cognitive style

A deep-seated, stable and often strong preference for certain ways of processing information, for example an analyst as opposed to a holist style. Analysts try to approach tasks one bit at a time; holists like to see the big picture first.

collaborative group work

Learning activities in which learners work together on a task (not children sitting in groups while individually undertaking identical tasks). Some writers stipulate a difference between collaboration and cooperation but this has not gained wide acceptance and the terms are generally used interchangeably.

community of educational enquiry

A group focused on enquiring into an aspect of education. Often involving participants from a range of disciplines and sectors and electronic communication – for example, through a **virtual research environment (VRE)**.

community of practice

A group of individuals engaged in a common role or activity such as a group of tailors, insurance salesmen or mathematics teachers. Communities of practice socialize new members into particular norms, values and ways of working and thinking.

constructivism

This is a theory – a metaphor – of how knowledge is acquired and developed: the idea that knowledge needs to be actively constructed by the learner. It is the dominant view of knowledge acquisition in current educational theory with implications for active learning, learner autonomy and a critical approach to **transmission teaching**. See also **radical constructivism** and **social constructivism**.

contingent teaching

Teaching in which support is provided when learners experience difficulties, but is gradually withdrawn as they begin to show understanding and success. An important strategy in early education.

cooperative group work

Another term for **collaborative group work**.

corpus callosum

A thick bundle of nerve fibres linking the right and left hemispheres of the brain, which suggests that (contrary to some **neuromyths** about left- and right-brained thinking) there is continual and significant communication between different sides of the brain during many important tasks and activities.

CPD

Continuing professional development. Generally refers to formally organized professional learning. Recent analyses have highlighted tensions between individual teacher initiatives, provision by professional bodies (such as a General Teaching Council) and policy-driven staff development; and have suggested a need to balance these forms of CPD.

critical pedagogy

Pedagogy that looks critically at education and society in relation to social justice and aims to raise learners' critical consciousness about oppressive social conditions and so contribute to their eventual personal liberation.

critical periods

The idea that certain aspects of human development must take place at a certain stage. Animals were known to have critical periods, for example for social bonding (imprinting) in birds and the concept was extended to humans. But it is now widely thought that there may be **sensitive periods** (optimal times for certain kinds of learning) rather than critical periods in human educational and social development. Associated with the Frankfurt School of sociology and the educational work and writings of Paulo Freire, Michael Apple, Henry Giroux and others.

cross-curricular teaching

Teaching where the focus of learning (a theme or topic) involves more than one subject area. The basis and extent of curricular integration can vary.

curriculum integration

The merging of ideas from different subject areas or disciplines in studying an issue. The nature of such integration and its desirability remain a matter of debate.

dialogic teaching

An approach to interactive teaching that emphasizes relatively open, high-level and probing questioning and a positive teacher role. It aims to develop clear understanding of concepts and subject matter.

dendrite

Branch-like extension of the **neuron** body. It receives information from other neurons. ('Dendrite' comes from a Greek word for tree-like.)

de-professionalization

The perception that new demands on the teaching role make traditional teaching qualities and skills redundant or accord them low priority and value, leading teachers to feel incompetent and experience a loss of autonomy.

differentiation

The strategy of providing different teaching and learning arrangements for particular learners in order to match diverse levels of knowledge and skills in a class. Differentiation can be by task, expected outcome, teacher support and other means. Widely championed, but critics note a danger that low attaining learners will not be effectively challenged.

digital divide

Refers to the gap in access to ICT facilities between various groups such as industrialized and developing countries, rich and poor, urban and rural dwellers. There is also a divide between those who are skilled and confident users and those who have access but have only rudimentary competence and experience; and school and home facilities often differ markedly.

discourse

The typical language, verbal interaction and associated values and norms of a culture, professional, occupational or social group – its particular customs and systems of thinking and talking.

dyscalculia

Inability to perform arithmetic operations despite standard teaching, adequate intelligence and opportunity. Assumed to be caused by some neurological impairment.

dyslexia

A disorder involving a difficulty in learning to read despite standard teaching, adequate intelligence and opportunity. Recent research suggests learners with dyslexia have non-standard approaches to processing phonological information.

dyspraxia

A difficulty in carrying out any complex sequence involving motor coordination, assumed to have a neurological origin.

EEG

Electroencephalogram. Uses electrodes to measure the brain's activity. EEGs are proving very helpful in studying reading because they can reflect the direct electrical activity of neurons at the time of stimulation, for example when a child sees a word on a flashcard.

emotional intelligence

Emotional awareness, ability to express emotions appropriately and to relate to others with compassion and empathy. A popular idea but criticized by educational philosophers when taken to imply a simple set of skills without acknowledging the complex value issues raised by emotional engagements.

empirical evidence

Evidence from observation, sense experience or experimental studies and surveys – in contrast to logical deduction or speculation. 'Empirical' derives from a Greek word for experience.

environment for learning

A term used in two senses: factors in the physical environment that affect learning (heat, lighting and so on); and aspects of teacher-learner relationships and roles that affect the quality of learning.

evidence-based teaching

The idea that teaching and educational policies should be based squarely on findings from research aiming to test alternative approaches or the effectiveness of particular approaches. Research using **randomized controlled trials** (RCTs) is especially valued.

experiential learning

Learning by reflection on experiences or, incidentally, through various experiences.

extended professional

A teacher interested in professional development issues and roles beyond routine classroom teaching competence.

fMRI

Functional magnetic resonance imaging. A type of brain scan that detects changes in blood chemistry and flow in the brain. It provides a way of mapping increases in brain activity in various areas in response to particular stimuli and when particular mental tasks are undertaken.

formative assessment

Assessment that aims to guide and support the learning process, especially by providing feedback on various aspects of learning. Formative in the sense of 'building up' the learner as opposed to just measuring learning.

generative topics

Issues, themes, concepts, and ideas that provide enough depth, significance, connections and variety of perspectives to promote deep understanding in learners. 'Rainforests', 'revolution' and 'the concept of zero' are examples. A feature of the **teaching for understanding** approach.

globalization

The worldwide spread of commercialized activities, transnational agencies, communications and influences that lead people to become consumers in society; and the growth of 'supra-territorial' or transworld relations between people. Critics express concern about inequality, cultural loss and economic exploitation while advocates claim better access to health, education and so on.

heutagogy

Self-determined learning. A relatively new concept developed in vocational learning contexts involving **ICT** and distance learning. The term has been concocted from roots linking to the Greek for 'self' and 'leading' and by contrast with **pedagogy** and **andragogy** to take account of learning needs and opportunities stemming from **ICT** and the explosion and diversity of knowledge in the world today.

ICT

Information and communication technology. An umbrella term that now includes any electronic communication device – not only computers and the internet but radio, television, digital cameras, mobile phones and associated applications such as email, videoconferencing, wikis and social networking sites.

incidental learning

Unplanned, unintended learning achieved in the course of other learning or activities. Many now consider its role in school learning has been significantly underestimated.

inter-disciplinary studies

Studies that draw on ideas and skills from more than one discipline. Sometimes called transdisciplinary studies.

jigsaw groups

Groups formed to share developing expertise. Thus if each of four groups studies a different aspect of a topic and then new groups are formed based on one member from each of the original groups, the different learning of the original groups can be shared. An example of **collaborative group work**.

kinaesthetic learners

Learners who prefer to learn in ways involving physical actions such as role play, manipulation of objects, touching, movement and field trips.

latent learning

Learning, often unconscious, that remains dormant – for example, a young child learning, by observing an adult, how to tighten a nut or set a place at table but not expressing this knowledge for a considerable period.

learning how to learn

A problematic though increasingly utilized idea. Often treated as if it were an identifiable skill but recent research questions this and suggests that developing learning practices which promote autonomy might meet the aims behind the concern for learning how to learn.

learning style

A preferred way of approaching a learning task or receiving information. A term often used interchangeably with 'cognitive style' though some writers try to stipulate differences.

left-brained thinking

A popular idea but a **neuromyth** based on the misconception that higher-level thought processes are strictly divided into roles that occur independently in different halves of the brain. This myth is based on an exaggeration of research findings on hemispherical specialization in the brain. It is suggested that left-brained thinking is thinking which focuses on rational, logical, analytic, objective thinking and that some people have a decided preference for or bias towards such thinking.

long-term memory

Final phase of memory in which information can be stored for from a few hours up to a lifetime.

message system

Bernstein's view of education as a social institution having three message systems (curriculum, pedagogy and assessment) which (often implicitly) convey messages about what is to count as proper knowledge, proper ways of gaining knowledge and proper ways of assessing learners' knowledge. Bernstein argued that these messages reflect power differences, typically work to the disadvantage of already disadvantaged groups, and serve to reproduce social and cultural inequalities.

metacognition

Metacognition is 'thinking about thinking' and involves awareness of one's own thinking and learning processes. This second-order level of thinking includes, for example, planning how to approach a learning task and self-evaluating one's teaching progress. Encouraging metacognition is widely regarded as central to the development of effective learning.

mirror neurons

Neurons that mirror observed behaviour. They have been shown in monkeys to become active when a monkey makes a grasping action but also when the monkey merely observes a similar action by another monkey or human. May help explain why learning from observation is typically easier than from verbal descriptions.

mode of teaching

A form or type of teaching, based on the theory that there are four basic, distinct forms, each with a distinctive means of learning, leading to distinctive teacher and learner roles, assessment, teaching skills and resources.

model of teaching

Generally, a representation of the process of teaching. In the theory of Joyce and Weil a model of teaching means a type or strategy of teaching – for example, discovery learning or collaborative group enquiry.

MRI

Magnetic resonance imaging. A non-invasive technique, which creates images of the structures in a living human brain. It works by combining a strong magnetic field and radio frequency impulses. **MRI** is used to study brain structures while **fMRI** is used to explore the functions of different brain areas.

multiple intelligences

Howard Gardner's theory that there is not just one general intelligence but rather different kinds of intelligence such as verbal/linguistic, musical, spatial, mathematical and so on. The theory is popular in the learning styles movement but questioned by several educational philosophers, psychologists and researchers.

myelin sheath

A covering of fat and protein that protects an axon and speeds up transmission of electcial impulses. Myelination occurs as the brain develops, in some areas of the brain into adolescence.

neuromyth

A misconception, originating in misunderstanding or exaggeration of evidence established by brain research. Examples are left- and right-brained thinking and the idea that we use only 10 per cent of our brain capacity.

neuron

Nerve cell (brain cell) specialized for transmitting information. Neurons are the basic building blocks of the nervous system – the brain and other nerves in the body.

neuroscience

Scientific study of the structure and functioning of the brain and nervous system.

parietal lobe

A large region of the cortex (outer crust) at the top of the back of the brain. Has an important role in spatial and mathematical processing, among other functions.

pedagogy

In many educational contexts just academic jargon for teaching strategies and approaches. Increasingly however it is used to describe teaching strategies along with the theory underlying them. Used, especially by sociologists of education and in early education, to include assumptions about the nature of knowledge, learning and assessment, including questions of **social justice**.

performance of understanding

A report or demonstration that provides evidence of understanding. For example, a report back on a science experiment, or a historical investigation. A key feature of the **teaching for understanding** approach.

performativity

A focus on compliance with official policy expectations, typically set out in terms of targets and standards.

PET

Positron emission tomography. Uses radioactive tracers to produce three-dimensional coloured images of blood flow or metabolioc activity in the brain. This has proved helpful in studying the act of reading but the use of radioactive substances makes it unsuitable for studying children.

plasticity

Ability of the brain to change its structure and functioning to some extent as a result of experience. Neuroscience research throws up increasing evidence for this. The recognition of significant brain plasticity contrasts with older assumptions about the basic stability of the brain's structure after birth.

positivism

The view that objective knowledge is only possible through empirical research – that is by observing, measuring and experimenting. Critics point out that since the development of quantum physics this is not even an accurate account of scientific method and that all study of human interactions cannot validly be reduced to such approaches, but rather needs research approaches involving interpretation of actions and statements that take full account of human intentions and meanings.

practitioner research

Research undertaken by practising teachers, usually focused on their own classrooms or schools; often collaborative. Can involve **action research** or some other research methodology – such as experiment, survey or observational study.

problem-based learning

A form of enquiry learning in which small teams address a real-life problem and develop the analytic and intellectual skills and the disciplinary knowledge relevant to solving it. It aims to make learners aware of operating factors in the real world and to motivate further disciplined study. Widely used in medical education and now in other fields. Not now viewed as a complete approach to vocational or professional learning in any field.

productive pedagogies

Teaching and wider educational strategies associate with Queensland's 'New Basics' approach. The focus is on deep learning, life relevance and **social justice**. Productive in the sense of effective in realizing these aims.

project method

Stemming from teaching developed in early twentieth-century America by Dewey and Kilpatrick, now typically refers to a teaching approach where learners solve a practical problem over a period of several days or weeks. It may involve, for instance, building a 'rocket', designing a playground or publishing a class newspaper. Project work focuses on applying as well as acquiring specific knowledge or skills, and on improving student involvement and motivation in order to foster independent thinking, self-confidence and social responsibility.

Project Zero

Harvard's noted educational research project, part of which focused on developing a **teaching for understanding** approach to learning through, initially, subject discipline-based tasks. Recently research has moved to considering inter-disciplinary studies.

radical constructivism

Influential in science and mathematical education, radical constructivists argue that all knowledge is constructed rather than discovered, and that it is impossible to tell (and quite unnecessary to know) if and to what degree knowledge reflects an objective reality. Radical constructivism holds that fitting knowledge to our experiences should be the basis for knowledge claims and the mechanism by which we learn.

RCT
Randomized controlled trial. A type of scientific experiment to test the effectiveness of different strategies. It involves random allocation of different strategies to sufficient groups or individuals to even out possible confounding factors.

reception learning
Learning from direct teaching that is well structured and clearly linked to learners' previous knowledge. Associated with Ausubel's work on meaningful learning. It should involve active critical reception not passive absorption of transmitted knowledge.

reciprocal teaching
A form of paired peer teaching shown to be an effective means of developing understanding and raising attainment.

recitation
A form of classroom interaction typified by a series of question and answer exchanges, originally designed to test understanding of a set text but now, especially in North America, referring to question and answer teaching generally.

reflective practice
Professional practice developed through careful reflection on evidence from learners, and thinking about and critically analysing one's own teaching.

reflexive practice
Directing reflections on teaching back at oneself – relating professional development issues to one's own personal history and attitudes and the wider context in which one works.

restricted professional
A teacher with a narrow, traditional view of the teacher's role as confined to competence in standard classroom teaching on the basis of strong subject knowledge and skills.

rich tasks
Assessable and reportable tasks students undertake and in which they display their understandings, knowledge and skills through performance in trans-disciplinary activities that have an obvious connection to the wider world. They are presented to learners as themes such as 'disaster' or 'pictures at an exhibition'.

right-brained thinking
Thinking which is creative, intuitive and imaginative – in contrast to so called **left-brained thinking** but equally based on a **neuromyth** about brain hemisphere functioning.

scaffolding
Temporary support from a teacher (in the form of structuring into manageable portions, offering hints, modelling how to proceed) for a learner undertaking a task, which eventually the learner should be able to do unaided. As learner confidence grows the scaffolding can be reduced.

sensitive periods

Times in a child's growth at which certain developmental events can most helpfully occur for successful development, such as emotional attachment and language exposure. Many, if not most, mental skills do not appear to have sensitive periods for their development. What were considered **critical periods** are now seen generally as sensitive periods.

short-term memory

A phase of memory whereby a limited amount of information may be held for up to a few minutes and will be lost if not consolidated into 'long-term' memory. Now often referred to as 'working memory'.

social constructivism

An approach to **constructivism** that places an emphasis on the role of social interaction and particularly talk with others in developing knowledge.

social justice

An umbrella term which includes a concern for equality and for removing discrimination in relation to gender, social class, sexuality, race, ethnicity and so on.

social pedagogue

A term used for workers in youth education and early education in Europe and widely discussed in the UK as a way of strengthening the early years workforce. A social pedagogue supports the development of the whole child, and all aspects of their life skills.

social pedagogy

A term emerging in studies of collaborative group work which emphasizes the difference between traditional teaching based on interactions between a teacher and individuals pupils – an individualized pedagogy – and a (social) pedagogy which aims to exploit the potential of collaborative group learning.

storyline

An approach to integrated or inter-disciplinary study within a story framework created by teacher and learners. The narrative involves 'key questions' which lead learners to investigate real problems within the created story context.

symbol processing

A view of learning as assimilating information about the world, manipulated and processed in a mechanical way somewhat analogous to computer processing. Contrasted with a constructivist view of learning.

synapse

A gap between two neurons (brain cells) or other nerves that is the site of transfer of information from one cell to another.

synaptic density

A number of synapses are associated with any given neuron. This can vary considerably. The more synapses per neuron the richer the ability to handle information.

synaptic pruning

In brain development unused synapses tend to be eliminated.

synthetic phonics
Teaching letter sound matches and immediately getting students to use this knowledge to read and spell regular words by blending sounds together – synthesizing them, hence synthetic phonics.

teaching for understanding
An approach that provides teachers with a language and structure for teaching, based on a performance view of understanding and ensuring opportunities for learners to demonstrate that they understand information, can expand upon it, and apply it in new ways.

teaching style
Preferred approach to organizing and interacting in teaching contexts, usually viewed as a contrast between formal and informal style preferences.

technicist
A conception or approach which implies that teaching is just a set of straightforward techniques which can be mastered through training, like physical or routine skills; and that systematic scientific studies can determine which techniques are most effective.

thematic teaching
Teaching focused not on a given subject discipline such as mathematics, history or chemistry, but on a theme or topic such as 'Vikings', 'water' or 'aircraft'.

topic work
Another name for thematic teaching.

transdisciplinary studies
Another name for cross-curricular or inter-disciplinary studies.

transmission teaching
Direct teaching, usually of structured knowledge.

VAK
Short for visual, auditory, kinaesthetic. Refers to a classification of supposed learning style preferences, recently very popular in schools but now regarded as based on a **neuromyth**. Most learning appears to be multi-modal, not reliant on a single sensory mode.

VRE
Virtual research environment. An electronic forum whereby a group of researchers such as a community of educational enquiry can share ideas and together write research papers.

Wernicke's area
A brain area involved in understanding language and producing meaningful speech.

whole-class interactive teaching
A modern form of direct teaching usually characterized by phases of whole-class discussion, pupil participation and assertive questioning.

ZPD
Zone of proximal development. Variously defined but commonly viewed as a range of achievements stretching from tasks one can do unaided to what one can achieve with support.

References

Alexander, R. (2000) *Culture and Pedagogy*. Oxford: Blackwell.

Alexander, R. (2006) *Towards Dialogic Teaching*, 3rd edn. Cambridge: Dialogos.

Alexander, R. (2008a) 'Culture, dialogue and learning: notes on an emerging pedagogy', in N. Mercer and S. Hodgkinson (eds) *Exploring Talk in School*. London: Sage, pp. 91–114.

Alexander, R. (2008b) *Essays on Pedagogy*. London: Routledge.

Alexander, R. (2008c) *Towards Dialogic Teaching*, 4th edn. Cambridge: Dialogos.

Alexander, R. (ed) (2010) *Children, Their World, Their Education*. Lndon: Routledge.

Alexandrou, A., Field, K. and Mitchell, H. (eds) (2005) *The Continuing Professional Development of Educators*. Oxford: Symposium.

Allen, J., Potter, J., Sharp, J. and Turvey, K. (2007) *Primary ICT*, 3rd edn. Exeter: Learning Matters.

Anning, A. (2006) 'Early years education: mixed messages and conflicts', in D. Kaseem, E. Mufti and J. Robinson (eds) *Education Studies*. Maidenhead: Open University Press, pp. 5–17.

Apple, M. W. and Beane, J. A. (2007) *Democratic Schools: Lessons in Powerful Education*. London: Heinemann.

Ashton, J. and Elliot, R. (2007) 'Juggling the balls – study, work, family and play: student perspectives on flexible and blended heutagogy', *European Early Childhood Education Research Journal*, 15(2): 167–81.

Atherton, J. S. (2009) *Learning and Teaching; Bloom's Taxonomy*, www.learningandteaching.info/ learning/bloomtax.htm, accessed 10 June 2009.

Atkinson, T. and Claxton, G. (eds) (2000) *The Intuitive Practitioner*. Maidenhead: Open University Press.

Austin, H., Dwyer, B. and Freebody, P. (2003) *Schooling the Child*. London: RoutledgeFalmer.

Ausubel, D., Novak, J. D. and Hanesian, H. E. (1968) *Educational Psychology*, 2nd edn. New York: Holt, Rhinehart & Winston.

Bahktin, M. (1981) *The Dialogic Imagination*. Austin, TX: University of Texas Press.

Baines. E., Blatchford, P. and Chowne, A (2007) 'Improving the effectiveness of collaborative group work in primary schools: effects on science attainment', *British Educational Research Journal*, 33, (5): 663–80.

Baines, E., Blatchford, P. and Kutnick, P. (2009) *Promoting Effective Group Work in the Primary Classroom*. Abingdon: Routledge.

Banks, F., Leach, J. and Moon, B. (1999) 'New understandings of teachers' pedagogic knowledge', in J. Leach and R. Moon (eds) *Learners and Pedagogy*. London: Paul Chapman, pp. 89–110.

Barnes, D. (2008) 'Exploratory talk for learning', in N. Mercer and S. Hodgkinson (eds) *Exploring Talk in School*. London: Sage, pp. 1–16.

Barrow, R. (1990) *Understanding Skills*. London: Althouse Press.

Bartlett, S. and Burton, D. (2007) *Introduction to Education Studies,* 2nd edn. London: Sage.

Beard, C. and Wilson J. P. (2006) *Experiential Learning*, 2nd edn. London: Kogan Page.

Becta (2006) *2020Vision: Report of the Teaching and Learning in 2020 Review Group*. Coventry: Becta.

Bell, S. and Harkness, S. A. (2006) *Storyline*. Royston: United Kingdom Literacy Association.

Bell, S., Harkness, S. and White, G. (eds) (2008) *Storyline*. Glasgow: University of Strathclyde.

Bennett, N. (1976) *Teaching Styles and Pupil Progress*. London: Open Books.

Bennett, N. and Dunne, E. (1992) *Managing Classroom Groups*. Hemel Hempstead: Simon & Schuster.

Bennett, S., Maton, K. and Kervin, L. (2008) 'The digital natives debate: a critical review of the evidence', *British Journal of Educational Technology*, 39(5): 775–86.

BERA (2001) 'Report on the methodological seminar on Hay/McBer enquiry into teacher effectiveness', *Research Intelligence*, 76(July): 5–9.

Berliner, D. C. (1994) 'Teacher expertise', in B. Moon and A. S. Mayers (eds) *Teaching and Learning in the Secondary School*. London: Routledge, pp. 107–13.

Bernstein, B. (1973) *Class, Codes and Control*, vol. 1. London: Routledge.

Bernstein, B. (ed) (1977) *Class, Codes and Control: Towards a Theory of Educational Transmissions Volume 3*. London: Routledge & Kegan Paul.

Biggs, J. (2003) *Teaching for Quality Learning at University*, 2nd edn. Maidenhead: Open University Press.

Black, P., Harrison. C., Lee, C., Marshall, B. and Wiliam, D. (2003) *Assessment for Learning*. Maidenhead: Open University Press.

Blakemore, S-J. and Frith, U. (2005) *The Learning Brain*. Oxford: Blackwell.

Blatchford, P., Kutnick, P., Baines, E. and Galton, M. (2003) 'Towards a social pedagogy of classroom group work', *International Journal of Educational Research*, 39: 153–72.

Blythe, T. (ed.) (1998) *The Teaching for Understanding Guide*. San Francisco: Jossey-Bass.

Borich, G. D. (2006) *Effective Teaching Methods*, 6th edn. Upper Saddle River, NJ: Pearson Education.

Boyd, B. (2005) *CPD: Improving Professional Practice*. Paisley: Hodder Gibson.

Bridges, D. (1979) *Education, Democracy and Discussion*. Windsor: NFER.

Bridges, D. (1988) 'A philosophical analysis of discussion', in J. T. Dillon (ed.) *Questioning and Discussion: a Multidisciplinary Study*. Norwood, NJ: Ablex, pp. 15–28.

Broadfoot, P. (2007) *An Introduction to Assessment*. London: Continuum.

Brooks, V. (2004) 'Learning to teach and learning about teaching', in V. Brooks, I. Abbot and L. Bills (eds) *Preparing to Teach in Secondary Schools*. Maidenhead: Open University Press, pp. 7–17.

Brown, A. L. and Palinscar, A. S. (1989) 'Guided, cooperative learning and individual knowledge acquisition', in L. B. Resnick (ed.) *Knowing, Learning and Instruction*. Hillsdale, NJ: Lawrence Erlbaum Associates, pp. 393–412.

Brown, S. and McIntyre, D. (1993) *Making Sense of Teaching*. Buckingham: Open University Press.

Brownhill, B. (2002) 'The Socratic method', in P. Jarvis, (ed.) *The Theory and Practice of Teaching*. London: Kogan Page, pp. 70–78.

Bruer, J. (1997) 'Education and the brain: a bridge to far', *Educational Researcher*, 26(8): 4–16.

Bruner, J. S. (1960) *The Process of Education*. Cambridge, MA: Harvard University Press.

Bruner, J. S. (1961) 'The act of discovery', *Harvard Educational Review*, 31(1): 21–32.

Bruner, J. S. (1996) *The Culture of Education*. Cambridge, MA: Harvard University Press.

Bullock, K. and Muschamp, Y. (2006) 'Learning about learning in the primary school', *Cambridge Journal of Education*, 36(1): 49–62.

Burke, L. A., Williams, J. M. and Skinner, D. (2007) 'Teachers' perceptions of thinking skills in the primary curriculum', *Research in Education*, 77(May): 1–13.

Burns, C. and Myhill, D. (2004) 'Interactive or inactive? A consideration of the nature of interaction in whole class teaching', *Cambridge Journal of Education*, 34(1): 41–9.

Burton, D. (2007) 'Psycho-pedagogy and personalised learning', *Journal of Education for Teaching*, 33(10): 5–17.

Campbell, J., Kyriakides, L., Muijs, D. and Robinson,W. (2004) *Assessing Teacher Effectiveness*. London: RoutledgeFalmer.

Capel, S., Leask, M. and Turner, T. (eds) (2000) *Learning to Teach in the Secondary School: A Companion to School Experience*. London: Routledge.

Carlgren, I., Klette, K., Myrdal, S., Schnack, K. and Simola, H. (2006) 'Changes in Nordic teaching practices: from individualised teaching to the teaching of individuals', *Scandinavian Journal of Educational Research*, 50(3): 301–26.

Carr, D. (1999) 'Is teaching a skill?' Paper presented to the Philosophy of Education Society, New Orleans, July.

Carr, D. (2003a) *Making Sense of Education*. London: Routledge.

Carr, D. (2003b) 'Philosophy and the meaning of "education"', *Theory and Research in Education*, 1(2): 195–212.

Carr, D. (2007) 'Toward an educationally meaningful curriculum: epistemic holism and knowledge integration revisited', *British Journal of Educational Studies*, 55(1): 3–20.

Carr, D. and Skinner, D (2009) 'The cultural roots of professional wisdom: towards a broader view of teacher expertise', *Educational Philosophy and Theory*, 41(2): 141–54.

Cassidy, C., Christie, D., Coutts, N., Dunn, J., Sinclair. C., Skinner, D. and Wilson, A. (2008) 'Building communities of educational enquiry', *Oxford Review of Education*, 34(2): 217–35.

Child, D. (2008) *Psychology and the Teacher,* 8th edn. London: Continuum.

Cigman, R. and Davis, A. (2009) *New Philosophies of Learning*. Chichester: Wiley/Blackwell.

Clark, C. M. and Yinger, R. J. (1987) 'Teacher planning', in J. Calderhead (ed.) *Exploring Teachers' Thinking*. London: Cassell.

Cockcroft, W. H. (1982) *Mathematics Counts*. London: HMSO.

Coffield, F., Moseley, D., Hall, E. and Ecclestone, K. (2004) *Learning Styles: A Systematic and Critical Review*. London: Learning and Skills Development Agency.

Cohen, J., McCabe, E. M., Michelli, N. M. and Pickeral, T. (2009) 'School climate: research, policy, practice and teacher education', *Teachers College Record*, 111(1): 180–213.

Collins, A., Brown. J. S. and Newman, S. E. (1989) 'Cognitive apprenticeship: teaching the crafts of reading, writing and mathematics', in L. B. Resnick (ed.) *Knowing, Learning and Instruction*. Hillsdale, NJ: Lawrence Erlbaum Associates, pp. 453–94.

Conlon, T. (2008) 'The dark side of GLOW: balancing the discourse', *Scottish Educational Review*, 40(2): 64–75.

Conlon, T. and Simpson, M. (2003) 'Silicon Valley versus Silicon Glen: the impact of computers upon teaching and learning: a comparative study', *British Journal of Educational Technology*, 34(2): 137–50.

Conway, P. F. and Clark, C. M. (2003) 'The journey inward and outward: a re-examination of Fuller's concerns-based model of teacher development', *Teaching and Teacher Education*, 19(5): 465–82.

Cowie, H. and Ruddock, J. (1998) 'Learning through discussion', in N. Entwistle (ed.) *Handbook of Educational Ideas and Practices*. London: Routledge, pp. 803–812.

Croll, P. and Hastings, N.(1996) *Effective Primary Teaching*. London: Fulton.

Cuban, L. (2001) *Oversold and Underused: Computers in the Classroom*. Cambridge, MA: Harvard University Press.

Daniels, H. and Porter, J. (2007) *Learning Needs and Difficulties Among Children of Primary School Age: Definition Identification: Provisions and Issues* (Primary Review Research Survey 5/20). Cambridge: University of Cambridge Faculty of Education.

David, T. (2006) 'The world picture', in G. Pugh and D. Bernadette (eds) *Contemporary Issues in the Early Years*, 3rd edn. London: Sage, pp. 35–48.

David, T. and Powell, S. (2007) 'Beginning at the beginning', in J. Moyles (ed.) *Beginning Teaching: Beginning Learning*, 3rd edn. Maidenhead: Open University Press, pp. 13–23.

Davis, A. (2004) 'The credentials of brain-based learning', *Journal of Philosophy of Education*, 38(1): 2–35.

Davis, R. A. (2007) 'Putting the community back into inquiry based learning. Why inquiry based learning should look back as well as forward', *New Zealand Journal of Teachers' Work*, 4(2): 99–104.

Dearden, R. F. (1984) *Theory and Practice in Education*. London: Routledge.

de Bono, E. (1976) *Teaching Thinking*. London: Temple Smith.

de Bono, E. (1991) *Six Action Shoes*. London: Harper Collins.

Della Sala, S. and Beyerstein, B. L. (2007) 'Introduction', in S. Della Sala (ed.) *Tall Tales about the Mind and Brain*. Oxford: Oxford University Press, pp. xvii–xxxvii.

Derry, J. (2009) 'Technology-enhanced learning: a question of knowledge', in R. Cigman and A. Davis (eds) (2009) *New Philosophies of Learning*. Chichester: Wiley/Blackwell, pp. 142–55.

Dewey, J. (1938) *Experience and Education*. New York, NY: Macmillan.

DfES (Department for Education and Skills) (2004) *A National Conversation About Personalised Learning*, www.publications.teachernet.gov.uk, accessed 20 July 2008.

DfES (Department for Education and Skills) (2007) *Pedagogy and Personalisation*. London: DfES.

Diamond, J. B. (2007) 'Where the rubber meets the road: rethinking the connection between high stakes testing policy and classroom instruction', *Sociology of Education*, 80 (October): 285–313.

Dillon, J. T. (1982) 'The effect of questions in education and other enterprises', *Journal of Curriculum Studies*, 14(2): 127–52.

Dillon, J. T. (1985) 'Using questions to foil discussion', *Teaching and Teacher Education*, 1(2): 109–21.

Dillon, J. T. (1988a) *Questioning and Teaching*. London: Routledge.

Dillon, J. T. (ed.) (1988b) *Questioning and Discussion: a Multidisciplinary Study*. Norwood, NJ: Ablex.

Dillon, J. T. (1994) *Using Discussion in Classrooms*. Buckingham: Open University Press.

Dillon, J. T. (1998) 'Using diverse styles of teaching', *Journal of Curriculum Studies*, 30(5): 503–14.

Dobbs. S. M. (1998) *Learning in and Through Art*. Los Angeles, LA: The J. Paul Getty Museum.

Doddington, C. and Hilton, M. (2007) *Child-Centred Education*. London: Sage.

Doyle, W. (1986) 'Classroom organisation and management', in M. C.Wittrock (ed.) *Handbook of Research on Teaching*, 3rd edn. New York, NY: Macmillan, pp. 392–431.

Driver, R. (2004) *Making Sense of Secondary Science: Research into Children's Ideas*. London: Routledge.

Drucker, P. F. (1962) *The Effective Executive*. London: Heinemann.

Dweck, C. (2007), *Mindset*. New York: Random House.

Education Queensland (2001) *New Basics: Rich Tasks*. Brisbane: Education Queensland.

Eisner, E. W. (1979) *The Educational Imagination*. London Macmillan.

Elias, J. L. (1979) 'Andragogy revisited', *Adult Education*, 29: 252–5.

Entwistle, N. (1981) *Styles of Learning and Teaching*. Chichester: Wiley.

Enwistle, N. (1987) *Understanding Student Learning*. London: Hodder & Stoughton.

Entwistle, N. and Peterson, E. (2004) 'Learning styles and approaches to studying', *Encyclopedia of Applied Psychology*, Vol. 2, pp. 537–42.

Eraut, M. (1994) *Developing Professional Knowledge and Competence*. London: Falmer.

Ericsson, K. A. (1996) *The Road to Excellence: The Acquisition of Expert Performance in the Arts and Sciences, Sports and Games*. Mahwah, NJ: Lawrence Erlbaum.

Fielding, M. (2007) 'Personalisation, education and the totalitarianism of the market', *Soundings*, December.

Filer, A. and Pollard, A. (2000) *The Social World of Pupil Assessment*. London: Continuum.

Fontana, D. (1995) *Psychology for Teachers*, 3rd edn. London: Macmillan.

Fox, R. (2001), 'Constructivism examined', *Oxford Review of Education*, 27(1): 23–35.

Frame, B. (2008) 'Storyline, a cross-curricular approach: its capacity for promoting and fostering a thinking classroom', in S. Bell, S. Harkness and G. White (eds) *Storyline*. Glasgow: University of Strathclyde, pp. 127–37.

Fredriksson, U. and Hoskins, B (2007) 'The development of learning to learn in a European context', *The Curriculum Journal*, 18(20): 127–34.

Freire, P. (1970) *Pedagogy of the Oppressed*. New York, NY: Continuum.

Fuller, F. F. (1969) 'Concerns of teachers: a developmental characterization', *American Educational Research Journal*, 6: 207–26.

Fumoto, H., Hargreaves, D. J. and Maxwell, S. (2004) 'The concept of teaching: a reappraisal', *Early Years*, 24(2): 179–91.

Gage, N. L. (1978) *The Scientific Basis of the Art of Teaching*. New York: Teachers College Press.

Galton, M. (2007) *Learning and Teaching in the Primary Classroom*. London: Sage.

Galton. M. and Macbeath, J. (2008) *Teachers Under Pressure*. London: Sage.

Galton, M. and Simon, B. (eds) (1980) *Progress and Performance in the Primary Classroom*. London: Routledge & Kegan Paul.

Galton, M. and Williamson, J. (1992) *Group Work in the Primary Classroom*. London: Routledge.

Galton, M., Hargreaves, L., Comber, C., Wall, D. and Pell, A. (1999) *Inside the Primary Classroom: 20 Years On*. London: Routledge.

Gamoran, A. (2002) *Standards, Inequality and Ability Grouping in Schools*.

Edinburgh: University of Edinburgh, CES.

Geake, J. (2008) 'Neuromythologies in education', *Educational Research*, 50(2): 123–34.

Giroux, H. (2006) *The Giroux Reader*. Boulder, CO: Paradigm.

Glaser, R. (1999) 'Expert knowledge and processes of thinking', in R. McCormick and C. Paechter (eds) *Learning and Knowledge*. London: Paul Chapman, pp. 112–35.

Glasgow, N.A. and Hicks, C.D. (2003) *What Successful Teachers Do*. Thousand Oaks, CA: Corwin.

Grandy, R. E. (2007) 'Constructivism and objectivity: disentangling metaphysics from pedagogy', in R. Curren (ed.) *Philosophy of Education: An Anthology*. London: Blackwell, pp. 410–16.

Gordon, S. C. (1963) *A Century of West Indian Education*. London: Longman.

Goswami, U. (2008) 'Reading, dyslexia and the brain', *Educational Research*, 50(2): 135–48.

Goswami, U. (2009) 'Principles of learning, implications for teaching: a cognitive neuroscience perspective', in R. Cigman and A. Davis (eds) *New Philosophies of Learning*. Chichester: Wiley/Blackwell, pp. 26–43.

Grant, N. (1969) *Society, Schools and Progress in Eastern Europe*. Oxford: Pergamon.

Grimmett P. P. and Mackinnon A. M. (1992) 'Craft knowledge and the education of teachers', *Review of Educational Research*, 18: 385–456.

GTCE (2006) *Report on the PELRS Project*, www.gtce.org.uk, accessed 12 July 2008.

GTCE (2007) *Commitment: The Teachers' Professional Learning Framework*. Birmingham: GTCE.

Hadow Report (1931) *Report of the Consultative Committee on the Primary School*. London: HMSO.

Haggarty, L. (ed.) (2002) *Teaching Mathematics in Secondary Schools: A Reader*. London: Routledge.

Hamilton, D. (1982) *In Search of Structure*. Edinburgh: Scottish Council for Research in Education.

Hammersley, M. (2002) *Educational Research, Policymaking and Practice*. London: Paul Chapman.

Hammersley, M. (ed) (2007) *Educational Research and Evidence-based Practice*. London: Sage.

Hammond, M. *et al.* (2009), 'Why do some students make very good use of ICT: an exploratory case study', *Technology, Pedagogy and Education*, 18(1): 59–73.

Harre, R. (2002) *Cognitive Science*. London: Sage.

Harris, A. (1998) 'Effective teaching: a review of the literature', *School Leadership and Management*, 18(2): 169–83.

Hartley, D. (2007) 'Personalisation: the emerging "revised" code of education?' *Oxford Review of Education*, 33(5): 629–42.

Hartley, D. (2008),'Education, markets, and the pedagogy of personalisation', *British Journal of Educational Studies*, 56(4): 365–81.

Hase, S. and Keynon, C. (2007) 'Heutagogy: a child of complexity theory', *Complicity*, 4(1): 111–18.

Hastings, N. (1998) 'Change and progress in primary teaching'. in C. Richards and P. H. Taylor (eds) *How Shall we School our Children?* London: Routledge, pp. 148–59.

Hastings, N. and Wood, K. C. (2002) *Reorganising Primary Classroom Learning*. Buckingham: Open University Press.

Hatch, T., White, M. E. and Capitelli, S. (2005) 'Learning from teaching: what's involved in the development of classroom practice?', *Cambridge Journal of Education*, 35(3): 323–31.

Hay McBer (2001) 'Research into teacher effectiveness', in F. Banks and A. S. Mayes, A.S. (eds) *Early Professional Development for Teachers*. London: Fulton/The Open University.

Hayes, D. (2003) *Planning, Teaching and Class Management in Primary Schools*. London: David Fulton.

Hayes, D. (2008) *Foundations of Primary Teaching*, 4th edn. London: Routledge.

Hayes, D., Mills, M. Christie, P. and Lingard, B. (2006) *Teachers and Schooling Making a Difference*. Crows Nest, NSW: Allen & Unwin.

Higgins, P. (2008) 'Why indoors? The role of outdoor learning in sustainability, health and citizenship. Inaugural Lecutre, University of Edinburgh, October.

Hoban, G. F. (2002) *Teacher Learning for Educational Change*. Buckingham: Open University Press.

Hopkins, D. (2007) *Every School a Great School*. Maidenhead: Open University Press.

Howard-Jones, P. (2008) 'Education and neuroscience', *Educational Research*, 50(2): 119–22.

Howard-Jones, P. (2009) 'Philosophical challenges for researchers at the interface between neuroscience and education', in R. Cigman and A. Davis (eds) *New Philosophies of Learning*. Chichester: Wiley/Blackwell, pp. 26–43.

Howard-Jones. P. and Pickering, S. (2005) *Collaborative Frameworks for Neuroscience and Education*. London: TLRP.

Howard-Jones, P., Winfield, M. and Crimmins, G. (2008) 'Co-constructing an understanding of creativity in drama education that draws on neuropsychological concepts', *Educational Research*, 50(92): 187–202.

Hoyle, E. (1972) 'Educational innovation and the role of the teacher', *Forum*, 14: 42–4.

Hutchinson, C. and Hayward, L. (2005) 'The journey so far: assessment for learning in Scotland', *The Curriculum Journal*, 16(2): 225–48.

Ireson, J. (2008) *Learners, Learning and Educational Activity*. London: Routledge.

Jackson, P. (1968) *Life in Classrooms*. Eastbourne: Holt, Rinehart & Winston.

James, M. (2008) *Only Connect! Improving Teaching and Learning in Schools*. London: Institute of Education.

James, M. and Pollard, A. (eds) (2006) *Improving Teaching and Learning in Schools: a Commentary by the Teaching and Learning Research Programme*. Swindon: ESRC.

James, W. (1903) *Talks to Teachers on Psychology and to Students on some of Life's Ideals*. New York: Holt.

Jarvis, P. (2002) *The Theory and Practice of Teaching*. London: Kogan Page.

Johnson, S. (2001) *Teaching Thinking Skills*. Philosophy of Education Society of Great Britain. Northampton: University of Northampton.

Johnston, D. W. and Johnson, R. T. (1993) *Circles of Learning: Cooperation in the Classroom*. Edina, MN: Interaction Book Company.

Johnston, J. (1996) *Early Explorations in Science*. Buckingham: Open University Press.

Jollife, W. (2007), *Cooperative Learning in the Classroom*. London: Paul Chapman.

Jones, L. (2003) 'The problem with problem-solving', in D. Haylock (ed.) *Enhancing Primary Mathematics Teaching*. London: Routledge, pp. 86–97.

Joyce, B. (1978) 'A problem of categories: classifying approaches to teaching', *Boston University Journal of Education*, August: 67–95.

Joyce, B. and Weil, M. (1986) *Models of Teaching*, 3rd edn. London: Prentice-Hall International.

Keddie, A. and Mills, M. (2007) 'Teaching for gender justice', *Australian Journal of Education*, 51(2): 205–19.

Keynes, J. M. (1935) *The General Theory of Employment, Interest and Money*. Cambridge: Cambridge University Press.

Kirk, G. (1973) 'A critique in some arguments in the case for integrated studies', *Scottish Educational Studies*, 4(2): 95–102.

Kirkwood, M. (2005) *Learning to Think: Thinking to Learn*. Paisley: Hodder Gibson.

Kirschner, P., Strijbos, J-QW and Kreijns, K. (2004) 'Designing integrated collaborative e-learning', in W. Jochems, J. van Merrienboer and R. Koper (eds) *Integrated E-Learning*. London: RoutledgeFalmer, pp. 24–38.

Knowles, M. (1970) *The Modern Practice of Adult Education. Andragogy versus Pedagogy*. New York: Associated Press.

Knowles, M. (1979) 'Andragogy revisited, Part 2', *Adult Education*, 30: 52–3.

Kolb D. A. (1984) *Experiential Learning Experience as a Source of Learning and Development*. Upper Saddle River, NJ: Prentice Hall.

Kutnick, P., Blatchford, P.and Baines, E. (2003) 'Pupil groupings in primary school classrooms: sites for learning and social pedagogy?' *British Educational Research Journal*, 28(2): 187–206.

Kryiacou, C. (1995) 'Direct teaching', in C. Desforges, (ed.) *An Introduction to Teaching*. Oxford: Blackwell, pp 115–31.

Kyriacou, C. (2007) *Essential Teaching Skills*, 3rd edn. Cheltenham: Nelson Thornes.

Laurillard, D. (1993) *Rethinking University Teaching: A Framework for the Effective Use of Educational Technology*. London: Routledge.

Lave, J. and Wenger, E. (1991) *Situated Learning: Legitimate Peripheral Participation*. Cambridge: Cambridge University Press.

Lawton, D. and Gordon, P. (2002) *A History of Western Educational Ideas*. London: Woburn Press.

Leach, J. and Moon, B. (eds) (1999) *Learners and Pedagogy*. London: Paul Chapman.

Leach, J. and Moon, B. (2008) *The Power of Pedagogy*. London: Sage.

Learning and Teaching Scotland (2005) *Let's Talk About Pedagogy*. Glasgow: LTScotland.

Leinhardt, G. (2001) 'Instructional explanations: a commonplace for teaching and location of contrast', in V. Richardson (ed.) *Handbook of Research on Teaching*, 4th edn. Washington, DC: American Educational Research Association.

Lewis, A. and Norwich, B. (2005) *Special Teaching for Special Children?* Maidenhead: Open University Press.

Lingard, B., Hayes, D. Mills, M. and Christie, P. (2003) *Leading Learning*. Maidenhead: Open University Press.

Livingstone, S. and Helsper, E. (2007) 'Gradations in digital inclusion: children, young people and the digital divide', *New Media and Society*, 9(4): 671–96.

Lumby, J. and Foskett, N. (2004) *14–19 Education, Policy Leadership and Learning*. London: Sage.

McCormick, R. (1999) 'Practical knowledge: a view from the snooker table', in R. McCormick and C. Paechter (eds) *Learning and Knowledge*. London: Paul Chapman, pp. 112–35.

McCormick, R. and Murphy, P. (2000) 'Curriculum: the case for a focus on learning', in B. Moon, S. Brown and M. Ben-Peretz (eds) *Routledge International Companion to Education*. London: Routledge, pp. 204–34.

MacDonald, A. (2004) 'Collegiate or compliant? Primary teachers in post-McCrone Scotland', *British Educational Research Journal*, 30(3): 413–33.

McGuiness, C. (2005) 'Teaching thinking: theory and practice', in P. Tomlinson, J. Dockrell and P. Winne (eds) 'Pedagogy – teaching for learning', *British Journal of Educational Psychology*, monograph series 11, no. 3, pp. 107–126.

McNiff, J. (1988) *Action Research*. London: Macmillan.

Martin, M. (2007) *Building a Learning Community in the Primary Classroom*. Edinburgh: Dunedin Academic Press.

Mayall, B. (2003) *Sociologies of Childhood and Educational Thinking*. London: London University Institute of Education.

Mercer, N. and Littleton, K. (2007) *Dialogue and the Development of Children's Thinking*. Abingdon: Routledge.

Milbank, J. (2006) *Theology and Social Theory*, 2nd edn. Oxford: Blackwell.

Moon J. A. (2004) *A Handbook of Experiential and Reflective and Experiential Learning*. London: RoutledgeFalmer.

Moore, A. (2000) *Teaching and Learning: Pedagogy, Curriculum and Culture*. London: RoutledgeFalmer.

Moore, A. (2004) *The Good Teacher*. London: RoutledgeFalmer.

Moreno, A. and Martin, E. (2007) 'The development of learning to learn in Spain', *The Curriculum Journal*, 18(2): 175–93.

Morgan, C. and Morris, G. (1999) *Good Teaching and Learning: Pupils and Teachers Speak*. Buckingham: Open University Press.

Mosely, D. Baumfield, V., Elliot, J., Gregson, M., Higgins, S., Miller J. and Newton, D. (2005) *Frameworks for Thinking*. Cambridge: Cambridge University Press.

Mosston, M. and Ashworth, S. (1990) *The Spectrum of Teaching Styles: From Command to Discovery*. New York, NY: Longman.

Moyles, J. (ed.) (2007) *Beginning Teaching, Beginning Learning*, 3rd edn. Maidenhead: Open University Press.

Muijs, D. and Reynolds, D. (2005) *Effective Teaching*, 2nd edn. London: Sage.

Munn, P. (2008) 'Building research capacity collaboratively: can we take ownership of our future?', *British Educational Research Journal*, 34(4): 413–30.

Myhill, D. (2006) 'Talk talk talk: teaching and learning in whole class discourse', *Research Papers in Education*, 21(1): 19–41.

Newman, F.M. *et al.* (1996) *Authentic Achievement: Restructuring Schools for Intellectual Quality*. San Francisco, CA: Jossey-Bass.

Nikitina, S. (2006) 'Three strategies of interdisciplinary teaching: contextualising, conceptualising and problem-centring', *Journal of Curriculum Studies*, 38(3): 251–71.

Noddings, N. (2007) *Philosophy of Education*, 2nd edn. Boulder, CO: Westview Press.

North Yorkshire County Council/Dialogos (2007) *Talk for Learning* (DVD). Northallerton: North Yorkshire County Council/Dialogos.

OECD/CERI (2007) *Understanding the Brain: The Birth of a Learning Science*. Paris: OECD.

Orlando, J. (2009) 'Understanding changes in teachers' ICT practices: a longitudinal perspective', *Technology, Pedagogy and Education*, 18(1): 33–44.

Palmer, J.A. (ed) (2001) *Fifty Modern Thinkers on Education*. London: Routledge.

Papastephanou, M. and Angeli, C. (2007) 'Critical thinking beyond skill', *Educational Philosophy and Theory*, 39(6): 604–21.

Passmore, J. (1980) *The Philosophy of Teaching*. London: Duckworth.

Paterson, L. (1998) 'The civic activism of Scottish teachers: explanations and consequences', *Oxford Review of Education*, 24(3): 279–302.

Peacock, C. (1990) *Classroom Skills in English Teaching*. London: Routledge.

Pedder, D. (2006) 'Organisational conditions that foster successful classroom promotion of learning how to learn', *Research Papers in Education*, 21(2): 171–200.

Petty, G. (2004) *Teaching Today*, 3rd edn. Cheltenham: Nelson Thornes.

Petty, G. (2006) *Evidence Based Teaching*. Cheltenham: Nelson Thornes.

Phillips, D. C. (2007) 'The good, the bad and the ugly: the many faces of constructivism', in R. Curren (ed.) *Philosophy of Education: An Anthology*. Oxford: Blackwell, pp. 398–409.

Plowman, L., McPake, J. and Stephen, C. (2008) 'Just picking it up? Young children learning with technology at home', *Cambridge Journal of Education*, 38(3): 303–19.

Pollard, A. (2002), *Reflective Teaching*. London: Continuum.

Pollard, A. (2007) 'The UK's Teaching and Learning Research Programme: findings and significance', *British Educational Research Journal*, 33(5): 639–46.

Powell, J. L. (1985) *The Teacher's Craft*. Edinburgh: Scottish Council for Research on Education.

Prashnig, B. (2006) *Learning Styles and Personalised Teaching*. London: Network Continuum.

Prensky, M. (2001a) 'Digital natives, digital immigrants', *On the Horizon*, 9(5): 1–6.

Prensky, M. (2001b) 'Do they really think differently?', *On the Horizon*, 9(6): 1–10.

Prensky, M. (2007) 'How to teach with technology: keeping both teachers and students comfortable in an era of exponential change', in *Emerging Technologies of Learning*, Vol. 2. Coventry: Becta.

Pring, R. (1971) 'Curriculum integration', in R. Hooper (ed.) *The Curriculum: Context, Design and Development*. Edinburgh: Oliver & Boyd, pp. 265–72.

Pring, R. (1976) *Knowledge and Schooling*. London: Open Books.

Pring, R. (2004) *Philosophy of Education*. London: Continuum.

Pring, R. (2007a) 'Reclaiming philosophy for educational research', *Educational Review*, 59(3): 315–30.

Pring, R. (2007b) *John Dewey*. London: Continuum.

Pritchard, A. (2007) *Effective Teaching with Internet Technologies*. London: Paul Chapman.

Quay, J. (2004) 'Knowing how and knowing that: a tale of two ontologies', In A. Brookes (ed.) *Conference*

Papers of the International Outdoor Education Research Conference: Connections and Disconnections. Bendigo: Latrobe University, pp. 2–13.

Reedy, G. B. (2008) 'PowerPoint, interactive whiteboards, and the visual culture of technology in schools', *Technology, Pedagogy and Education,*17(2): 143–62.

Reynolds, D., Treharne, D. and Tripp, H. (2003) 'ICT: the hopes and the reality', *British Journal of Educational Technology,* 34(2): 151–68.

Riley, J. (2007) *Learning in the Early Years,* 2nd edn. London: Sage

Roby, T. (1988) 'Models of discussion', in J. T. Dillon (ed.) *Questioning and Discussion: A Multidisciplinary Study.* Norwood, NJ: Ablex, pp. 163–91.

Rogers, C. and Kutnick, P. (1990) *The Social Psychology of the Primary School.* London: Routledge.

Rogoff, B. (1990) *Apprenticeship in Thinking: Cognitive Development in Social Context.* Oxford: Oxford University Press.

Rollett, B. A. (2001) 'How do expert teachers view themselves?' in F. Banks and A. S. Mayes (eds) *Early Professional Development for Teachers.* London: Fulton.

Rousseau, J-J. (1911) *Emile.* London: Dent.

Sachs, J. (2002) *The Activist Teaching Profession.* Buckingham: Open University Press.

Savin-Baden, M. and Wilkie, K. (eds) (2004) *Challenging Research into Problem-Based Learning.* Maidenhead: SRHE/Open University Press.

Schön, D. (1983) *The Reflective Practitioner.* London: Temple Smith.

Schwab, J. J. (1978) *Science, Curriculum and Liberal Education.* Chicago: University of Chicago Press.

Scott, D. (2008) *Critical Essays on Major Curriculum Theorists.* London: Routledge.

Scottish Committee on Primary Education (1987) *Some Aspects of Thematic Work in Primary Schools.* Dundee: Scottish Consultative Council on the Curriculum.

Scottish Consultative Council on the Curriculum (2000) *Direct Interactive Teaching.* Dundee: Scottish Consultative Council on the Curriculum.

Scottish Education Department (1950) *The Primary School in Scotland.* Edinburgh: HMSO.

Scottish Education Department (1965) *Primary Education in Scotland* ('The Primary Memorandum'). Edinburgh: HMSO.

Scottish Education Department (1980) *Learning and Teaching in Primary 4 and Primary 7.* Edinburgh: HMSO.

Scottish Executive (2004) *A Curriculum for Excellence.* Edinburgh: Scottish Executive.

Scottish Executive (2007) *A Curriculum for Excellence: Building the Curriculum (2) Active Learning in the Early Years.* Edinburgh: Scottish Executive.

Scottish Executive (2008) *Curriculum for Excellence,* www.ltscotland.org.uk/curriculumforexcellence/experiencesandoutcomes, accessed 20 July 2009.

Shaker, P. and Ruitenberg, C. (2007) 'Scientifically based research, the art of politics and the distortion of science', *International Journal of Research and Method in Education,* 30(2): 207–19.

Sharp, J., Ward, S., and Hankin, L. (eds) (2006) *Education Studies.* Exeter: Learning Matters.

Sharples, D. (1990) 'Teaching styles and strategies in the open-plan primary school', in N. Entwistle (ed.) *Handbook of Educational Ideas and Practices.* London: Routledge.

Shulman, L. S. (1987) 'Knowledge and teaching: foundations of the new reform', *Harvard Educational Review,* 57(1): 1–22.

Siraj-Blatchford, I. (1999) 'Early childhood pedagogy: practice, principles and research', in P. Mortimore (ed.) *Understanding Pedagogy.* London: Routledge, pp. 20–45.

Siraj-Blatchford, I. and Siraj-Blatchford, J. (2006) *A Guide to Developing the ICT Curriculum for Early Childhood Education.* Stoke-on-Trent: Trentham.

Skidmore, D. (2006) 'From pedagogical dialogue to dialogic pedagogy', *Language and Education*, 14(4): 283–96.

Skinner, D. (1973) 'Streaming in a communist country: the case of Czechoslovakia', *Scottish Educational Studies,* 4(2): 103–14.

Skinner, D. (1994),'Modes of teaching', in G. Kirk and R. Glaister (eds) *5–14: Scotland's National Curriculum.* Edinburgh: Scottish Academic Press, pp. 26–49.

Skinner, D. (2005) *Get Set for Teacher Training.* Edinburgh: Edinburgh University Press.

Slavin, R. E. (1995) *Cooperative Learning. Theory, Research and Practice.* Boston, MA: Allyn & Bacon.

Smith, C. and Easton, L. (2009) 'A new concept of teacher–researcher?' in J. McNally and A. Blake (eds) *Improving Learning in a Professional Context.* London: Routledge, pp. 27–40.

Smith, G. F. (2002) Thinking skills: the question of generality, *Journal of Curriculum Studies*, 34(6): 659–78.

Smith, H. J., Higgins, S., Wall, K. and Miller, J. (2005) 'Interactive whiteboards: boon or bandwagon? A critical review of the literature', *Journal of Computer Assisted Learning*, 21: 91–101.

Smylie, M. and Perry, G. (1998) 'Restructuring schools for improving teaching', in *International Handbook of Educational Change.* Dordrecht: Kluwer.

Somekh, B. (2006a) *Action Research.* Maidenhead: Open University Press.

Somekh, B. (2006b),'New ways of teaching and learning in the digital age', in A. Moore (ed.) *Schooling, Society and Curriculum.* London: Routledge, pp. 119–29.

Stenhouse, L. (1967) *Culture and Education.* London: Nelson.

Stenhouse, L. (1975) *An Introduction to Curriculum Research and Development.* London: Heinemann.

Stenhouse, L. (1977) 'Skill in forms', *British Journal of Teacher Education,* 3(3), pp. 239–242.

Stephen, C., Cope, P., Oberski, I. and Shand, P. (2008) ' "They should try to find out what the children like": explaining engagement in learning', *Scottish Educational Review*, 40(2): 17–28.

Taber, K.S. (2007) *Classroom-based Research and Evidence-based Practice.* London: Sage.

Thomas, G. (2007) *Education and Theory*. Maidenhead: Open University Press.

Thomas, G. and Pring, R. (2004) *Evidence-based Practice in Education.* Maidenhead: Open University Press.

TLRP (2006) *Neuroscience and Education: Issues and Opportunities*, TLRP commentary. London: Teaching and Learning Research Programme.

Varma, S. and Schwartz D. L. (2008) 'How should educational neuroscience conceptualise the relationship between cognition and brain function? Mathematical reasoning as a network process', *Educational Research*, 50(2): 149–61.

Watkins, C., Carnell, E. and Lodge, C. E. (2007) *Effective Learning in Classrooms.* London: Paul Chapman.

Wegerif, R. (2008) 'Dialogic or dialetic? The significance of ontological assumptions in research on educational dialogue', *British Educational Research Journal*, 34(3): 347–61.

Winch, C. (2009a) 'Learning how to learn: a critique', in R. Cigman and A. Davis (eds) (2009) *New Philosophies of Learning.* Chichester: Wiley/Blackwell, pp. 277–292.

Winch, C. (2009b) 'Gilbert Ryle on knowing how and the possibility of vocational education', *Journal of Applied Philosophy*, 26(1): pp. 88–101.

Wiske, M. S. (ed.) (1998) *Teaching for Understanding.* San Francisco, SF: Jossey-Bass.

Witkin, H. A., Moor, C. A., Goodenough, D. R. and Cox, P. W. (1977) 'Field dependent and field independent cognitive styles and their educational implications', *Review of Education Research*, 47(1): 1–64.

Wood, E. (2007) 'New directions in play: consensus or collision?' *Education 3–13*, 35(4): 309–20.

Wood, H. and Wood, D. (1983) 'Questioning the pre-school child', *Educational Review*, 35: 149–62.

Woods, P. (1996) 'The art and science of teaching', in P. Woods (ed.) *Researching the Art of Teaching*. London: Routledge.

Wragg, E. C. and Brown, G. (1993) *Explaining*. London: Routledge.

Wrigley, T. (2006) *Another School is Possible*. Stoke-on-Trent: Trentham.

Wurdinger, S. D. (2005) *Using Experiential Learning in the Classroom*. Oxford: Scarecrow Education.

Wyse, D. and Styles, M. (2007) 'Synthetic phonics and the teaching of reading: the debate surrounding England's Rose Report', *Literacy*, 41(1): 35–42.

Yelland, N. J. (2005) 'Curriculum practice and pedagogies with ICT in the information age', In N. J. Yelland (ed.) *Critical Issues in Early Childhood*. Buckingham: Open University Press, pp. 224–42.

Xu, R.T. (2007) 'How do Chinese students learn and study?, *TLA Interchange*, 1. University of Edinburgh.

Index

ability and ability groups 125
accelerated learning 136, 153
action and experience 23, 57–67
action learning 59, 64, 65, 153
action research 147–151, 153
active learning 57–9, 62, 153
activity methods 58
adolescence 134–5
adult education 120–1
affordance 105, 153
aims and values 5, 8, 19, 20, 113, 126–7, 146, 149
Alexander, R. 2, 9, 15, 25–6, 37, 46, 48, 52, 62, 115, 117, 122–3, 142, 146
Alexandrou, A. 144
algebra 135
alignment 153
Allen, J. 58, 105, 107
amygdala/ae 135, 153
andragogy 120–1, 123, 153
Angeli, C. 98
Anning, A. 118
Apple, M. 14, 120
art education 73
Ashton, J. 121
Ashworth, S. 121
assessment 23, 36, 41–2, 65, 76, 95–6
assessment for learning 43, 154
    see also formative assessment
Atherton, J. 41
Atkinson, T. 59
Austin, H. 14,
Ausubel, D. 40
authentic assessment/tasks 96, 154
autonomy
  see independent learning
axon 154

Baines, E. 15, 83
Bakhtin, M. 52
balance in teaching 24–5, 82
Banks, F. 92, 122
Barnes, D. 70
Barrow, R. 10
Bartlett, S. 29
baseball 60
basic school 2
Bastin, M. 127, 131, 135
Beane, J. 14, 120
Beard, C. 25, 61

Becta 88
behaviourism 8, 13, 154
Bell, S. 94
Bennett, N. 20, 83–4
Bennett. S. 109
BERA (British Educational Research Association) 21
Berliner, D. 142
Bernstein, B. 15, 117, 119
Beyerstein, B. 130
Biggs J. 40
Black, P. 19, 43
Blakemore, S-J. 126, 134
Blatchford, P. 83, 143
blended learning 121, 154
Blythe, T. 95
Borich, G. 21
Bourdieu, P. 15
Boyd, B. 141
brain gym 129, 136, 154
brain imaging studies 126, 129, 132
brain plasticity 129, 135, 161
brain-based learning 28, 126, 154
Bridges, D. 48–9, 52, 55
broadbanding 83
Broadfoot, P. 14
Broca's area 132, 154
Bronfenbrenner, U. 118
Brooks, V. 143
Brown, A. 63
Brown, G. 25, 38
Brown, S. 18–9
Brownhill, B. 52
Bruer, J. 127
Bruner, J. 11, 69, 72
Bullock. K. 99
Burke, L. 98
Burns, C. 82
Burton, S. 29, 88

Campbell, J. 7
Capel, S. 30
Carlgren, I. 88
Carnegie, Dale 130
Carr, D. 9, 10, 13, 15, 82, 92, 142, 144
Cassidy, C. 14
charismatic teachers 30
Chartered Teacher 145
Child, D. 69

China 40
Cigman, R. 128
civic activism 149
Clark, C. 19, 142
class organisation
    see organisation of teaching
class size 82–3
classroom climate 21, 22, 154
    see also learning environment
classroom layout 88–9
Claxton, G. 59
Cockcroft Report 59
co-construction 154
Coffield, F. 28
cognition 155
cognitive apprenticeship 63, 66, 155
cognitive neuroscience 125, 131, 136, 155
cognitive psychology 8, 125–6, 136
cognitive style 27, 155
Cohen, J. 89
collaborative group work 25, 42, 83–5, 90, 155
collaborative story making 92, 94
Collins. A. 63
common sense 11, 23
community of educational enquiry 14, 151, 155
community of philosophical enquiry 53
community of practice 155
competence 144
compliance 144
Confucian heritage cultures 40
Conlon, T. 108
constructivism 58, 70–1, 77, 83, 109, 112, 155
radical 71, 161
social 71, 83, 163
contingent teaching 155
Conway, P. 142
cooperative group work
    see collaborative group work
corpus callosum 130–1, 155
cost/benefit 6
Cowie, H. 48
CPD (continuing professional development)
    144–6, 151, 156
craft knowledge 9, 11, 16, 19, 126
critical pedagogy 119–20, 156
critical periods 129, 134–5, 156
Croll, P. 88
cross-curricular teaching 92, 156
Cuban, L. 108
Curriculum for Excellence 2, 57, 62, 75, 91, 100
curriculum integration 92, 156

Daniels, H. 16
Davis A. 127–8
Davis R. 50
David, T. 134
Dearden, R. 99

de Bono, E. 28, 97
Della Sala, S. 130
dendrites 128, 156
de-professionalization 156
Derry, J. 109
Dewey, J. 58, 61, 69, 72, 93, 117
dialogic teaching 23, 37, 46–50, 52–5, 59, 161
Diamond, J. 6
didactic teaching 93
didactics 122
DfES (Department for Education and Skills) 21,
    87, 105
differentiation 41, 85, 162
digital divide 156
digital generation 109
digital immigrants/natives 109–10
Dillon, J. T. 20 25, 42–3, 50–1, 54–5, 72
direct teaching 23, 26, 31, 35–45, 47–8, 58, 69,
    82–3, 120–1
discourse 157
discovery learning 68–70
discussion 20, 23, 46–56, 68
Dobbs, S. 73,
Doddington, C. 88
Doyle, W. 13
Driver, R. 74
Drucker, P. 5
dual route theory 133
Dunne, E. 83–4
Durkheim, E. 117
Dweck, C. 13
dyscalculia 157
dyslexia 132–3, 157
dyspraxia 157

early education 37, 110–11, 118–19, 123, 134
Eastern Europe 2, 87
economics 11
Edgerton, D. 108
education and schooling 8, 10, 15, 17
EEG 157
effective teaching 18–19
effectiveness 5–7, 21, 37–8
efficiency 5–7, 38
Einstein, A. 130
Eisner, E. 9
Elias, J. 120
Elliot. R. 121
Emile 68, 86
emotional intelligence 13, 157
empirical evidence 157
enquiry 23, 58–9, 61, 68–78, 93–4, 121
Entwistle, N. 20, 28–30, 89
environmental studies 37
Eraut, M. 143
Ericsson, E. 143
Europe 118

evidence-based teaching 157
experiential learning 58–9, 61, 65–6, 157
expertise 10, 141–3
explaining 36, 38–9, 43, 44
exploratory talk 48, 52, 83
extended professional 145, 157

field dependence /independence 29–30
Fielding, M. 88
Filer, A. 14
5–14 programme (Scotland) 62
Fmri 158
folk psychology 11
Fontana, D. 13
formal/informal styles 29
formative assessment 41–4, 158
Foskett, N. 60
Foucault, M. 15
14–19 education 60
Fox, R. 70–1
Foxfire approach 61
Frame, B. 98
Frankfurt School 120
Fredrickson, U. 99
Freire, P. 15, 117, 120
Frith, U. 126, 134
Froebel Institute 62
Fumoto, H. 118

Gage, N. 8–9
Galton, M. 8, 20, 38, 41, 63, 69, 83, 87, 146
Gamoran, A. 83
Geake, J. 29
generative topics 95, 158
Giroux. H. 120
Glaser, R. 143
Glasgow, N. 145
globalization 158
good teaching 21–2
Gordon, P. 26
Gordon, S. 97
Goswami, U. 138
Grandy, R. 71
Grant, N. 86
Grimmett, P. 9
group size 84
GTCE (General Teaching Council for
    England) 110, 145–6
guided discovery 70, 77

Hadow report 58, 62
Haggarty, L. 29
Hamilton, D. 93
Hammersley, M. 9, 14, 145
Hammond, M. 112
Harkness, S. 94
Harre, R. 127

Harris, A. 20
Hartley, D. 88, 108
Hase, S. 121
Hastings, N. 86, 89
Hatch, T. 148, 154
Hayes, Debra 2, 6, 119
Hayes, Dennis 5, 39
Hayward, L. 43
Herbart, J. H. 26
heutagogy 120–1, 123, 158
Hicks, C. 145
Higgins, P. 61
high attainers 85
High/Scope 62
Hilton, M. 88
hippocampus 133
history 73–4
Hoban, G. 149
Holofernes 115
Hopkins, D. 20
Hoskins, B. 99
Hoyle, E. 145
hothousing 129
Howard-Jones, P. 19, 125–6
Humanities Curriculum Project 69
Hutchinson, C. 43

ICT (Information and communication
    technology) 38–9, 44, 73–4, 77, 86, 88, 95,
    97, 105–113, 116, 158
incidental learning 158
inclusion 81
independent learning 86, 99
infusion 98
integrated day 88
intelligence 13, 82,125
interactive whiteboards 111–12
inter-disciplinary studies 91–2, 100, 137, 158
Ireson, J. 83

Jackson P. 13
James, M. 22, 59, 99, 143, 146
James, W. 8, 130
Japan 40
jigsaw groups 158
Johnson, S. 97
Johnston, D. 83
Johnston, J. 74
Johnston, R. 83
Jollife, W. 83–4
Jones, L. 75
Joyce, B. 20
juggling 135

Keddie, A. 16, 119
Keynes, J. M. 11
Keynon, C. 121

Kilpatrick, T. 69
kinaesthetic learners 158
Kirk, G. 92
Kirkwood, M. 97
Kirschner, P. 105
knowing how/that 63–4
Knowles, M. 120–1
Kolb, D. 61
Korea 40
Kutnick, P. 83, 85
Kyriacou, C. 41, 58, 69

language 37, 75, 132
latent learning 159
Laurillard, D. 86
Lave, J. 71
law 10
Lawton, D. 26
Leach, J. 105–6, 114–15, 117, 122–3
Learning and Teaching Scotland 118
learning by doing 59
learning environment 88–9, 157
learning how to learn 98–100, 159
learning outcomes
    sharing 19
    prespecification 19, 69
learning out-of-school 2, 12
learning styles 27–8 , 31, 136, 159
left-brained thinking 130–1, 159
Leinhardt, G. 38
lesson phases 26, 39
Lewis, A. 16
lifelong education 134
Lingard, B. 15
Literacy 131–3
literacy hour 5–6
Littleton, K. 48, 50
long-term memory 159
Love's Labours Lost 115
Lumby, J. 60

Macbeath, J. 146
McCormick, R. 60, 98, 115 117
Macdonald, A. 144
McGuiness, C. 98
McIntyre, D. 18–9
Mackinnon, A. 9
Macmurray, J. 88
McNiff, J. 147
Makarenko, A. 86
Man: A Course of Study 69
Martin, E. 99
Martin, M. 83–5,
mathematics 37, 75, 131–2, 135
Mayall, B. 14
medicine 10, 12
Meno 86

Mercer, N. 48, 50, 83
message system 116, 119–20 123, 159
metacognition 97, 99, 159
Mills, M. 16, 119
mirror neurons 159
mixed ability 85
modelling 36, 38
models of teaching
    see teaching (models of)
modes of teaching
    see teaching (modes)
Moon, B. 105–6, 114–15, 117, 122–3
Moon, J. 144
Moore, A. 30, 144
Morgan, C. 30
Morris, Albert 9
Morris, G. 30
Morrison, A. 25
Mortimore, P. 21
Mosely, D. 98
Mosston, M. 121
Moyles, J. 89
Mozart, W. 26
MRI 160
Muijs, D. 21, 26, 37, 40, 62
multimodal learning 28
multiple intelligences 160
Murphy, P. 115, 117, 123
Muschamp, K. 99
Munn, P. 15
myelinisation 134
myelin sheath 160
Myhill, D. 48, 52, 82

National Curriculum (England) 20–1, 25, 83, 91
National Literacy Strategy 26
National Numeracy Strategy 26, 39
neuromyths 28, 129–30, 160
neurons 160
neuroscience 125, 160
New Basics 96,
Newman, F. 96
Noddings, N. 69
normal desirable states 18
Norwich, B. 16

OECD/CERI 127, 130–2, 134
one best way 22
organisation of teaching 23, 25, 35–6, 64–5, 82–3
    whole class 20, 24–25, 35–7, 39, 82–3, 88–90, 164
    group 25, 39 83–5
    individual 25, 42, 86–8, 95
Orlando, J. 112
outdoor education 61

Pacific Rim 86

Palinscar, A. 63
Palmer, J. 15
Papastephanou, M. 98
parietal lobe 132, 167
passive learning 40, 43, 46, 61
Paterson, L. 149
Peacock, C. 25
Passmore, J. 6
pedagogy 108–9, 114–24, 160
    see also productive pedagogies
    dimensions 115
    invisible 119
pedagogues 115, 118
pedagogical content knowledge 122
Pedder, D. 99
PELRS (Pedagogies with e-learning resources) 110
performance of understanding 65, 95, 160
performatativity 160
Perry, G. 6
personalized learning 87–8
PET 161
Peterson, E. 28, 89
Petty, G. 25, 41, 43, 47
Phillips, D. 71
philosophy 11, 13, 130–1, 141
philosophy for children 53, 55
Piaget, J. 11, 70, 77
plasticity
    see brain plasticity
Plato 86
play 57–8, 62, 111, 118
Plowden Report/era 44, 47, 58, 83, 86
Pollard, A. 2, 14, 21–2, 146
Porter, A. 16
Positivism 161
Postman, N. 108
Powell, J. 23
Powell, S. 134
PowerPoint 109, 116
practitioner research 161
Prashnig, B. 89
Prensky, M. 109–10
Pring, R. 8–9, 13–4, 25, 43, 60, 72, 92, 95, 119
Pritchard, A. 106
problem based learning 161
problem-solving 70, 75, 93
productive pedagogies 117, 161
professional development 144–5
professional learning frameworks 145–6
project method 161
project work 72, 91–2
Project Zero 95–6, 105, 161
psychology 12, 13
Pythagoras' theorem 86

Quay, J. 61
Queensland 2, 100,119, 123

questioning 38, 41–4 50–2, 63, 72
    types of 41–2
    from pupils, 72
    alternatives to 50–1
question and answer 26, 44, 47

randomised controlled trials (rcts) 10, 162
reading 11, 132–3
reception learning 35–6, 40–1, 162
reciprocal teaching 66, 162
recitation 35, 50, 162
Reedy, G. 112
reflective practice 61–2, 64, 145, 143–4, 149, 162
reflexive practice 144, 149, 162
religious education 75
research, policy and practice 14
restricted professional 145, 162
Reynolds, D. 21, 26, 37, 40, 62, 108
rich tasks 96–7, 162
right brain thinking 129–30, 162
Roby, T. 52
Rogers, C. 83
Rogoff, B. 63
Rollett, B. 142
rote learning 40
Rousseau, J-J. 68, 86
Ruddock, J. 48
Ruitenburg, C. 6

Sachs, J 149
scaffolding 132, 162
Scandinavia 2, 88
Schon, D. 143
schooling
    see education and schooling
Schwab, J. 63
Schwartz, D. 132
science 74
SCOPE (Scottish Committee on Primary
    Education) 92
Scott, D. 69
Scotland 25, 62, 66, 82, 91, 94
Scottish Education Department 59, 62, 82, 100
Scottish Executive 2, 57,
Scottish Primary Memorandum 59, 82, 94
self esteem 13
sensitive periods 134, 163
setting 83
Shaker, P. 6
Shakespeare 26, 115
shared joint thinking 39
Sharples, D. 88
short-term memory 163
Simon, B. 20, 87
Simpson, M. 108
single route theory (reading) 133
Siraj-Blatchford, I. 39, 111

Siraj-Blatchford, J. 111
Skidmore, D. 55
Skinner, D. 10, 25, 37, 82, 142
Shulman, L. 122
Smith, H. 115–16
Smylie, M. 6
snooker 63
social anthropology 9, 11
social justice 8, 15, 16, 107, 163
social pedagogy 89, 124, 163
social pedagogues 123–4, 163
sociology 11, 13, 14
Socrates 52–3, 86
Socratic teaching 52
Somekh, B. 110, 149
Soviet Union 87–8
split brain experiments 130
Stenhouse, L. 25–6, 48, 52, 69, 72, 145
Stephen, C. 61
Storyline 94–5, 100, 163
streaming 83
Styles, M. 6
symbol processing 163
synapses 163
synaptic density 163
synaptic pruning 163
synthetic phonics 5–6, 164
subject knowledge 122–4
subject teaching 91, 97, 100

Taber, K. 145
tacit learning 59, , 63
teaching (conceptions of) 7–8
   as art 7–8, 12
   as craft 12, 17
   as form 25, 26
   as moral practice 7–8, 10, 12
   as profession 8, 10
   as science 7–8, 10, 12
   as skill 7–8, 10, 12,
   as technology 7, 15
   as vocation 8, 10
   models of 20, 160
   styles of 19–20, 23, 30–2, 126, 164
teaching modes 23- 31, 81–2, 97, 109, 112, 121, 159
   see also action and experience, dialogue, direct teaching
   discussion, enquiry
teaching for understanding 95–6, 164
teaching principles 22
teaching/research tensions 147–8
technicist view 10, 30, 144, 164

technology 10, 108, 113
ten percent myth 129–30
The Winter's Tale 26
thematic teaching 92–3, 100, 164
theory and practice 11
TLRP (Teaching and Learning Research Project) 2, 22, 99, 126, 135
topic webs 92–3,
topic work 164
thinking skills 28, 97–8, 100
Thomas, G. 9, 14, 43, 60
3-18 perspective, 2, 78n
traditional and progressive teaching 20, 24
transdisciplinary study 128, 164
transmission teaching 35, 164

UK 2, 44, 83, 91, 114–15, 117, 122–3
USA/North America 2, 21, 35, 61, 83, 95–6, 117, 120, 122

VAK (visual, auditory, kinaesthetic) 28–9, 129, 164
Varma, S. 132
vocational education 121
VRE 164
Vygotsky, L. 71

Watkins, C. 58
Weil, M. 20
Wenger, E. 71
Wernicke's area 137, 164
whole class interactive teaching
   see organisation of teaching
Williamson, J. 83
Wilson, J. 25, 61
Winch , C. 60, 99
Wiske, M. 95
Witkin, H. 29
Wood, D. 50
Wood, H. 50
Wood, K. 89
Woods, P. 9
Wragg, E. 25, 38, 42
Wrigley, T. 5
Wurdinger, S. 61
Wyse, D. 6

Xu, R. 40

Yelland, N. 110
Yinger, R. 19

ZPD (zone of proximal development) 71, 164